The Illustrated Book of
Songs

The Illustrated Book of Songs

Colm Boyd

Illustrated by Patricia Ghijsens-Ezcurdia

LUSTER

Content

Introducing *The Illustrated Book of Songs*

"... The show must go o-o-on! The show must go o-o-on! Ye-e-ah! Inside my heart is breaking ..." My heart really *was* breaking. This house party was going to shit. And it had all been going so well: the ice had been well and truly broken; people were letting loose. My friend the host had prepared an immaculate playlist of bonafide bangers and thundering throwbacks. The floor was full, shoulders were being shimmied, imaginary buttocks were being slapped. And then as one song ended, I saw the culprit, knowingly, stealthily, making her way to the laptop. A brief moment of silence. And then the opening strains of a new song. But no rockin' riffs or thumping beats here. Just those heartbreakingly dark synths of Queen's *Show*. You've gotta be kidding me.

Please understand, I love Queen. But this song? Here? Now? Surely it was time to rock the casbah, to shake it like a polaroid picture, maybe even to go-shawty-it's-your-birthday. It was certainly, definitely not the time to reflect on the resilience of the human spirit in the face of impending death. I was furious. Just who exactly was this infiltrator who had taken it upon herself to single-handedly ruin the evening? How could anybody be so tone-deaf to the mood of the room? And why was everybody ... hugging, and ... swaying, and ... singing along? Oh my God, they were all loving it! And nobody more than the infiltrator herself. I felt a rush of resentment mixed with something like admiration. There's probably a word in German for that.

When you start to write a book about songs, you quickly realise that people take their music very personally indeed. One woman's Bob Dylan is another man's Adele, and the first half of this sentence will mean something entirely different for everybody. It's not just about people's musical tastes; it's more like a sense of parental protectiveness over the songs we love. This has led to many conversations with friends these past few months along the lines of the following:

Friend: Which list are you working on at the moment?

Me: Songs about getting dumped.

Friend: Oh, cool. Like, *Don't Speak*.

Me: Yeah! That song's not on there though.

Friend: What?? But that's my *song!*

Me: I think you'll find it was actually a young Gwen Stefani and No Dou- …

Friend: But that's my *song!*

To select the songs for this book, we've gone for a team effort. I've suggested some, my editor Tania has done the same, we've both spoken to fellow music fanatics to get further ideas. From the resulting pool of lists and songs, we've selected the ones you'll read about in this book. Some are old, some more recent; many are well-known, some will hopefully be new to you. As a guiding principle, we've chosen songs that could in some way be called "classics". In certain cases, this is obvious: nobody would argue against the legendary status of a hit like *Born to Be Wild*. But for newer tracks, we've selected them on the basis of being modern classics or at least having the potential to be.

The songs we've chosen are diverse. They're from different musical genres. Some have amazing musicality, some have lyrics worthy of a Nobel Prize for Literature. Some deal with death, others deal with zebras, one deals with prostitute frequenting chess players in Bangkok. Some of the songs tell their tale within the track itself, others have required some detective-like delving into how – or why – they came to exist.

The thing that all the songs in this book have in common is that, for one reason or another, they tell a fascinating story. In researching them, I have gasped, I have wept, I have snorted with laughter, I have scrambled to check information from various different sources while exclaiming, "Is that *actually* true?" And it usually is.

Writing this book has been an amazing journey. For the songs I already knew and loved, it's made me love them a bit more. For the songs that have been suggested to me, it's helped me discover many new favourites to add to the playlist of my life. Reader, I wish you the same wild ride.

— ***Colm Boyd***

How to Listen to *The Illustrated Book of Songs*

Time to sit back, break out your smartphone and put on your headphones. You'll find all this book's songs on Spotify. To make them easier to find, you can scan the codes provided. The codes are located under the title of each list throughout the book.

How to Scan and Play the Spotify Codes in 5 easy steps

1. Open the Spotify app on your smartphone
2. Tap **SEARCH** in the menu at the bottom of the screen (tap twice).
3. Tap the **CAMERA** icon
   If you haven't yet allowed Spotify access to your camera, please do so.
4. Point your camera at a Spotify Code
   or if you saved the code image to your phone's photo gallery, you can tap **SELECT FROM PHOTOS**.
5. Press **PLAY** ▶

See a helpful video of how it works at
www.spotifycodes.com/index.html#video

Alternatively you'll also find the songs on YouTube or other streaming/download services.

WORDS
MAKE YOU
THINK.
MUSIC
MAKES YOU
FEEL.
A SONG
MAKES YOU
FEEL A
THOUGHT.

— YIP HARBURG

Beginnings
Songs with an Amazing Intro

Let's Go Crazy
Prince and The Revolution

"Dearly beloved, / We are gathered here today / To get through this thing called 'life'." To the tune of sombre(ish) electric organ, the High Priest of Pop begins his 1984 classic by asking us to lend him our ears so that he may take us all to church. Hallelujah! But let's remember, this is a Prince song, so the particular brand of holiness is not for the faint-hearted. As the serene sermon of the song's intro morphs into bangin' 80s funk-rock, the opening verse gets down to the nitty gritty. Prince tells us how he recently phoned up his lady friend for a chat but was greeted with a remarkably filthy-sounding "Ah! Ff! Ah! Ff!" What to do now that he knows his girl is cheating? To go crazy, obviously; to get nuts; to "look for the purple banana / Until they put us in the truck ..." The message appears to be that life is tough, so you're going to need a healthy dose of madness just to get through it. "But", you ask, "what was that thing about the purple bana-" Oh for goodness sake! This is a *Prince* song!

Blue Monday
New Order

Rapid gunfire drum machine. A synth melody, slowly growing. A suddenly stonkin' beat. Badass guitar, presumably strummed by some snarling cowboy. Monastic chanting. Every element building and building until *Blue Monday*'s epic intro finally peaks with some gloriously pissed-off Mancunian in monotone: "How does it feel to treat me like you do?" Now, that's a way to make an entrance. But why so annoyed, Bernard? It seems the singer has had enough. The lyrics appear to be aimed at a master manipulator, an expert at what a therapist might call *gaslighting* (where you cause a person to doubt their own emotions, hence the song's classic line "Tell me now, how do I feel?"). When New Order's label first released the track in 1983, they foolishly opted for a fancy record sleeve that cost more to manufacture than they could charge in stores. The track became a huge hit, quickly selling 500,000, and making a net loss of £50,000. Bassist Peter Hook is stoic about the whole thing. He says that whenever he runs into the multi-millionaire likes of Bono or Chris Martin, he reflects on how "they don't have an iota of what we've got – which is respect." Careful, Peter, this is how pop divas get into battle.

A MULATTO, AN ALBINO, A MOSQUITO, MY LIBIDO.
— NIRVANA

Smells Like Teen Spirit
Nirvana

Alert! Abandon beer and make a beeline for the mosh pit. From the opening riff of Nirvana's 1991 grunge anthem, there's barely time to register before a thumping drumbeat (1-2-3-4!). And then suddenly that mild-mannered guitar turns into the roar of a particularly hairy beast. Kurt Cobain made no secret of the fact that, from its outset, the track was kind of a rip-off: partly inspired by the Pixies; partly a reworking of Boston's *More Than a Feeling* (but sadly with less air guitar and smaller hair). While most fans agree that the song is loosely about teen rebellion, many think that we shouldn't read too much into the mind-boggling lyrics, such as Kurt's famous chorus-warbling "A mulatto, an albino, a mosquito, my libido / Yeah!" Just to indulge speculation, it's been suggested that those lines might be a game of opposites: as mulatto (dark) is to albino (light), a mosquito (tiny) is to Kurt's sex-drive (voracious!). One meaning that Kurt was clearer about was the song's title. Apparently, a friend of his had written "Kurt smells like teen spirit" on the wall of his house (because nothing says *grunge* like grubby scrawl on a wall). Kurt found the line profound, and used it as inspiration to write

Nirvana's hit. Only later did he discover that the friend had been referring to *Teen Spirit*, the brand of deodorant that Kurt's then-girlfriend used to wear.

Kids
MGMT

A (mercifully) brief clip of excited kids shrieking a countdown. A hard beat. A simple, Atari-like electro tune. Suddenly, a backing melody, but this time played by approximately *every synth on the entire planet*, leading to blissful release, tears of euphoria, bed-wetting (for those of us brave enough to admit it ...). And then, not quite done with emotional impact, a tale of damp-eyed nostalgia: "You were a child / Crawling on your knees toward it." While *Kids* (2008) keeps its message subtle, the song seems to be a sort of warning. The lyrics take us on a journey from joyful, harmless childhood to our capacity for destruction at a later age. The chorus centres around a heartfelt reminder to enjoy life, but not at a cost: "Control yourself / Take only what you need from it." A useful mantra for the next time you're home alone and rip open a family-size bag of *Doritos*.

Crazy in Love
Beyoncé ft. Jay-Z

Is there a person alive who has not sashayed down an imaginary runway, finger-lickin' and booty-shakin', as the opening horns of *Crazy in Love* start to blare? If you have reacted to that question with a scornful frown, then shame on you, dear reader. Shame on you. For you see, Beyoncé's 2003 anthem does not just kick off with a clever intro; rather, it sparks some primeval response. As Pavlov's hounds salivated to the sound of a bell, human beings of the 21st century must not deny the hip-thrusts and hair-flips demanded by this fanfare of trumpets, booming drums and Beyoncé's "Uh-oh-uh-oh-uh-oh". Those horns were the idea of producer Rich Harrison, who sampled them from a little-known soul track from the 70s (*Are You My Woman*, by The Chi-Lites). In a stroke of genius, he had the idea to just repeat the horns on a loop, throw in a cowbell, and get Queen Bey to help him come up with a storyline. Given that *Jayoncé* were just in the early stages of their romance, it seemed fitting to go for a tale of losing one's senses: "Got me looking, so crazy, my baby / I'm not myself lately, I'm foolish, I don't do this!" Music's greatest power couple was born, as was Beyoncé's solo career.

Setting the Scene
Iconic Opening Lines

Into My Arms
Nick Cave

Sitting down to write a hopelessly romantic love song, it was perhaps not the most obvious choice to go for the opening line "I don't believe in an interventionist God". Akin to kicking off an email to your boss with a pondering on why men have nipples, the connection is not immediately clear. And yet, Nick manages to pull it together. In *Into My Arms* (1997), Nick tells his lover that if such a God were to exist, he would ask him/her/it "not to intervene when it came to you". What follows is a near-holy song, where the singer's religion is the simple adoration that he feels for his lover. A track that manages to leap from intellectual furrowed-brow to teary-eyed abandonment. Good save, Nick.

Tom Traubert's Blues (Four Sheets to the Wind in Copenhagen)
Tom Waits

Speaking of tear-jerking, even just the opening strings of this 1976 classic are enough to unstiffen the most rigid of upper lips. A ravaged-sounding Waits then weighs in: "Wasted and wounded, it ain't what the moon did / Got what I paid for now." The song tells the sad tale of Tom Traubert, a heavy-drinking drifter who finds himself in a cold and foreign land from which he will probably never find his way back home. The chorus of the song incorporates the Australian folk song *Waltzing Matilda*. Waits says that this song reminded him of an Australian soldier "far away from home and drunk on the corner with no money, lost". While the opening line hints that Tom's tragedy might be all of his own making, it's impossible not to feel heartbroken for the lonely Aussie pining for a homeland that he may never see again.

The Sound of Silence
Simon & Garfunkel

"Hello darkness, my old friend / I've come to talk with you again." At the age of 21, Paul Simon's chosen spot for songwriting was his bathroom, its tiled floor providing the perfect echo chamber for his guitar and voice. To help his concentration, he used to turn off the light and sing to – you've guessed it – the darkness. What follows from this iconic line is an equally classic folk hit, described by Art Garfunkel as "the inability of people to communicate with each other ... so what you see around you are people unable to love each other." In pop culture, the term "Hello darkness, my old friend" is often used as a means of ironically greeting a familiar surge of depression. The perfect line for the next time you dribble some ketchup down your newly-washed shirt.

Common People
Pulp

In Pulp's playful takedown of upper-class pretensions, singer Jarvis Cocker begins by setting the scene: "She came from Greece, she had a thirst for knowledge / She studied sculpture at Saint Martin's College / That's where I / Caught her eye." The song goes on to marvel at the world of this spoilt little rich girl, who wants nothing more than to experience the daily shitshow of life for folks without a hefty trust fund (granted, the song phrases this in a more poetic way). Why would she want that, you ask? Because she fancies Jarvis and also happens to think that "poor is cool", especially when you hold an opt-out card. Originally released in 1995, the song attracted some unexpected press during the 2015 Greek financial crisis. Rumours abounded that the girl in the song was Danae Stratou, wife of Yanis Varoufakis, the former finance minister of Greece.

> *IS THIS THE REAL LIFE? IS THIS JUST FANTASY?*
>
> — QUEEN

Bohemian Rhapsody
Queen

It could be argued that Queen's 1975 masterpiece has two opening lines. The song's intro ponders "Is this the real life? Is this just fantasy?" Post intro, the song begins in earnest with the monumental "Mama, just killed a man / Put a gun against his head, pulled my trigger, now he's dead." And thus begins the operatic, comedic rollercoaster which would become one of the most famous songs of all time. Entire documentaries have been made about lyrical interpretations. Most commentators agree that the song is about a man who confesses to a murder, and his subsequent trial. Is it all a metaphor for Freddie's sexuality? Is much of the song nonsense? Oh, who cares? As a true classic, *Bo Rap* is what you make it.

Stand by Your Man
Tammy Wynette

"Sometimes it's hard to be a woman ..." The classic opening line of Tammy's 1968 country hit was hard to argue with. It's the rest of the song that caused the controversy. What makes womanhood so tough? "... giving all your love to just one man ..." With the rising tide of Women's Lib of the late 60s, feminists saw red. Here they were trying to dismantle the patriarchy while the airwaves were filled with a catchy ballad telling them to stand by their men. Throughout her life, Tammy always defended the song as simple a message of acceptance. If we're looking to evaluate the singer's feminist credentials, though, perhaps we should consider how she lived. Four times divorced, Tammy was no Stepford Wife. She married her first husband, Euple, while still in high school and they soon had three kids. Euple was not the most supportive, and eventually Tammy decided to leave him and go earn some money by singing. As she drove away, he told her, "Dream on, baby!" Years later, Euple showed up at one of Tammy's concerts and queued for an autograph. And he got one, of sorts: Tammy signed, "Dream on, baby."

Famous Blue Raincoat
Leonard Cohen

How many songs owe their inspiration to a restless mind at the witching hour? "It's four in the morning, the end of December / I'm writing you now just to see if you're better." We find Leonard penning a letter to the friend who betrayed him. Get ready to munch some popcorn while involuntarily exclaiming things like "He *didn't*!", because this is a tale of *telenovela*-level deceit. Leonard's letter describes the affair between his girlfriend and his friend, the subsequent fallout, the singer's attempt at forgiveness. There is much debate about whether *Famous Blue Raincoat* (1971) is truly addressed to a former friend or if it relies on the old self-as-other metaphor, with Leonard singing to his past self. Almost as iconic as the opening is the song's closing line, lest the listener forget that they have been listening to a letter set to music: "Sincerely, L. Cohen".

Feast Your Ears!
Songs about Food

Lollipop
The Chordettes

Apparently, this 1958 classic was inspired by one of the songwriters arriving to the studio late because his daughter had gotten a lollipop stuck in her hair. With lollipops in mind, his co-writer got to work on a cheerful ditty centred around such a funny-sounding word. How to turn that into a hit? Well, obviously some romance needed to be introduced: "He loves to kiss me / 'Til I can't see straight / Gee, my Lollipop is great! / I call him / Lollipop, lollipop ..." The song has seen many recordings, but the most successful internationally was the all-female barbershop quartet version by The Chordettes. These days, singing about your man's lollipop would sound obscene, but not as much so as the mention of a high-sugar snack. Will the coming years bring yet another cover version, updated for modern palates to some sort of lactose-free kefir stick? Good luck with that rhyme scheme.

Bakerman
Laid Back

"Bakerman is baking bread / Bakerman is baking bread." Laid Back's 1989 hit united people all over the world (well, mainly Europe) in their love for a freshly baked loaf. The song's chilled-out, steady-as-she-goes vibe and lyrical repetition bring to mind the busy bakerman stretching, pulling, kneading, slapping ... wait, is this really about bread? Might the singer's insistence that "The night train is coming" be something other than a simple stating of facts about the arrival of a late train while the baker rhythmically whacks his slippery batter against the countertop? The answer, it would seem, is in the ears of the beholder. Whether the song makes you hungry or horny (or if you're truly twisted, both), the video holds no clues as to the intentions behind the lyrics. In a shocking foray into the sphere of "sense of humour", Lars von Trier directed the classic clip of the Danish group singing and playing their instruments, all while plummeting towards the earth in skydiving gear.

Caramel
John Grant

Tempting as it might be to pledge one's undying devotion to actual caramel, it probably makes for a more emotionally engaging song to just use the sugary treat as simile: "My love is the rarest jewel / And he grounds me with his love / My love – he is rich like caramel ..." The food references end after the first few lines, as John moves on to describing his love in much less culinary terms, like shelter and healing. In interviews, the singer has been very open about his troubled past, growing up gay in an orthodox Methodist family in the American Midwest of the 70s. Having battled with substance abuse and mental-health issues, John seems to have written *Caramel* (2010) as a poem to the lover who has become his rock amid the chaos, a sort of sweet ending. Like a nasty meal followed by a surprisingly delicious crème brûlée.

Frim Fram Sauce
Diana Krall

"I don't want French-fried potatoes, red, ripe tomatoes / I'm never satisfied / I want the frim fram sauce / With the aussen fay and chifafah on the side." "Ah, yes," nod the foodie Instagrammers, "chifafah is, like, *so* hot right now." Not so fast, douchebags. Diana Krall's 1993 track is actually an old jazz standard, famous for its silly, made-up lyrics. Originally popularised by Nat King Cole back in the 40s, *Frim Fram Sauce* is a tale of craving, when just that one dish will hit the spot. The restaurant may offer a whole menu of delights, but Diana can only be sated by that frim-fram-aussen-chifafah thing. Is it all a bit of cheeky innuendo? Possibly. And yet, it's just so easy to imagine overhearing some grandiose diner insisting, "Yah, I'm gonna go for the frim fram, but make sure the aussen isn't over-fayed and did I mention that I cannot *abide* a limp chifafah?"

I DON'T WANT FRENCH-FRIED POTATOES, RED, RIPE TOMATOES.

— DIANA KRALL

Old Whore's Diet
Rufus Wainwright ft. Anohni

"An old whore's diet / Gets me goin' in the mornin'." While it's not immediately apparent what the breakfast of an elderly prostitute might consist of, Rufus clearly has mixed emotions on the issue. The 2004 song moves from wistful ballad to fun reggae-strumming, to poignant violins with the added vocal of Anohni (formerly of Antony and The Johnsons), to funereal organ and an eventual climax of wailing pandemonium. Jesus, Rufus, we can assume this isn't a strawberry pop-tart you're talking about. So, what could it be that fires up Rufus's pistons every morn? His official explanation is that the lyrics were inspired by a time he found himself eating old, cold Chinese food from a hotel fridge. Hmm. Fans point out that an old whore's diet may not be quite so innocent. How to put this? Apparently, a more aged sex worker will often need to perform certain ... favours ... to stay popular. Bon appétit!

Chin-Chin!
Songs about Drinks

Horchata
Vampire Weekend

Warm sunshine, a cool glass of *horchata* and a special somebody to share it with. Thus begins Vampire Weekend's 2009 song about everybody's favourite sweet, Spanish beverage (at least the booze-free ones). It seems the singer has left the cold winter behind to go sit amongst the palm trees: "In December, drinking horchata / I'd look psychotic in a balaclava". Thankfully, the rhyming changes after those lines, sparing us descriptions of any potential follow-up drinks (*kiwi guava*? ... *cup of java*??). Anyhoo, while enjoying the tropical breezes, the singer seems to meet a love interest. But, as is the nature of most holidays, he soon returns to the cold concrete jungle and is doomed to forever question what might have been: "Oh, you had it but oh, no, you lost it / Looking back, you shouldn't have fought it." Nothing sweet about the taste of regret.

Gin and Juice
Snoop Dogg ft. Dat Nigga Daz

"Rollin' down the street, smokin' indo / Sippin' on gin and juice, laid back / With my mind on my money / And my money on my mind." Long before gin was being mixed with rose petals at your local, exposed-brick hipster bar, it was the staple liquor of a much cooler clique. In his 1994 classic, Snoop Dogg tells us all about his drink of choice and the lifestyle that surrounds it. For Snoop, gin goes hand in hand with house parties, sex, smoking weed and just cruising with his homies. And of course, gin is also a status symbol that sets you apart as the flushest of partygoers (hence the "money on my mind"). In what may have been a very early example of product placement in rap, Snoop even namedrops his favourite gins. In one verse, he arrives at a party with *Seagrams*; in the next, he's sipping on *Tanqueray*. That's a "*Tanqueray* and chronic", by the way, as opposed to a *Schweppes*. In 2018, Snoop Dogg broke the world record for the largest Paradise Cocktail, a five-hundred-litre mix of gin, apricot brandy and orange juice. It is unclear whether he shared it out or guzzled it himself.

Tequila
The Champs

Has ingesting tequila ever seemed so innocent? Playful guitar, a light drumbeat, a fun saxophone riff that kind of makes you want to do the twist. Like a midnight round of shots, it all seems so jolly and painless. The 1958 song's only hint towards the sinister is the gravelly, sneered voice which utters the word "Tequila", like a cartoon devil sitting on your left shoulder. That voice came from the song's sax player, Danny Flores. He was also the one who wrote the song, which largely came about from a jam session based on a simple Cuban beat. The label originally saw the track as simple filler, a B-side to a different song that seemed to have more commercial appeal. And yet, it was *Tequila* that caught people's attention. As one of the few largely instrumental songs to hit number one in the US, it proves an important point about the public's fondness for getting trolleyed.

Born Slippy (NUXX)
Underworld

Pounding techno is never the most likely to go mainstream. And yet, in the summer of 1996 *Born Slippy* dominated the airwaves, not least in the UK. Over that thumping beat, it wasn't easy to make out what Underworld frontman Karl Hyde was bellowing, except for one repeated line: "Shouting, 'Lager, lager, lager, lager'…" As a people who tend to enjoy a tipple or two, Brits quickly adopted the song as their new National Anthem of Drinking. It's ironic, really, given that Karl says that the lyrics were inspired more by problem drinking than merriment. What first seem like drunken ramblings, turn into a hazy story: "… squatting pissed in a tube hole / At Tottenham Court Road, I just come out of The Ship / Talking to the most blonde I ever met …" Karl says that he wrote the lyrics after a night of boozing at The Ship pub in London's Soho. The song is basically a torrent of his jumbled, self-loathing thoughts as he found himself stumbling to the tube station to catch his train home. As for the reasons behind the bender: Karl had won money at the greyhound track that day. The dog's name was Born Slippy.

Milkshake
Kelis

The year was 2003, a time when otherwise-sane human beings would spontaneously burst into a wholly unprovoked, "My milkshake brings all the boys to the yard / And they're like, 'It's better than yours'". While milkshakes were still popular in those heady, lactose-fuelled days, it's probably safe to say that most people questioned whether the song was actually about milky refreshment. Would a peppermint-fudge combo really get the boys so excited? Would Kelis truly be so boastful to the other girls about her superior blending techniques? The singer herself clarified the issue when, in an interview, she defined her *milkshake* as "the essence of a woman". That solves that, then. The track was co-written by Pharrell Williams, who says that he was inspired by Middle-Eastern music. In a move that could have shaken the foundations of musical history, the song was originally offered to Ms. Britney Spears, but she turned it down. Maybe Britney isn't much of a foodie – unlike Kelis, who is a Cordon Bleu-trained chef and has released her own cookbook.

MY MILKSHAKE BRINGS ALL THE BOYS TO THE YARD.

— KELIS

Got a Light?
Songs about Smoking

Cigarettes and Coffee
Otis Redding

"It's early in the morning / About a quarter till three / I'm sitting here talking with my baby / Over cigarettes and coffee". If anybody could do late-night, pour-your-heart-out smoothness, it was Otis. Released on *The Soul Album* (1966), *Cigarettes and Coffee* is a dreamy description of one of life's most elusive treasures: the perfect moment. As Otis and his lady friend sit up into the night, he tells her how much better his life is with her in it, even how he wants to marry her, all as the wee hours pass by and coffee leads to cigarette leads to coffee (and so on). Time almost stands still as Otis and his girl simply bask in each other's company. No mention here of the heart-stopping panic that will surely grip them as the excessive caffeine truly takes hold. Neither must we dwell on the moment they finally kiss, the evening's antics having soured their teeth into yellowed stalks. Apologies to all Otis fans, but such matters need to be pointed out.

Don't Smoke in Bed
Nina Simone

While most "smoking" songs ponder the luxurious appeal of a good ol' puff, Ms. Simone begs to differ. *Don't Smoke in Bed* has been recorded by many singers over the decades, but few can compare to Nina's stark, seething version (1958). With just the piano to accompany her, Nina sets the scene of a wife who has had enough. She's left a note and her wedding ring on the bedside table and is off to start a new life. She reveals the concluding lines of her *Dear John* letter: "Don't look for me / I'll get a hand / Remember darling / Don't smoke in bed." The "hand" she refers to is presumably a way of saying that she'll find herself a new suitor. As for the no-smoking warning, most fans take this as a reference to her husband's cheating. The symbol of the bed runs throughout the song as a possible metaphor for their marriage. Has the husband been failing to cover his tracks? (Cheaters take note: hide your butts!) And of course, we all know that smoking in bed is a risky business which means it could all end in flames. Sounds like it already has.

Cigar
Tamino

In Amsterdam's Van Gogh Museum, there hangs a rather macabre portrait called *Skull with Burning Cigarette*. The oil-on-canvas features a simple skull with a lit cigarette clenched between teeth. Tamino first saw the painting when he was just 18. He interpreted that clench as a smile, the smouldering cigarette a sign of a man who had lived well, satisfied his urges, and died free of regrets. *Cigar* (2017) is Tamino's own reflection on the lessons he can take from the smoking skull. To hell with rule-following, maybe life is about indulgence. At the end of the track, the singer speaks directly to his bony muse: "You, look at me now / With that burning cigar hanging out of your mouth / And it seems all a lie, what they've told me so far." While the song is a real gem, it is not entirely insignificant that Tamino is an über-talented, 20-something-year-old Belgian-Egyptian who also happens to be a fashion model. Would the song's message of shameless decadence sound quite as romantic coming from a middle-aged builder named Mick trying to justify his morning Egg McMuffin? Maybe not.

Sympathique
Pink Martini

"Je ne veux pas travailler / Je ne veux pas déjeuner / Je veux seulement l'oublier / Et puis je fume." ("I don't want to work / I don't want to eat / I just want to forget / And so, I smoke.") At first listen, you'd be forgiven for thinking this song was recorded at some 1930s Parisian ballroom. Such was the intention of American group Pink Martini, who make tracks in the style of certain places and times. *Sympathique* is actually from 1997, though the lyrics are a reworking of an old French poem (*Hôtel* by Guillaume Apollinaire). The song tells a tale of a woman who sits prisoner-like in her room, suffering from a bad case of lovesickness. Has her lover left her? Or is she pining for a love unrequited? Either way, she is determined to ponder the issue in a way that seems almost impossibly French: through fabulously pouty smoking.

The High Life
Songs about Drugs

Cocaine
Eric Clapton

Some songs hide behind metaphor while others, well, they say it all in the title. *Cocaine* was written and recorded by JJ Cale in 1976 but is better known for the Eric Clapton version from the following year. The singer begins by introducing us to his date for the evening (shall we call her Charlene?): "If you want to hang out / You've got to take her out / Cocaine." Although the song's slick groove may have you reaching for your stash, Clapton claims that the song is, in fact, a warning against drugs. Now that, ladies and gentlemen, is what they call a boner-killer. Aware of the confusion that might be caused by advising people not to do drugs while singing a really cool song literally called COCAINE, Clapton altered the song in live performances by adding the line "that dirty cocaine". Because nobody would *ever* want to do anything dirty ...

The Needle and the Damage Done
Neil Young

In *Cocaine*, Eric Clapton keeps repeating the hook "She don't lie", presumably as a reminder that highs come at a cost. Neil Young offered a similar sentiment in his 1972 classic, sadly reflecting on the devastation that heroin had brought to the lives of those around him. Neil says that he wrote the song about a bandmate who was hooked on heroin, and who ultimately died from it after the song's recording. "I hit the city and I lost my band / I watched the needle take another man / Gone, gone, the damage done." The timing of the track's release was significant. For many, the early 70s were a hangover period, when "the damage done" was becoming apparent to all. While not many eyebrows can be raised at Neil Young singing about smack, the same cannot be said for Andrea Corr (of The Corrs), who did a cover version in 2007.

Because I Got High
Afroman

Most people can't claim to enjoy the idle ramblings of a giddy stoner. No, Chad, we *can't* prove that we don't live in *The Matrix*. And yet, somehow, *Because I Got High* became an international sensation in 2001. Perhaps it was because we had never before heard anything quite like its unfiltered, ridiculous telling of a pothead lifestyle. In between croaks and chuckles, our baked narrator sings about all the things he would have done if it hadn't been for weed: "I was gonna clean my room until I got high / I was gonna get up and find the broom, but then I got high". You get the idea. While the song gets into slightly darker territory (our narrator starts selling dope and missing child support payments), it doesn't take from the song's status as a stoner anthem for college dorms across the world.

WHITE LINES. BLOWING THROUGH MY MIND.

— GRANDMASTER FLASH & THE FURIOUS FIVE

White Lines (Don't Do It)
Grandmaster Flash & The Furious Five

Trend alert: funky, danceable songs about doing drugs which claim to be actually about not doing drugs. As the grandmaster raps about the pros and cons of snorting lines (well, mainly the pros), melodic backing vocals remind us that it's not all fun and games: "White lines / Blowing through my mind / High price / For us to unwind." Listeners keen to improve their street slang might learn a thing or two from the track's thesaurus-like references to cocaine: blow, rock, freebase, snow, and of course the song's climactic "Sugar! Cane!" The track was released in 1983 and even had an unofficial video directed by film student Spike Lee, offering a glimpse of the impossibly cool New York underground scene. If all that doesn't put the kids off drugs, really, what will?

Lipstick Marks
Songs about the Other Woman

If I Were Your Woman
Gladys Knight & the Pips

Gladys has got it bad. In her 1970 soul classic, she's in love with a man but he has no time for her, distracted as he is by some no-good hussy who doesn't appreciate him: "You're like a diamond / But she treats you like glass / Yet you beg her to love you / But me, you don't ask." It's unclear whether Gladys is already involved with this guy (and thus, the other woman) or just lovesick from a distance. Whatever the case, the singer pledges her undying love. Her male backing vocalists egg her on, singing the provocations of her love interest: "If you were my woman … What would you do?" Careful, Gladys. Remember what Groucho Marx said about how we never want to belong to any club that would have us as a member.

Back to Black
Amy Winehouse

For many fans, *Back to Black* (2007) is the song that defined Amy Winehouse. An old-school soul classic full of heartache, vice and stark-but-playful lyrics. Amy was quite straightforward about the inspiration for the song. She had broken up with her boyfriend, Blake, and he had gotten back with the girl he'd left for her. It's a matter of perspective to decide who "the other woman" is here, Amy or Blake's new (formerly old) gal? Either way, Amy is devastated: "You went back to what you knew / So far removed from all that we went through / And I tread a troubled track … I'll go back to black." It's a question for the ages to decide just what Amy's *black* is. Depression? Alcohol-fuelled numbness? A drug reference? Sad as the track may be, fans will remember its accompanying video as the moment when Amy's beehive hairdo truly came into its own. Grandmothers around the world wondered why the hairspray aisle was suddenly full of youngsters.

Call Your Girlfriend
Robyn

Super producer Max Martin has said that, these days, when he meets budding new popstars, they walk into his office, put Robyn's 2010 album *Body Talk* on the table and say "I wanna make this!" And it's not hard to see why. *Call Your Girlfriend* is just one example of the electropop album's ability to make the listener want to dance through the tears. On this track, Robyn plays the role of the other woman, pleading with her new lover to end things with a current girlfriend: "Call your girlfriend / It's time you had 'the talk' / Give your reasons / Say it's not her fault". Now before we get all high and mighty and start pointing at individual fingers to list off our thoughts on home-wreckin' Robyn, let us pause for a moment. If the song really is so catty, why does it make you want to choke up? Is it Robyn's pained vocals suggesting that she knows it's all a fantasy? Or is it the creeping sense that the singer herself may have been at the receiving end of "the talk" on more than a few occasions?

YET YOU BEG HER TO LOVE YOU. BUT ME, YOU DON'T ASK.

— GLADYS KNIGHT & THE PIPS

Jolene
Dolly Parton

Ravishing redhead Jolene must surely hold the dubious accolade of being country music's most famous other woman. Dolly tells it to her straight: "I can easily understand / How you could easily take my man / But you don't know what he means to me, Jolene." We could well wonder why Dolly isn't addressing the issue with her wayward man rather than some pretty stranger, but it was the 70s, and Jolene makes for a better musical hook than a name like "Hank, Hank, Hank, *Ha-a-ank*". Dolly says that the inspiration for the song's narrative came when she noticed a leggy redhead flirting with her husband at the bank. In an interview with NPR, Dolly recalled her jealousy towards the other woman, saying that the sight of her made Dolly question what her husband saw in "some little short, sawed-off honky like me". A humble heart of gold, perhaps? Dolly for president!

The Green-Eyed Monster
Songs about Jealousy

Why Can't I Be You?
The Cure

Frontman Robert Smith has said that he wrote this 1987 song after a fan asked him the exact question which ended up as the title. Anybody who has ever been to a Cure concert will know how much fans idolise Smith, imitating his goth style, wild hair and red lipstick. Here, idolising turns to infatuation, with the singer expressing his wish to actually *be* the person who he fancies. The song features an interesting take on flirtatious envy: "I'll run around in circles until I run out of breath / I'll eat you all up or I'll just hug you to death". Believe it or not, such lyrics led to accusations of satanism from some critics in the US. Note to teenagers: in attempting to attract a mate, it's not always the best look to admit to a deep, aching jealousy towards them. Unless you can turn it into a cool song like this one, which just might get you laid.

Who Is He (And What Is He to You)?
Bill Withers

When it comes to giving a jealous stare, ain't nobody withers like Bill Withers withers. In his 1972 classic, the singer finds himself trying to make sense of his shifty-acting partner. As the two walk down the street, they pass a man who gives Bill cause for suspicion. A subtle glance here, a minor gesture there, suddenly Bill finds himself putting it all together, leading to love rivalry's most iconic verse: "When I add the sum of you and me / I get confused and keep coming up with three / You're too much for one man but not enough for two / Dad-gum-it, who is he, and what is he to you?" As well as being a masterpiece of soulful funk, what also stands out about this early-70s track is Bill's defence of men as emotional creatures. His partner assumes that, as a man, Bill doesn't have much intuition. Bill retorts, "Is that what you really think or are you wishin'?" Withering indeed.

I'd Rather Go Blind
Etta James

Jealousy never seems too far away from misery. Like so many songs that have become classics, *I'd Rather Go Blind* (1968) started off as a B-side and from there, gained popularity due to vocals and lyrics that packed a punch. Etta spots her love talking to another girl and confesses "I would rather go blind, boy / Than to see you walk away from me." Etta co-wrote the song with her friend Fugi, who was in prison at the time. Fugi has said that he wrote the mournful lyrics in a state of grief, not knowing when he was going to be released. Etta stated that the song was about both her love life and her "personal ways". Some think this could be a reference to the heroin habit she struggled with for many years, giving the song an even more tragic twist. Despite the fact that we have surely all, at some point, engaged in verbal exchanges with our bag of smack, the record label chose not to push this slightly less relatable interpretation of the song.

Mr. Brightside
The Killers

Has indie music ever dealt with jealousy in purer form than The Killers did in this 2005 anthem? Singer Brandon Flowers allows his thoughts to fester, imagining his lover cheating and driving himself really quite mad: "Jealousy, turning saints into the sea / Swimming through sick lullabies, choking on your alibis". Is Brandon himself the saint, forced into retreat by ugly jealousy? Are the sick lullabies his own bitter songs, like this one? One thing that is for sure is that Brandon is miffed. No more looking on the bright side, time to see things as they are. Some fans have pointed out fun word play in the initial verse, when Brandon is having awful visions of his lover doing the deed with another fellow: "… and my stomach is sick / And it's all in my head, but she's touching his / Chest. Now, he takes off her dress now." Giving the song's rhyming scheme, it's quite possible that Brandon wanted us to expect him to say a body part other than "chest".

That Look You Give That Guy
Eels

Eels singer Mark Everett has said that this song is his favourite from their 2009 album *Hombre Lobo*. And it's not hard to see why. Simple, understated, heart-rending, the song is the story of a love that will probably never be. He sees his love interest walking around with some other guy and allows himself to dream: "That look you give that guy / I wanna see / Looking right at me / If I could be that guy / Instead of me …" No furious male rivalry here, just an envious love from afar for somebody he suspects might be out of his league. Kind of an indie music version of *Cyrano de Bergerac*, but without the protrusive nose or the weird incest (OK, this analogy is a stretch). Speaking of French influences, this Eels track is a version of the 80s French classic *Le Coup de Soleil* by Richard Cocciante.

JEALOUSY, TURNING SAINTS INTO THE SEA.

— THE KILLERS

It's Not You, It's Me
Songs about Getting Dumped

Song for the Dumped
Ben Folds Five

Some people deal with a break-up by pondering, taking a teary-eyed glance at what might have been. Others prefer a good old rant. *Song for the Dumped* (1997) is exactly what the title says it is. Singer Ben says that the song came about when the band's drummer, Darren, objected that Ben sometimes wrote overly complicated lyrics. As a joke, Darren took Ben's notebook and wrote a break-up track that could certainly never be accused of complexity: "Give me my money back / You bitch / I want my money back / And don't forget / To give me back my black t-shirt." A simple reminder that, emotions aside, break-ups can also mean the loss of your most prized items of clothing.

I Can't Make You Love Me
Bonnie Raitt

Warning: *I Can't Make You Love Me* should only be consumed in appropriate doses. While the recently dumped may feel the urge to play it on repeat, this option is to be treated with extreme caution. Indeed, Bonnie herself says that she recorded the vocals in just one take, admitting that it would have been impossible for her to recapture the emotion.

The 1991 song is a sad acceptance of a relationship's final moments: "I'll close my eyes, then I won't see / The love you don't feel when you're holding me / Morning will come and I'll do what's right / Just give me 'til then to give up this fight." One of the songwriters, Mike Reid, said he got the idea for the lyrics from a news report he had read about a drunk man who had shot at his girlfriend's car. When the judge asked him if he could take any lessons from the situation, he replied, "I learned, Your Honour, that you can't make a woman love you if she don't."

Hurt
Timi Yuro

"You said your love was true / And we'd never, ever, ever part / Now you want someone new / And it breaks my heart." Lyrically, Timi Yuro's 1961 hit sounded much like many radio hits of the time. What was remarkable was her voice, belting and whispering in almost equal measure. In glorious melodrama, the song describes the devastation of finding out that an ex-lover has moved on. The track had many versions over the years, with even Elvis taking a shot at it. The King himself was reportedly a huge fan of fellow Vegas entertainer Timi, and he regularly performed *Hurt* at concerts in the mid-70s, his final years. On various occasions, he ended the song by holding the climactic final note for a full seven seconds while collapsing to his knees in overwhelmed emotion. Can you even imagine? What a time to have been alive!

Someone Like You
Adele

Adele says that this is the song that she will be remembered for. Coming at the end of her 2001 album *21*, which features sassy break-up hits like *Rolling in the Deep* and *Rumour Has It*, Adele admits that she wrote *Someone …* "because I was exhausted from being such a bitch". No room for posturing here, just a heartfelt goodbye: "'Don't forget me', I beg / 'I'll remember', you said / Sometimes it lasts in love / But sometimes it hurts instead." According to the singer, the lyrics are about an ex-boyfriend who she imagined she would one day marry. He left her and soon got engaged to another woman. She describes as "the horrible-est feeling" the realisation that he wanted marriage, just not with her. Poor Adele, condemned to a life of global success, unimaginable wealth, a new family of her own and great hair. The winner really does take it all.

Go Your Own Way
Fleetwood Mac

Written by the band's lead male singer, Lindsey Buckingham, *Go Your Own Way* (1976) is a bitter F-you to the girlfriend who has decided to leave him. Slightly awkward that the girlfriend in question was Stevie Nicks, the band's lead female singer. The verses of the song are sung by Buckingham, but Stevie joins in for the chorus, essentially having to tell herself to get stuffed. She told *Rolling Stone* that she took particular offence at the song's line "Packing up, shacking up's all you wanna do". Disliking the implication that she just wanted to shack up with different men, Stevie asked her ex to change the line. He refused. If you watch video performances of the song, you may notice Stevie banging that tambourine a little harder than she needed to.

Crying
Roy Orbison

Lots of songs do heartbreak, but few like *Crying*. Roy Orbison's 1961 classic is a benchmark song about the one that got away. Roy sings about running into an old flame he just can't let go of: "When you said, 'So long' / Left me standing all alone / Alone and crying / Crying ..." The song has seen many versions over the years, but few singers can match Roy's majestic vocal range, from deep bass to sharp falsetto. As friend and collaborator Bob Dylan wrote in his autobiography, Orbison's range "made you want to drive your car over a cliff. He sang like a professional criminal." If Bob's calling you a criminal, you know you're doing something right.

Over and Out
Songs about Saying Goodbye

Je Suis Venu Te Dire Que Je M'en Vais
Serge Gainsbourg

Serge Gainsbourg wasn't *exactly* an asshole. He just wanted you to think that he was. The master provocateur revelled in the role of being France's most notorious womaniser, the man who looked Whitney Houston in the eye on live television and told the audience, "I want to fuck her!" With huge talent and a knowing sense of humour, Serge was seen by the French (and many others) as a genius, his arrogance wholly justifiable. At first listen, *Je Suis Venu …* (1973) sounds like the cold farewell of a schmuck: "Je suis venu te dire que je m'en vais / Et tes larmes n'y pourront rien changer / Comme dit si bien Verlaine au vent mauvais / Je suis venu te dire que je m'en vais." ("I came to tell you that I'm leaving / And your tears can't do anything about it / As Verlaine said so well, 'on an ill wind' / I came to tell you that I'm leaving."). As the song progresses, we hear a woman sob and sniffle as she tries to imagine how she will possibly get by without Serge and his massive ego. But why, then, does the song sound so genuinely heart-breaking? Might there be more to the narrator than his frosty veneer? That Verlaine quote is from an old French poem about death. Given that Serge wrote the song soon after suffering a heart attack, might this goodbye not be quite a callous as it seems?

Leaving on a Jet Plane
John Denver

It was the late 60s, commercial air travel was becoming more commonplace and the airwaves were filled with a sweet ballad about jet planes. The song was written and recorded by Denver, though the more popular version was performed by Peter, Paul and Mary. As the innocent goodbye-track of choice for dewy-eyed grandmothers, it's a little bit surprising that the second verse deals with the thorny issue of infidelity: "There's so many times I've let you down / So many times I've played around ... they don't mean a thing". While floppy-haired, bespectacled John came across as a very wholesome country boy, it seems he was a bit of a dark horse. During a dispute over assets following his first divorce, apparently John took a chainsaw and cut the marital bed in half! Anyway, hellraiser or not, John will always be remembered as the smooth, heartfelt voice behind classics such as *Leaving on a Jet Plane*. The song took on a more tragic twist in 1997, when John died after his single-seat plane crashed into the sea.

November Rain
Guns N' Roses

OK, time for the goodbye song to end all goodbye songs. At nine minutes long, *November Rain* (1992) packs it all in: emotive piano with sweeping strings; a crescendo of chorus chants; towering guitar solos. And then there's Axl's bare, lonesome soul: "... nothing lasts forever / And we both know hearts can change / And it's hard to hold a candle / In the cold November rain." He seems to be resigning himself to something. Axl and his girl have decided to put things on pause and he's faced with a metaphorical winter of wondering if they can figure it out. Judging by the anguish of the music, this is one break that never got untaken. After almost seven minutes, the emotional wrenching seems to be coming to an end when the piano picks up again and suddenly, we're launched into what many consider to be one of the greatest guitar solos ever. The marvellously ridiculous accompanying video shows Slash atop a piano, making sweet love to his guitar (not literally).

... NOTHING LASTS FOREVER. AND WE BOTH KNOW HEARTS CAN CHANGE ...

— GUNS N' ROSES

Reportedly, during shooting, Slash found himself standing near a crew member and asked him what his role was. The worker replied, "I'm the production designer, *slash* art director, *slash* prop man ..." Slash cut him off: "I'm just Slash." Epic.

Orly
Jacques Brel

Goodbyes don't get much sadder than stoic French uttered over a moody piano. At first, *Orly* (1977) seems like a simple tale of a sad parting. Jacques is at Orly airport (for the sake of romanticism, let's allow that to evoke an image of 70s chic rather than budget flights and cold paninis). The singer finds himself watching a couple as they bid each other adieu: their embrace, their gazes, their whisperings, their final separation. The list of observations, recounted with building passion, takes on a more profound meaning when we consider how close Brel was to death at the time of writing. He wrote and recorded the song when his cancer had reached a point of no return. "La vie ne fait pas de cadeau / Et nom de Dieu / C'est triste Orly le dimanche." ("Life doesn't hand out gifts / And, by God, / Orly is sad on a Sunday."). Within a year, Brel would make his own sad departure, leaving *Orly* as his farewell to the world.

Hey, That's No Way to Say Goodbye
Leonard Cohen

Oh, Leonard. Can't you just lie to her? As break-up tunes go, *Hey, That's No Way to Say Goodbye* (1967) really shouldn't be that sad. Nobody is exactly getting dumped, no wild accusations are flying across the room. Leonard and his lady have simply come to a point where they need to call it a day. The track begins with romantic nostalgia: "I loved you in the morning, our kisses deep and warm / Your hair upon the pillow like a sleepy golden storm". We then discover that this is to be the couple's final morning, with Leonard quietly explaining that their relationship has run its course. It's just the way things go. As his lover's eyes fill with tears, Leonard softly agrees that saying goodbye really shouldn't feel this tough. Leonard, do the woman a favour. Tell her you're off to join the army or to rescue chimpanzees in the Congo. Because with a song like this, she is *never* getting over you.

Gin 'n' Tears
Songs to Cry Along with While Drunk and Lonely

Lilac Wine
Nina Simone

What to do when the love of your life is no longer around? Get sozzled, obviously. (Disclaimer: the suggestion to drink excessively does not necessarily reflect the views of all medical practitioners, just the fun ones.) While younger readers may be more familiar with the Jeff Buckley version of *Lilac Wine*, he himself described Nina's 1966 rendition as the only one that matters. Her wavering voice really hits home, telling the tale of a woman who drinks sweet wine to allow herself just a flash of a joy she once knew: "When I think more than I want to think / Do things I never should do / I drink much more that I ought to drink / Because it brings me back you." Interestingly, lilac wine actually exists, made from the fermented flowers of a lilac tree. It must be pretty strong stuff. As it takes hold on our song's narrator, passions build and daydreaming turns to lament ("Where's my love?"). It all tails off to a tearful end, the singer waiting for a love that we suspect will never arrive.

One for My Baby (And One More for the Road)
Frank Sinatra

OK, now it's Frank's turn to discover that Whiskey 'n' Woe is not the sweetest cocktail. In his 1947 cover of *One for My Baby* ... (it was initially popularised by Fred Astaire), we find Frank in a bar in the wee hours, pouring his heart out to barman Joe. Frank drowns his sorrows as he recalls the memory of his ex-lady. Has Fat Tony sent her to sleep with the fishes? Intriguing a story as that would make, we can assume this was a more mundane type of break-up. Frank asks Joe to line up the drinks, two at a time, one to the memory of his ex-doll and one for the road. Perhaps the saddest moment of the song is towards the end, when the singer realises: "Joe, I know you're getting anxious to close / Thanks for the cheer / I hope you didn't mind / My bending your ear". Poor Frank: a man deserted, his only companions the booze and the bar.

A Case of You
Joni Mitchell

Who even needs alcohol for a quick buzz? Especially if, like Joni, you get all the inebriation you need from a certain special someone. Well, Joni, time for an AA meeting. In *A Case of You* (1971), that special someone is no longer around and the singer is finding it hard to kick the habit. She looks back on what they had and sees that, like a bottle of booze, her lover should have been issued with a warning label, but damn did it all taste good: "Oh, you are in my blood like holy wine / You taste so bitter and so sweet / Oh, I could drink a case of you, darling / And I would still be on my feet." Set to heart-rending guitar chords, it seems like this is one addiction that's still got the singer truly in its grip. Perhaps the Betty Ford Clinic does a special on toxic exes.

The Piano Has Been Drinking
Tom Waits

Where other singers talk about getting tipsy and forlorn, trust Tom Waits to deliver a number about getting all-out legless. In his 1976 classic, Tom sings in a boozy slur with even the piano sounding like it's being played by clumsy, drunken fingers. Guess that explains the title. As the song gets going, our plastered pianist lists muddled observations of the bar. These range from the humorous ("And the lightman's blind in one eye / And he can't see out of the other") to the more ambiguous ("And the newspapers were fooling / And the ashtrays have retired"). Might our bar crooner have been getting bad reviews in the press? Might he be singing to a near-empty house? By the end of the song, the merry clown is starting to sound a bit life-weary. Let's hope he gets some sort of applause. And let's hope the owner fixes that dodgy piano.

Formidable
Stromae

Picture the scene: the most famous popstar in the country is wandering the streets in a drunken stupor. Some onlookers ask him if he's OK; one woman guides him out of the way of an oncoming tram. A depressing number of people just record videos of him on their phones, wondering if they're capturing 2013's equivalent of Britney's head-shaving meltdown. That popstar was Stromae, the Belgian singer behind international hits *Alors On Danse* and *Papaoutai*. And that drunken walkabout in Brussels was, well, fake. The drunkenness was all an act, partly a promo for Stromae's song *Formidable*, partly a social experiment to see if people are still capable of empathy. In the track, Stromae takes on the character of a drunk man who walks the streets, recounting his formerly "formidable" life to strangers walking by: "Oh bébé – oups ! – mademoiselle ... J'suis célibataire, depuis hier putain ! / J'peux pas faire d'enfant et bon c'est pas – Eh reviens !" ("Hey babe, oops, Miss ... I've been single since yesterday, fuck! / I can't have kids but well, it's not – Hey, come back!") Oversharing? Undoubtedly. But this guy is devastated, so let's not judge too harshly. Both song and video are a reminder that, behind every slurred rambling, there's a truly sad tale yearning to get out.

There's a Tear in My Beer
Hank Williams & Hank Williams Jr.

Kick open the saloon doors and tip your hat for a cold brew, it's time to hang with some lonesome cowboys. As a true country classic, *There's a Tear ...* suggests a very Nashville way to ward off the melancholy of a love departed: by getting all tanked up. "I'm gonna keep drinkin' til I can't move a toe / And then maybe my heart won't hurt me so / There's a tear in my beer / 'Cause I'm crying for you, dear ..." Country superstar Hank Williams originally recorded the song in the 1950s but never released it and, sadly, died soon after. In 1988, a patchy copy of the recording was found, so Hank's son decided to sing the missing parts to create a duet. The accompanying video uses the (dubious) wonder of 1980s special effects to bring father and son back together. Two lonesome cowboys reunited, but in a non-*Brokeback*, family sort of way.

OH, I COULD DRINK A CASE OF YOU, DARLING. AND I WOULD STILL BE ON MY FEET.

— JONI MITCHELL

What a #$@&%!
Songs about Being a Complete and Utter Asshole

Charmless Man
Blur

"He thinks his educated airs, those family shares will protect him / That we'll respect him ... There's the model of a charmless man." Blur's 1996 hit is basically a three-and-a-half-minute eyeroll at self-importance. Singer Damon Albarn finds himself in a rather one-way conversation with some rich toff who won't stop droning on about his wealth, his private education and his VIP friends. Much debate has been provoked by the line "I think he'd like to have been Ronnie Kray / But then nature didn't make him that way." Does the moneyed man wish he was a feared gangster like Ronnie Kray? Or is the song a dig at Britpop rival Brett Anderson of Suede? Kray was rumoured to be gay, and Anderson had famously described himself as a bisexual who had never had a gay experience (many people thought he was just trying to sound cool). Was Britpop capable of such playground bickering? Of course it was!

GMF
John Grant

The G is for greatest; the rest, you can figure out yourself. John Grant begins by admitting that social niceties are not for him: "I'm usually only waiting for you to stop talking so that I can / Concerning two-way streets, I have to say that I am not a fan." The song continues with the grandiose ramblings of an egomaniac. The singer says that he wrote the 2013 track as a reflection on low self-esteem and then overcompensating for that with arrogance. Beneath the surface, the self-loathing is evident, with references to Grant's religious upbringing being at odds with his gayness (as exemplified in the rather unambiguous line, "I should not be attracted to males"). The song seems to be addressed to a partner, an infuriating *love me if you must, but you knew I was trouble*. Yes, people, John is *that* ex-boyfriend.

I'm a Man You Don't Meet Every Day
The Pogues

As with most folk songs, *I'm a Man ...* has gone through many incarnations over the decades, or even the centuries. Some consider it to be a simple Scottish-Irish drinking song about an unusually generous man: "So come fill up you glasses of brandy and wine / Whatever it costs, I will pay." The man boasts of his wealth, his land, his soldiers. The Pogues' 1985 version went darker. Sung by the group's female bassist, Cait O'Riordan, the original punks of Irish trad added in a verse where the man casually tells his fellow drinkers "I took out my dog and him I did shoot ..." Could it be that the rich man's generosity is all just an attempt to mask the fact that he's an A-grade a-hole?

Asshole
Denis Leary

No double meanings here, in what is surely the archetypical asshole song. Comedian Denis Leary released the track in 1993, offering a glimpse into the world of a thoroughly awful individual: "I drive really slow in the ultrafast lane ... I use public toilets and piss on the seat ... Sometimes I park in handicapped spaces ... I'm an asshole!" Leary's bonehead is also specifically American, guzzling cheeseburgers and then wiping his mouth with the stars and stripes. In a sign of the times, Leary updated the lyrics for a performance on *The Late Late Show* in 2016. The revised version replaced the central chorus line with "Trump's an asshole". Who ever said satire had to be subtle?

Tearjerker
Chilly Gonzales & Jarvis Cocker

If only the walls could talk. In 2016, composer Chilly teamed up with Jarvis to create *Room 29*, a collection of songs describing the imagined goings-on in suite number 29 at a classic Hollywood hotel. In *Tearjerker*, the room is not a happy place. The singer's girlfriend is waiting at an airport as he entertains another lover at the hotel. The jerk in question admits his wrongdoing, telling himself "You are a tearjerker / You don't need a girlfriend / You need a social worker." Between the sad melody and the singer's self-mockery, we almost begin to feel sorry for him. Until he tells his lover that their rendezvous needs to end by 10 a.m., so he doesn't miss the hotel breakfast. What a keeper.

It Is What it Is
Songs about Acceptance

You Can't Always Get What You Want
The Rolling Stones

A decade of excess, then the harsh light of reality. Many regard The Stones' 1969 classic as a sort of sad awakening at the end of the Swingin' Sixties. Each verse tells a story of hope thwarted: a love affair turns bitter; a political protest is quashed; Mick Jagger scores some drugs only to be reminded of their dark side. And yet, each chorus comes back to acceptance: "You can't always get what you want … But if you try sometimes / Well, you just might find / You get what you need." Though bleary-eyed and disillusioned, Mick was in the mood for learning lessons. The song was apparently an attempt by The Stones to create their own version of The Beatles' epic, orchestral *Hey Jude* from the previous year. Mick had wanted to include a full gospel choir, but (fittingly) there was none available so they ended up using the classical-based London Bach Choir instead. No complaints came from Keith Richards, who himself had been a choirboy as a youngster. Who would have thought that the angelic young Keith would grow up to be the mascara-smudged bad boy who would one day tell a journalist, "The strangest thing I've tried to snort? My father. I snorted my father." (Apparently, he mixed dad's ashes with some coke and did a quick line.)

You've Got the Love
The Source ft. Candi Staton

"Sometimes, I feel like throwing my hands up in the air / I know I can count on you … sooner or later in life, the things you love, you lose / But you've got the love I need to see me through." What is it about The Source's classic that makes acquiescence sound so uplifting? In blissful soul, Candi Staton lays out some inescapable facts of life: food, friends and patience will all run out. So if we're going to get through, we need to dig deeper. Perhaps we need to find God; perhaps we need to go beyond attachment to all things. Quite profound for a happy-house track. It seems the public were on board though, particularly in the UK where mixes of the song entered the charts in 1991, 1996 and 2006. The song began life back in the mid-80s, when Candi recorded it as a soul-gospel track to accompany a documentary film about the slimming efforts of the world's fattest man. Several years later, Candi struggled to recall the track when she got a phonecall to tell her that a dance mix of it had entered the UK charts. But she soon remembered, especially as the royalties flooded in. Love is all you need, but some dosh doesn't go astray.

I'VE LOOKED AT CLOUDS FROM BOTH SIDES NOW.

— JONI MITCHELL

Both Sides Now
Joni Mitchell

In the mid-60s, Joni Mitchell was on a flight reading the novel *Henderson the Rain King*. She got to the line, "We are the first generation to see clouds from both sides. What a privilege!", and she gazed out the airplane window. Thoughts started to bubble about how the wispy, dreamy clouds out there were the same things that brought rain and storms. Joni had an idea for a lyric: "I've looked at clouds from both sides now / From up and down, and still somehow / It's cloud illusions I recall / I really don't know clouds at all." In later verses, this reflection is applied to love, and finally to life. Written in her early 20s, the song seems to be Joni's growing acceptance that love and life (and clouds) all contain some good and some bad. And then there's all that messy in-between stuff that we'd rather not think about, our memories preferring to cling to illusions. The public lapped up Joni's verses, contrasting love with heartache, immense success with old friends turned bitter. The song went on the become one of her most beloved. In an age of Twitter rants and polarised politics, perhaps it's time for a re-release of Joni's reflection on humble not knowing.

No Easy Way Down
Dusty Springfield

In typically velvety style, Dusty begins *No Easy Way Down* (1969) with a simple anecdote. A child has been excitedly watching a balloon soaring through the sky, but is now feeling tearful as the balloon descends towards the ground.

Most child psychologists would recommend solving this situation by screeching, "Suck it up, weener!", but should we really be listening to the advice of underage therapists? Dusty takes a more enlightened route. She tells the child that, quite simply, what goes up must come down. As the sumptuous orchestra pushes her on, Dusty gets more reflective. She recalls the giddy heights of a past love, but also the subsequent cost: "We all like to climb to the heights of love / Where our fantasy world can be found / But you must know in the end / When it's time to descend / That there is no easy way down." For mournful Dusty, we need to accept that we basically all end up alone, a fact as inevitable as gravity. Sheesh. Suddenly the "weener" comment seems positively mushy!

Feelin' Frisky
Songs about Being Horny

Sexual Healing
Marvin Gaye

Possibly the most famous "sexy time" song of all time, *Sexual Healing* (1982) was also a comeback for Marvin, who had temporarily retired to Ostend (Belgium) to get away from a recent divorce, a nasty cocaine habit and financial difficulties. Far from wallowing in his woes while ruminating on a soggy *moules-frites*, the Motown star's mind was clearly on issues of a steamier nature. Perhaps Marvin's Belgian break included a vow of chastity, because the resulting lyrics pointed to a man truly on the edge: "Ba-aby, I'm hot just like an oven / I need some lovin' / And ba-aby, I can't hold it much longer / It's getting stronger and stronger ..." After a few months, Marvin returned to the States packin' a seven-inch that was about ready to explode (the song, obviously). *Sexual Healing* would go on to become the biggest hit of his career. If you really turn up the volume in the song's final fade-out, you'll hear Marvin plead to his lover, "Please don't procrastinate, it's not good to masturbate." Most readers will probably agree that the latter part of that message is (a) shocking, and (b) hopefully untrue.

Horny
Mousse T

Released in 1998, *Horny* marked a watershed in pop music, a moment when we as a people collectively agreed that it would be fun for us all to spend some time together in the gutter. "You got me horny in the morning and you kno-o-ow / I try to call you but I can't find the telephone / I sent a message through the Internet but it rejected / I wrote a letter and I sent it with the po-o-ost". Originally penned by Bob Dylan (not really), the song tells a tale of a lady who is simply ravenous. Actually, the lyrics were sung by three ladies: Birmingham duo Hot 'n' Juicy on the verse; New York vocalist Inaya Day on the chorus. Love it or hate it, a commentary on libido has rarely been so mainstream.

Perhaps it got by radio watchdogs because of the startling number of simpletons who thought the chorus was "Honey, honey, honey".

Push It
Salt-n-Pepa

Salt-n-Pepa have claimed that their 1987 smash is in fact not sexual. It is a simple rap number about dancing with a gentleman friend: "... you come here, give me a kiss / Better make it fast or else I'm gonna get pissed / Can't you hear the music's pumpin' hard like I wish you would? / Now push it / Push it good". The lyrics never elaborate on the "it" which these ladies are so willing to be pushed, or indeed pumped. But let's take it as a reference to the man's fetching personality. In the UK, the song initially had mediocre sales, not truly taking off until after a performance at Wembley as part of a show for Nelson Mandela's 70th birthday. Did *Madiba* himself, who reportedly saw a video of the show from his prison cell, appreciate Salt-n-Pepa's instruction to "get up on this"? Perhaps he did.

I'm on Fire
Bruce Springsteen

"Hey, little girl, is your daddy home? / Did he go away and leave you all alone? / I got a bad desire / Oh, oh, oh, I'm on fire." Hey, Bruce: 1985 just phoned to tell you that poetic licence died in the late 90s. These days, talking about girls and their daddies is a recipe for disaster. But anyway, we get it that Bruce is singing to a very *adult*, very *married* woman who he's got the hots for. Oh, the forbidden fruit. Apparently, Bruce wrote the music for *I'm on Fire* as a nod to the simple, country strumming of Johnny Cash. You might expect a moody, Johnny-inspired number to deal with something like God or death. Well, Bruce took us all by surprise and instead told a tale of waking up with his loins simply aflame after a dream about a lady who's off limits. And somehow, he makes it all sound genuinely classy. In the song's video, Bruce plays a mechanic who needs to fix the car of an admiring rich lady. Unfortunately, we don't actually get to see greased-up Bruce tightening those nuts or cranking that shaft (might he also have muffled the backbox?), but the car is soon running like a dream. Lucky lady.

Relax
Frankie Goes to Hollywood

There are some songs that, with hindsight, seem so blatantly sexual that it's hard to imagine the public ever believed the lyrics to be about anything else. *Relax*, however, is not such a song. For you see, *Relax* (1983) was only ever about sex. With Holly Johnson's opening wail ("Mi-i-ine!") thoughts may turn to the neighbour's cat yowling at the moon for some other feline to come along and scratch this most unholy itch. Well, Holly himself must be red raw, as his wailing turns to grunts, sighs and the repeated instruction: "Relax, don't do it / When you want to go to it / Relax, don't do it / When you want to come." Ok, it's all a bit ambiguous, but we get the idea, especially as the track devolves into shrieks of "I'm coming!" (or for elderly listeners who might be hard-of-hearing, the eventual, simplified "*Come!*"). Oh, and just in case anybody was still not picking up on the intricacies, the record label accompanied the song's release with some equally demure ads in the press. They featured the band members decked out in leather vests, rubber gloves and sailor caps, along with the slogan "ALL THE NICE BOYS LOVE SEA MEN". Again, we can assume that the use of capital letters was to appeal to elderly, short-sighted fans.

If I Was Your Girlfriend
Prince

Of all Prince's many, many (many!) horned-up songs, *If I Was Your Girlfriend* offers perhaps the most unique perspective. Prince envisions that he could swap places with his lover's best female friend. He imagines the closeness to his lover that this would grant him: the secrets she'd tell him; the emotions she'd share. So far, so vanilla. But this is Prince, and the King of Kink is not one to disappoint. Thoughts of being his lover's lady friend soon turn friskier, and suddenly he is fantasising about washing her hair, tickling her, giving her a bath. By the end of the song, Prince has worked himself into a bawdy mess: "And would you, would you let me kiss you there? / You know down there where it counts?" Did nobody ever tell Prince that he may have held a slightly skewed view on the nature of female friendships?

Ladies (and Gentlemen) of the Night
Songs about Prostitution

Just a Gigolo
Bing Crosby

The world's oldest profession must have enjoyed quite a boom during the Roaring 20s, when this song was first written. *Just a Gigolo* originated as an Austrian poem about a former hussar who recalls his glory days during World War I, in contrast with his current life as a downtrodden gigolo. The poem was turned into a song in German, then in Italian. In 1931, Bing recorded an English-language version which included a new opening verse that reset the action of the song in a Paris café. Perhaps label executives thought France would be a more suitable setting for a scandalous tale of a working gentleman. Of course, it could be argued that the word "gigolo" might innocently refer to a hired dancer. But the song's lyrics (at least in Bing's version) make the sexual references surprisingly clear: "… as he strolls by ladies hear him say / 'If you admire me, hire me' … Just a gigolo … Paid for every dance / Selling each romance …" Ooh, monsieur!

Basket Case
Green Day

Feeling anxious? If so, *Basket Case* is either the worst or the best track that you could listen to, depending on your levels of recklessness. Green Day's 1994 punk anthem is one white-knuckled ride. Leadman Billie Joe Armstrong sings about his neuroses pushing him to breaking point, all as he tries to sort himself out: "I went to a shrink / To analyse my dreams / She says it's lack of sex that's bringing me down / I went to a whore / He said my life's a bore …" Upon the song's release, there was much discussion about pronouns. Billie set the record straight in 1995 when he came out as bisexual. He says that he decided to make the song's prostitute male as a challenge both to himself and to the listeners. A brave thing to do in the mid-90s.

Gender aside, the working guy in question doesn't seem to have much time for Billie's hysterical ramblings. Let's hope the poor fellow has never had to sit through a full Green Day album.

Roxanne
The Police

It's a story as old as time itself: boy meets girl, girl happens to be a sex worker, boy falls in love and gets wildly jealous about the fact that his girlfriend is a sex worker.
It's surprising Disney hasn't touched on this one yet. In this 1978 Police classic, Sting sings to Roxanne, a character in a similar vein to *La Traviata*'s Violetta (or *Pretty Woman*'s Vivian, if your cultural references are largely based around Julia Roberts movies, which is a perfectly valid way to live). "Roxanne / You don't have to wear that dress tonight / Walk the streets for money … I won't share you with another boy". Sting is in love, but in the charmingly judgemental sort of way. A few seconds into the track, you can clearly hear an odd piano sound and laughter. Apparently, that was Sting accidentally sitting on the piano keys in the recording studio. Oh, the tomfoolery! But worry not, the singer quickly recomposes himself and gets down to the urgent business of telling his beloved that she a ho.

ROXANNE. YOU DON'T HAVE TO WEAR THAT DRESS TONIGHT.

— THE POLICE

Queer
Garbage

Dust off grandma's nipple clamps and break out the family ball gag, Shirley Manson is here to whip the whole household into shape. In *Queer* (1995), the Garbage singer takes on the role of paid dominatrix. The band say the track was inspired by a novel called *Brotherly Love*, in which a father takes his son to a female prostitute so that she can "make him a man". No pressure here, kid. In *Queer*, the son is clearly not into it but the singer is not taking no for an answer (this was before Twitter invented *#ConsentIsSexy*): "This is what he pays me for / I'll show you how it's done / You'll learn to love the pain you feel / Like father like son". The song's chorus is a list of venomous insults spat at the boy, calling him queer, strange, lame, dumb. We never learn if Shirley's titillating seduction technique pays off. Perhaps not?

Private Dancer
Tina Turner

"All the men come in these places / And the men are all the same ... You keep your mind on the money / Keeping your eyes on the wall." Written by famed guitarist Mark Knopfler, Tina Turner claimed that she was shocked to discover that the song could be interpreted as a nod to prostitution. Really, Tina? A savvy soul superstar at the top of her game didn't realise that this very *private* dancer might have been a female escort, or at least a stripper? Perhaps Tina was just playing coy to appease the more conservative side of her fanbase. In recording, Knopfler didn't actually play guitar, the job instead going to fellow Brit Jeff Beck. Years later, Knopfler criticised the producers "drafting in Jeff Beck to play the world's second ugliest guitar solo." Ooohh. Guitar Legends: Face/ Off. Mark's bitchy comment also begs the question of which solo he thinks is the absolute worst. Another Jeff Beck number, perhaps?

Hey, Big Spender!
Songs about Rich People

Big Spender
Shirley Bassey

Shirley's 1967 hit is a love song in its purest form. That is, to a man's bulging wallet. *Big Spender* was originally written for the 1966 Broadway musical *Sweet Charity*, which told the story of a New York dancer named Charity. Her particular line of work was as an escort at a downtown ballroom, where she competed with other dancing ladies for the affections of the male clientele. Forget demure glances, Charity approached her potential clients with a sales pitch that was a little more direct: "So, let me get right to the point / I don't pop my cork for every man I see / Hey, big spender! / Spend a little time with me". With booming brass and a soaring finale, who better to take the song to the airwaves than Ms. Bassey herself? The public lapped up Shirley's saucy propositioning of a wealthy fellow, and the track quickly became one of her signature songs. She even sang it at a performance for Prince Philip's 80th birthday party back in 2001. No doubt Philip had previously been advised that the evening would include a song about female escorts, and had practised his look of bewilderment accordingly.

Killer Queen
Queen

As a man who certainly didn't beat around the bush, Freddie Mercury was really quite direct when it came to explaining *Killer Queen* (1974): "It's about a high-class call girl. I'm trying to say that classy people can be whores as well." Well alrighty, then. And what a firecracker this posh lady-of-the-night seems to be: "She's a Killer Queen / Gunpowder, gelatine / Dynamite with a laser beam / Guaranteed to blow your mind." Oh, is there anything this dame won't blow?! As for the slightly confusing mention of gelatine, apparently it can be mixed with gunpowder to make a sort of bomb. This explosive lady's clientele includes only the most A-list of womanisers ("Khrushchev and Kennedy"), ensuring she never runs dry on the Moët. Did the general public of the mid-70s realise that Queen's breakout hit was all about a high-end hooker? Maybe not. But with those camp harmonies and Freddie's vaudeville-style delivery, who could resist?

Money
Pink Floyd

Label executives must have a special facial expression reserved for when an established rock band suggest a new track about money. A kind of frozen smile, transmitting encouragement while internally shrieking at the notion of how to sell this to the squalid masses. Rockstars tend to be filthy rich; the public don't. Except in Luxembourg. In *Money* (1973), Pink Floyd let loose on the awfulness of rich people (a demographic the band had surely already joined by then). Maybe we could take it all as a sort of insiders' exposé. And guess what? You'd never have imagined but the 1% really *are* a bunch of greedy hogs: "Money, it's a hit / Don't give me that do-goody-good bullshit / I'm in the high-fidelity first-class travelling set / And I think I need a Lear jet." The song is instantly recognisable with its distinctive percussion of clinking coins and dinging cash registers. These days, such sound effects and lyrical content would be reserved for the likes of Drake and Kanye. Wait, does this mean that Pink Floyd are *street*?! Whatever next? Roger Waters in a pair of Timberlands?

> *MONEY, IT'S A HIT. DON'T GIVE ME THAT DO-GOODY-GOOD BULLSHIT.*
> — PINK FLOYD

Gold Digger
Kanye West ft. Jamie Foxx

Speaking of Kanye, no list about rich folk would be complete without at least a mention of the most humble man in hip-hop. Yes, that is sarcasm, and yes, *Gold Digger* (2005) is about exactly what you assumed it was about. Never one to downplay his dough, Kanye spells out the difficulties of trying to meet a girl who's not just looking to cash in. Feminists be damned, the rap's central verse tells the tale of Kanye's pal, duped by some chick into paying child support: "18 years, 18 years / She got one of your kids, got you for 18 years ... And on the 18th birthday, he found out it wasn't his?" When it first came on the radio, we should really all have tuned out and decided to have nothing more to do with this misogynistic upstart Mr. West. But that beat! Oh, screw morals! Suddenly, listeners around the world were head bopping and grinding, jabbering along: "Now, I ain't sayin' she a gold digger / But she ain't messin' with no broke niggas." Granted, most white people didn't actually utter the final word of that line, preferring instead to awkwardly look at the floor while shuffling arrhythmically. And modest Kanye, whose tiny ego was so in need of a boost, claimed his throne as the King of Rap.

Johnny and Mary
Robert Palmer

"Johnny's always running around / Trying to find certainty ..." Robert Palmer's electro classic from 1980 is undeniably ambiguous, but the basic idea seems clear: Johnny and Mary are a couple and they're not very happy, perhaps because of Johnny's philandering. And then there's the money. The couple seem to be suffering from a type of middle-class malaise ("Johnny thinks the world would be right / If it could buy truth from him"; he also promises Mary that they will move house when he "earns time", not money). Oh, the ennui of comfort, and other such First World problems. Johnny seeks significance with other ladies, Mary shrugs and figures a wayward husband is what she signed up for. Fans have often debated the inspiration behind the characters. Could Johnny be Palmer himself, who had already had a taste of success at the time of writing? Could it be a song about a politician and his trophy wife? Or could it even be about Adolf Hitler and Eva Braun, as the video might subtly suggest?

Making Ends Meet
Songs about Being Broke

Town Called Malice
The Jam

In 1982, there wasn't much to be happy about for working-class Brits. Unemployment was soaring, strikes were frequent, an uncompromising Margaret Thatcher was at the helm. Paul Weller says he wrote *Town Called Malice* about his hometown of Woking, on the outskirts of London. The town's decimated state seemed emblematic of a country struggling to adapt to modern ways. "Rows and rows of disused milk floats / Stand dying in the dairy yard": in an age of supermarkets, what role now for the formerly jolly milkman delivering bottles to doorsteps? Weller's town is a place of loneliness and struggle, where cash-strapped parents consider "To either cut down on beer or the kids' new gear / It's a big decision in a town called Malice ..." But it's not all doom and gloom. The lyrics remind the listener that change is in our own hands. Perhaps that's why the general feel of the song is so upbeat, with bassist Bruce Foxton admitting that his bassline bears more than a passing resemblance to Motown smash *You Can't Hurry Love*. Of course, it wasn't unusual for The Jam to get into matters of workers' rights and social justice. In 2008, Conservative Party leader David Cameron named The Jam's hit *The Eton Rifles* as one of his favourite songs, prompting a gobsmacked Paul Weller to publicly wonder, "Which part of it didn't he get?"

The Message
Grandmaster Flash & The Furious Five

"Don't push me 'cause I'm close to the edge / I'm tryin' not to lose my head." In the decades following the release of *The Message* (1982), its classic *Don't. Push. Me ...* line has been embraced by popular culture as a mantra for times of duress. It's become the kind of thing a kind-hearted schoolteacher might mutter to herself on an afternoon of particularly restless students, as she breathes deeply and envisions the cool bottle of Pinot

Grigio in the fridge back home. Listening to the full track though, it's clear that its subject matter is anything but trivial. As one of the first hip-hop tracks to focus on the less glamourous aspects of ghetto life, it doesn't hold back on the dark reality of inner-city poverty. The rap describes various desperate characters: a woman forced into prostitution; a man who has stolen from his mom; a kid who turns to crime, ends up in jail, gets raped and is eventually found hanging in his cell. Far from dreams of Cristal and Bentleys, the track describes the knife-edge of poverty in a society which offers no hope. In 2002, the track was selected to be added to the US Library of Congress, alongside other culturally significant recordings such as Orson Welles' *War of the Worlds* and Martin Luther King's *I Have a Dream* speech.

Money for Nothing
Dire Straits

In the early 80s, Mark Knopfler found himself in an appliance store which had a wall of televisions, all tuned to MTV. He spotted a store worker watching those videos of leather-clad rock gods with a sort of begrudging respect. The worker reflected out loud on how much money those stars must be earning without having to lift a finger. Knopfler got an idea. And thus was born the 1985 classic that would provide one of rock's most famous guitar riffs: "Now look at them yo-yo's, that's the way you do it / You play the guitar on the MTV / That ain't workin' that's the way you do it / Money for nothin' and chicks for free." Slightly offensive that the song's only reference to women was as a commodity, but then again, our narrator is hardly an enlightened one. Equally questionable is the song's second verse: "That little faggot got his own jet airplane / That little faggot, he's a millionaire". Those lines led to the verse being cut in most radio edits. Keen listeners will notice a familiar voice throughout the track. Dire Straits were in the process of recording it on Montserrat when along came Sting, who happened to be there on a windsurfing holiday (Sting gonna Sting). At the band's request, he sang the track's famous line "I want my MTV". Even keener listeners will notice that the line uses the melody of Sting's 1980 hit *Don't Stand So Close to Me*.

I Need a Dollar
Aloe Blacc

There's nothing like a recession to send songs about money issues soaring to the top of the charts. In 2010, the global financial crisis was in full swing, *austerity* was the buzzword of the day and companies were downsizing willy-nilly. Joblessness was something Aloe Blacc understood well, having been laid off from his job as a consultant in the early 2000s. Of course, such an event would send most of us into a frenzied job search, "liking" disgustingly motivational videos posted by people we hate on LinkedIn. But not Aloe. He took a deep breath and focused on what he loved most: making music. One of the results was *I Need a Dollar*, an old-style bluesy number inspired by the songs of the chain gang. The lyrics portray a man down on his luck: "I had a job but the boss man let me go / He said / I'm sorry but I won't be needing your help no more". As the song progresses, we understand the extent of the man's desperation, his only friends the whiskey and the wine. Around the world (though not, weirdly, in Aloe's native US) the track clearly struck a chord with hard-up radio listeners, and it became a huge hit. These days, Aloe Blacc doesn't even *have* a LinkedIn profile. Surely there is no greater measure of success.

Money's Too Tight to Mention
Simply Red

The 80s were certainly a boom time for songs about not having a pot to piss in. *Money's Too Tight ...* was originally a minor hit for US group The Valentines, who released it in 1982. Three years later, Simply Red did their own version and the song became a bonafide global smash, quite a feat for the UK group's first single. The tale is a familiar one: "I've been laid off from work / My rent is due / My kids all need / Brand new shoes". The singer seeks help from his bank and his family, but neither can ease his woes. He goes on to reflect on the politics behind his problems, pointing the finger at the free-market ideas of Reaganomics. Who knew that this catchy pop number included a critique of fiscal policies? But never fear, as the song fades, singer Mick Hucknall takes us back to more relatable ground: "I'm talkin' 'bout money, money ... I'm talkin' 'bout Ronnie, Ronnie ... Did the earth move for you, Nancy?" Presumably we are being asked to imagine the former First Couple discussing their hoarded riches as they lay in bed in post-coital bliss. Shudder.

Ever the Optimist
Songs about Maintaining Hope

We'll meet again
Vera Lynn

"We'll meet again / Don't know where / Don't know when / But I know we'll meet again some sunny day."
The year was 1939 and Brits were, understandably, embracing their inner stoicism. The war was beginning, the Nazis looked near-undefeatable, and Vera Lynn's song was filling the airwaves. Goodness knows how many stiff upper lips were tested to breaking point as soldiers waved their loved ones goodbye to the tune of Vera's deeply sad lyrics reminding everybody to keep smiling until "the dark clouds" were driven away. Of course, the song has gone down in history as one of the UK's most beloved. During the Cold War tensions of later years, it was part of a secret selection of recordings which were to be played from the bunkers in the days following a nuclear attack in Britain, as a means of boosting public morale. The UK government have neither confirmed nor denied whether any Cher tracks made it onto the same selection.

I Won't Back Down
Tom Petty

One Sunday morning in 1987, Tom Petty was having breakfast with his wife and daughter at his home in LA. Suddenly, they smelled smoke and fled the house. Tests later showed that a mystery arsonist had doused an outer staircase and set it alight. The house was destroyed. Soon after, Tom started work on his first solo album, with the fire as a major influence. In 1989, *I Won't Back Down* was released as the lead single. Its message of resilience was as simple as it gets: "... I'll stand my ground / Won't be turned around / And I'll keep this world from draggin' me down ... And I won't back down". Tom was shocked by the power of his track, saying that he'd even heard it had brought a girl out of a coma. The mantra of the chorus became especially pervasive after September 11th, 2001, when the track was revived by radio stations across the US. On a lighter note, Tom had a horrible cold on the day he recorded the track. George Harrison, who was in the studio to provide guitar and backing vocals, boiled some ginger and made Tom stick his head into the pot to inhale the steam. It seems it worked. Not a blocked nostril in earshot.

Move On Up
Curtis Mayfield

If ever there has been a track to make you want to do the conga for a full nine minutes, it's *Move On Up* (1970). The song's manic bongo and brass fanfare provide the perfect accompaniment to its uplifting message to just keep going: "Hush now, child / And don't you cry / Your folks might understand you / By and by / Just move on up ..." Parents and other people may not be on your side right now, but they'll come round. At the time, Chicago-native Curtis was better known for songs related to the Civil Rights movement, such as *People Get Ready*, recorded with The Impressions. In *Move On Up*, however, the message seems to be a more general call for optimism, despite it all. Interestingly, the song failed to chart in the US, but became a huge hit in the UK. Perhaps the Brits are more appreciative of a particularly lengthy conga (which enlightened people may refer to as an *ana*-conga).

Survivor
Destiny's Child

Ok, *Survivor* may not be the most subtle anthem about overcoming adversity. But an anthem, it is. Co-written by Beyoncé, the 2001 track is thought to be a sassy riposte to former members of Destiny's Child. Under the stern control of – umm – Beyoncé's dad, the girl group went through various line-ups. Three girls got kicked out before settling on the final Beyoncé-Kelly-Michelle combo which would take over the world. The ditched members were clearly far from well-wishing, so Beyoncé told it

to them straight: "You thought that I'd be stressed without you, but I'm chillin' / You thought I wouldn't sell without you, sold nine million / I'm a survivor ..." The song, like its video, was a play on the reality TV show of the same name, in which cast members were eliminated every week. Upon the song's release, the former members came out ready for battle and sued for defamation. But never fear, the lyrics remind us that Beyoncé and co will never stoop to the level of their enemies, with lines such as: "I'm not gon' compromise my Christianity". Such compromises were reserved for later tracks in the album, like *Nasty Girl*, a scathing put-down of some stank ho.

> *... I'LL KEEP THIS WORLD FROM DRAGGIN' ME DOWN ... AND I WON'T BACK DOWN.*
>
> — TOM PETTY

Don't Give Up
Peter Gabriel ft. Kate Bush

Pop music often treats the theme of perseverance with swagger and hand-on-hip (here's looking at you, Christina Aguilera). Peter Gabriel decided to go the other way. *Don't Give Up* (1986) is a moving tale about a man who has lost his job in Thatcher's recession-plagued Britain. With no clear place in the world, he travels back to his hometown and to his caring family. It seems to be the man's loved ones who speak to him in the song's chorus, with iconic vocals provided by Kate Bush: "Don't give up 'cause you have friends / Don't give up, you're not beaten yet ..." Peter wrote the song after seeing photos of America's Dust Bowl, which reminded him of run-down areas of the UK. Given that the inspiration for the song had its origins in the southern US, Peter initially asked Dolly Parton to sing the chorus. Unfortunately, Dolly was too busy. Perhaps she had a nip and tuck scheduled. That's not a dig, by the way. In Dolly's own immortal words: "It takes a lot of money to look this cheap."

Throwing in the Towel
Songs about Giving Up Hope

Goodbye to Love
The Carpenters

Ah, The Carpenters. Melodies breezy enough to accompany a deodorant commercial; lyrics dark enough to make Nine Inch Nails seem like Disney Mouseketeers. *Goodbye to Love* (1972) is really about as bleak as it gets. Amid dreamy strings and piano, Karen Carpenter has decided to throw in the towel: “I'll say goodbye to love / No-one ever cared if I should live or die / Time and time again the chance for love has passed me by / And all I know of love is how to live without it …” Of course, the lyrics took on an even sadder edge after Karen's death from anorexia-related complications in 1983. Newspapers reported that, after a brief and unhappy marriage, Karen had been due to sign divorce papers on the day she died. Musically, *Goodbye to Love* caused a stir when it was first released because of the soaring guitar solo that closes the song. Various easy-listening stations refused to play the track and some fans sent hate mail, criticising the group's venture into “hard rock”. It's interesting that people were more offended by some fuzz guitar rather than the jump-off-a-cliff lyrics.

Love Is a Losing Game
Amy Winehouse

There are break-ups that sting, and then there are ones that shatter your belief in humanity. Amy wrote much of her hit album (*Back to Black*) after her boyfriend Blake abandoned her for a previous girlfriend. Blake and Amy would later go on to get married, but this was still unknown to the devastated Amy who wrote *Love Is a Losing Game* (2007). The song is a tearful, sombre reflection on what on earth the point is in ever putting your heart on the line: “Over futile odds / And laughed at by the gods … Love is a losing game”. As with the rest of the album, this song was produced by industry guru Mark Ronson. He says that … *Losing Game* was the first track that he mixed for it, so he was nervous when he first played his edit back to

OVER FUTILE ODDS. AND LAUGHED AT BY THE GODS …

— AMY WINEHOUSE

Amy. She listened intently for the full three minutes. When it ended, she walked over to Ronson, put her arms around him and said, "'I love it ... Just take that fucking harp out, it sounds like some Mariah Carey shit."

Piece of My Heart
Big Brother and the Holding Company (with Janis Joplin)

From Janis's opening shrieks on this track ("Come on! Come on! Come on!"), you know the lady is not messing around. *Piece of My Heart* (1968) may be a song about resignation, but certainly not of the meek-and-mild kind. Janis has given up on the idea of her beau ever turning good, but rather than ditching him, she embraces her inner masochist: "... each time I tell myself that I, well I think I've had enough / But I'm gonna, gonna show you baby, that a woman can be tough ... Take another little piece of my heart now, baby." The classic song was originally a hit for soul singer Erma Franklin (Aretha's sister) the previous year. When Janis got her hands on it, she went for a much rawer sound and more bluesy ad lib, to the point where Franklin claimed she didn't even recognise it when she first heard it on the radio. The song's in-your-face message seemed suited to scraggly-haired Janis, the child-of-nature who clearly did not give a rat's ass what people thought of her. Janis's version became an even bigger hit than the original, and her signature tune, both before and after her death in 1970.

Lost Cause
Beck

While Beck is often thought of as the King of Quirk, his 2002 album *Sea Change* kept things low-key. He had split up with his girlfriend of nine years and wrote most of the album in the week following the break-up. *Lost Cause* became the lead single. We find Beck in gloomy form, torn but despondent over the girlfriend who seems to have cheated on him: "Your sorry eyes cut through the bone / They make it hard to leave you alone ... Baby you're a lost cause." From the singer's perspective, the woman he loves has revealed herself to be a narcissist whose love is purely selfish. And so, the song is a reluctant shrug, a sad acceptance that it's time to give up. Poor ol' Beck. The good news is that, a few years later, he married another woman and started a family. Bizarrely, Beck's mom used to work as a midwife and actually delivered the baby girl who would go on to become her daughter-in-law!

Fast Car
Tracy Chapman

Since its original release in 1988, *Fast Car* has become a staple on commercial radio. Sandwiched in between Britney bangers and Bieber ballads, it's easy to almost miss Tracy's profound tale of stuckness. The simple folk-rock number lays out a story about a young woman whose life is pretty miserable. Her mom has walked out, her dad is an alcoholic, she works a crummy job just to make ends meet. The only joy in her life is a man with a fast car, who grants her one fleeting glimpse of escape as they speed through the city: "I, I had a feeling that I belonged / I, I had a feeling I could be someone ..." Eventually, the two indeed use the car to move away. But the woman soon finds herself raising babies and paying bills, while the man drinks in bars. Is it all a poignant glance at a woman doomed to repeat the same mistakes? Or does the woman end up empowered by freeing herself from her loser boyfriend and her impossible dreams? Let's hope it's the latter, but the sorrowful guitar suggests that this is no fairytale.

The Bright Lights
Songs about Cities

Budapest
George Ezra

Songs become hits for a whole range of factors, often including a strong element of randomness. In 2013, at just 20 years old, relatively unknown British singer George Ezra released *Budapest* as a free promo track for his EP. In Italy, where the singer had never even visited, radio stations latched onto the song and it quickly became a favourite with listeners. From there, the song caught on and began to top the charts around the world. It only ever made it to number 19 in Hungary though. Could it be because the song has basically nothing to do with Budapest? George says that the track is about things he doesn't have and a place where he has never been: "My house in Budapest / My hidden treasure chest / Golden grand piano / My beautiful Castillo". He reasons that even if he had these things, he would trade them all to be with his love. Oh, the follies of youth!

Nantes
Beirut

Some people collect stamps, others are into sniffing glue. What floats Zach Condon's boat is cities, and particularly their names. Guess that's why he called his group Beirut. Many of the American band's songs take their titles from cities, and *Nantes* is obviously no exception. The track appears on the 2007 album *The Flying Club Cup*, in which each song aims to capture the feel of a different French city. Well, judging by the music and the lyrics, Nantes comes across as the kind of place you might hang out if you're in the mood for pensive gazing at the sea while some distant, jaunty accordion melody floats through the air. The lyrics are ambiguous, but it seems like Zach is reflecting on lost joy: "Well it's been a long time, long time now / Since I've seen you smile ..." A slow-burning, subtle song, the chorus is almost a proud declaration of a lack of drama: "Nobody raise your voices / Just another night in Nantes." Sounds like the perfect holiday destination for introverts with a penchant for a sea breeze (which, really, is all introverts).

New York State of Mind
Billy Joel

Billy Joel's love song to New York may not have the pizazz of Sinatra's, or the swagger of Jay-Z's, but it is filled to the brim with what Billy does best: pure heart. After a few years living in LA, he wrote this song about heading back home: "It was so easy living day by day / Out of touch with the rhythm and blues / But now I need a little give and take / The New York Times, the Daily News". One line in the song refers to travelling on a Greyhound bus along the banks of the Hudson. Billy says that it was in those exact circumstances when he first got the inspiration for the song. Although the track was never released as a single, it has become a classic through memorable live performances, including by other NY legends like Tony Bennett and Barbara Streisand. Who needs a platinum disc when you've already got a nod from Babs herself?

One Night in Bangkok
Murray Head

Ah, the 80s. A heady mix of funky strumming, soft electro, camp harmonies, offensive lyrics. And *One Night in Bangkok* has them all! This 1984 track is from the musical *Chess*, a tale of two rival grandmasters. One of these players raps about Bangkok, which is playing host to a tournament. He doesn't sound too impressed, complaining about the pollution, the tourists, the city's lack of culture for highbrow intellectuals like himself. If you haven't gathered by now, the song's narrator is basically a total cock, taking every chance to explain his superiority to the locals: "I'd let you watch, I would invite you / But the queens we use would not excite you." The rapped verses are juxtaposed with a chorus line that reminds the narrator that perhaps the true delights of Bangkok are little more ... visceral. And with no shortage of innuendo: "Tea, girls, warm and sweet / Some are set up in the Somerset Maugham suite ... One night in Bangkok makes a hard man humble ..." The whole thing was a bit much for Thai authorities, who banned the song in 1985.

Vesoul
Jacques Brel

Jacques Brel might not be very well known to non-Francophone readers. Basically, he was kind of like the Belgian Bob Dylan, but perhaps with a keener sense of the ridiculous. Equally unfamiliar may be Vesoul, a small city in eastern France. While this old medieval town has many attractions, its main claim is as the inspiration behind Brel's 1968 classic, music's most manic waltz. Not that the song tells us much about Vesoul itself. Rather, the verses are a storming rant from Jacques to his really-quite-unreasonable girlfriend who demands he take her to see Vesoul, Hamburg, Antwerp, Paris. At each destination, the lady bores easily and asks to leave, causing Jacques to snap: "Mais je te le dis / Je n'irai pas plus loin. / Mais je te préviens / Le voyage est fini!" ("But I'm telling you / I won't go any further. / But I'm warning you / This holiday is over!") Yes, Jacques has reached that moment in a couple's holiday when deep breaths no longer suffice and it is time, nay, *beyond* time to release a fiery tirade of grievances. Let it out, Jacques. Who ever would have thought that holiday rage could sound this pretty?

Walking in Memphis
Marc Cohn

In 1986, five years before this track would make it big, Marc Cohn was struggling. At 28 years old, he had come to the realisation that he "didn't have any great songs yet". What do you do when faced with an early mid-life? Go to Memphis, obviously. It turned out to be a good decision. What he found there was a type of awakening, and inspiration for the song that would make his career. He saw the statue of Blues legend W.C. Handy, he visited Graceland, he went to hear the Reverend Al Green preach. He had a sense of walking on air, with the line "walking with my feet ten feet off of Beale" referring to Beale Street, the home of Memphis Blues bars. One night, he went to see an elderly singer named Muriel performing at a café. She invited Marc, who is Jewish, on stage to sing gospel songs. That's what led to the song's standout line: "... she said, 'Tell me are you a Christian, child?' / And I said, 'Ma'am I am tonight!'" Is there a person alive who hasn't belted out that line, finger in the air, during a particularly zealous karaoke session? That mid-90s Cher cover version has a lot to answer for ...

TELL ME ARE YOU A CHRISTIAN, CHILD? AND I SAID, 'MA'AM I AM TONIGHT!'

— MARC COHN

Waving the Flag
Songs about Countries

The Last Living Rose
PJ Harvey

"Goddamn Europeans! / Take me back to beautiful England / And the grey, damp filthiness of ages ..." Recorded in 2010, the opening lines of this track now seem oddly prescient of Brexit Britain. We find PJ playing the role of firm patriot to her native land. She gushes about its rolling fog, its noble history, its foul alleyways, its minor issue of mass alcoholism. OK, so the tribute may be just a little tongue-in-cheek. And yet, we get the sense of a love-hate relationship between PJ and the *Land of the Rose* (as her homeland is sometimes nicknamed). The gorgeous glistening sunset on the Thames only serves to remind her of gold "hastily sold for nothing". Some suggest that line refers to the UK government's decision to sell its gold reserves at a very cheap price in the early 2000s. By the end of the song, the ode seems more like a lament for PJ's beautiful land, where everything is tradable for a quick buck.

Back in the USSR
The Beatles

In 1958, Chuck Berry scored a hit with *Back in the USA*, an upbeat number about a man returning from abroad to his glorious homeland of hamburgers, jukeboxes and good ol' rock 'n' roll. A decade later, things in the Land of the Free seemed a little less rose-tinted. JFK and Martin Luther King had been assassinated, the war in Vietnam was raging, blind patriotism was out of fashion. And so, The Beatles decided it was time to mess with people's minds a little. Paul McCartney set about writing *Back in the USSR* (1969) as a spoof of Chuck Berry's old hit. If Americans could claim that their land is simply the best, then so, surely, could everybody else. Even the Russians. The Beatles' song used all the clichés of American pop music (50s-style guitar solos, McCartney's best attempt at a Jerry Lee Lewis voice, surfer-dude harmonies about hot chicks) and simply applied them to the land of the mortal enemy: "Well, the Ukraine girls really knock me out / They leave the West behind / And Moscow girls make me sing and shout / That Georgia's always on my mi-mi-... mind." So, was the whole track just a joke? Sort of. But a wonderfully subversive one that sounds just as good all these decades later.

Donald, Where's Your Troosers?
Andy Stewart

Scotland: land of mystical mists and lovely lochs. Neither of these are relevant to *Donald, Where's Your Troosers.* The hit from 1960 (and again in 1989) is a deep reflection on an age-old question: what do Scotsmen actually wear under their kilts? The answer, it would seem, is that Scots like to feel the wind beneath their wings. To a sprightly accordion tune, Andy Stewart regales us with the tale of Donald, a humble fellow from the Isle of Skye who always dons a kilt, even if it's blowing up a gale: "Let the wind blow high, let the wind blow low / Through the streets in my kilt, I'll go / All the lassies say 'Hello / Donald, where's your troosers?'" Each verse adds yet another example of ladies left slack-jawed after catching a glimpse of Donald's high-flying kilt, with some of the later verses even delivered as an Elvis impersonation (spare yourself any attempt at common sense reasoning here). The only thing more bizarre than the song itself is that its biggest success was in Canada, where it went to number one. Perhaps Canadians share an affinity for those northern gusts.

Dreadlock Holiday
10cc

"I don't like cricket. Oh no. I love it!" *Dreadlock Holiday* first hit the airwaves in 1978 and has remained there since. These days, the song would ruffle a few feathers: a white guy singing about getting robbed by four black guys while he's on holiday in Jamaica. But let's give the singer the benefit of the doubt. It seems that the joke is on him, the white bloke, hopelessly trying to fit in with the locals by attempting a Jamaican accent and insisting on his love for cricket, reggae, Jamaica herself. One of the imaginary thieves tells the singer not to ignore his demands: "Don't you walk through my words / You got to show some respect". The song is accompanied by a hilarious video which, presumably due to budget restrictions, was filmed on a grey pebble beach in Dorset rather than the white sands of Montego Bay.

In the Dutch Mountains
Nits

Ah, the Netherlands. Big sky, whimsical windmill blades being gently stirred by those … mountain breezes? Ok, so maybe there's an element of irony in this song title. Nits (formerly The Nits) are a Dutch group who have been around since the mid-70s. *In the Dutch Mountains* (1987) was the track that first got them noticed in many European countries, its dramatic synths and poetic lyrics establishing the group as Amsterdam's own answer to The Waterboys.
The mountains in question appear to be the result of a rather vivid imagination: "I was born in a valley of bricks / Where the river runs high above the rooftops / I was waiting for the cars coming home late at night / From the Dutch mountains." Singer Henk Hofstede recalls how, as a child growing up in a suburban brick terrace, the maps at school would just show the Netherlands with its borders fading into blank space. Henk used to imagine that beyond his surroundings, there was a fairy-tale land of soaring hills. One has to wonder if, in a parallel universe, a young girl in the Swiss Alps was fantasising about some Dutch dykes (that's obviously a reference to Holland's sea walls, though a girl's fantasies are her own business).

Douce France
Charles Trenet

Tinkling piano? Check. Mellow vibes? Check. Blissful French? Undoubtedly. *Douce France* is the classic that makes you want to ride a bicycle through Provence with a hamper full of bread and cheese (apologies to any French readers rolling their eyes right now). Instantly recognisable, the song is a rosy memoir to the France of old: "Douce France / Cher pays de mon enfance / Bercée de tendre insouciance / Je t'ai gardée dans mon cœur." ("Sweet France / Dear land of my childhood / Held with tender carefreeness / I've kept you in my heart."). Charles wrote the song in 1943, when France was still under Nazi occupation. In fact, the authorities at the time suspected him of being secretly Jewish, his surname an anagram of the common Jewish name Netter. He was forced to deny this. In such dark times, who could blame the man for feeling a little nostalgic?

Bollywood Boulevard
Indian-Style Songs which Had Global Success

Jaan Pehechan Ho
Mohammed Rafi

Down at the Princes Club, something very odd is occurring. To a manic rock 'n' roll riff, a lady in a gold dress is shakin' and grindin' at a rate that could possibly be a health hazard. And it's not just her. Men in mariachi suits are getting just about as lit. Oh, and everybody's wearing black eye-masks. "Why?", you ask. Well, fans of old Bollywood have learned never to ask such a question. The classic scene, from the 1965 movie *Gumnaam*, is what introduced a global audience to the song *Jaan Pehechan Ho* and to its singer, Mohammed Rafi (the Indian superstar who voiced songs in countless Hindi films). Watching the scene these days, it's hard not to think that its aesthetic and sound must surely have served as inspiration for more than a few Tarantino movies, decades later. The song itself, with a title that roughly translates as "We should get to know each other", is Bollywood's own frenetic take on 60s rock 'n' roll. And these cats know how to jive. Just try not to strain a neck muscle when attempting to replicate the moves.

Jimmy
M.I.A.

"Jimmy, aaja!" Apparently, that translates as the much less romantic-sounding "Jimmy, c'mere!" Just as well M.I.A. avoided English for the central hook of her 2007 hit. The British-Tamil singer is a one of a very small number of singers who've managed to bring the sound of Bollywood to the international charts. *Jimmy*'s strong disco vibe basically divides listeners into two camps: those who know how to dance bhangra and those who *believe* they know how to dance bhangra. Warning: know thine camp. The song is actually a cover. The original comes from a 1982 Bollywood movie in which our humble Jimmy needs to represent Team India at an International Disco Competition. M.I.A. loved the song as a kid and used to earn pocket money by performing it at parties and gatherings around London. When she decided to record her own version, she rewrote the verses in English. Far from the South-Asian melodrama of the original, M.I.A. turned the song into a surprising story of an elusive war journalist (let's call him Jimmy) who she met in Africa: "When you go Rwanda, Congo / Take me on your genocide tour / Take me on a truck to Darfur ..." Who ever said Bollywood disco had to be a simple affair?

JIMMY, AAJA!

— M.I.A.

Get Ur Freak on
Missy Elliott

The year was 2001 and bedazzled denim was, unfortunately, a thing. Apart from some questionable choices from the video's wardrobe department, however, pretty much nothing else has aged about Missy's groundbreaking anthem. *Get Ur Freak on*, with its sparse musical style and Missy's in-your-face rap, set the tone for hip-hop music for years to come. As for the Indian influence, most of us were too busy to notice, distracted as we were by trying to engage in some primitive precursor to twerking. But the track's basic tune is based on a famous Punjabi melody, the instantly-recognisable six-note *din-din-din-din-din-din*. It's played on a tumbi, a stringed instrument common in bhangra music. How did Missy end up combining Indian folk music with rapping about her musical prowess? No idea, but the rest is history. In the inimitable words of Missy: "... ain't no stoppin' me / Copywritten, so don't copy me / Y'all do it, sloppily / And y'all can't come close to me". Hard to argue with that.

Tattva
Kula Shaker

With today's debate around cultural appropriation, Kula Shaker wouldn't last a second. If Selena Gomez wearing a bindi is enough to cause a Twitter storm, it's hard to imagine the youth of today embracing a group fronted by a white Londoner that mixed psychedelic rock with Indian instruments and spiritual Sanskrit lyrics. But it was the 90s. Kula Shaker were free to make, admittedly, wonderful songs in the mystical-rock style of The Beatles and Zeppelin before them. *Tattva* was their first hit and filled the airwaves with the cult-like chant "acintya bheda abheda Tattva". People who know about these things say that means something about the inconceivable nature of oneness and its opposite. Oh, that old trope! Groovy.

Jai Ho
A.R. Rahman

In 2008, there really was no stopping *Jai Ho*. Written for the final dance scene of the film *Slumdog Millionaire*, the track was lauded by critics as a standout musical moment. It then went on to be graced with a Grammy, an Oscar and even (brace yourself) a cover version by US girl group The Pussycat Dolls. A brave decision by those Pussycat ladies to record a track with the word *ho* in the title. Although you wouldn't have guessed it from the mainly English Pussycat version ("Jai ho / You are the reason that I breathe!"), the original song was a much more multilingual affair featuring a mix of Hindi, Urdu, Punjabi and Spanish. Apparently, "Jai ho" translates as something like "Long live victory", making it the perfect accompaniment for the movie's triumphant dance number where our hero and heroine, Jamal and Latika, dance their cares away at a very crowded railway station in Mumbai.

Pasito a Pasito, Suave, Suavecito
Non-English Worldwide Hits

Despacito
Luis Fonsi ft. Daddy Yankee and Justin Bieber

The setting was 2017, somewhere in an LA boardroom. A meeting was being held on how to further internationalise the success of *Despacito*, the recent runaway hit by Puerto Rican performers Luis Fonsi and Daddy Yankee. "J-Justin Bieber", stuttered the intern. "Justin Bieber!", exclaimed the execs. The intern hesitated: "... but can Bieber actually speak Spani...?" "Sssshhhh!", pouted the exec as she pressed her taloned finger to his lips, "Hush now." And so it was. Within a matter of months, people the world over were calling each other *mami* while confusedly giving orders to *sube, sube, sube*. For this, we will always be grateful.

Rock Me Amadeus
Falco

These days, it's quite hard to imagine a song in German hitting the number-one spot in the US, the UK, Canada and many other countries around the world. As wonderful a track as *Amadeus* is, might part of its success back in 1985 be related to the fact that the average radio listener could have mistaken the lyrics for English ones? Falco raps about a fellow named Amadeus, that's Wolfgang Amadeus Mozart to the rest of us. The rapid German rap is interspersed with English and phrases not a million miles from English: "Er war Superstar, er war populär ... Er war ein Virtuose, war ein Rockidol / Und alles rief: 'Come and rock me Amadeus!'" If we are to take 80s rap as a reliable source of information (and why wouldn't we?), it seems the late, great Mozart really was packin' some swagger. Falco's track suggests that the composer was a heavy-drinking ladies man with a serious cashflow problem. Actually, this depiction of Mozart as the original punk rocker of the 18th century seems about right. This was, after all, the man who wrote a composition in the late 1700s famously titled *Leck mich im Arsch* (rough translation, *Lick My Arse*)!

La Vie en Rose
Grace Jones

How many incarnations has the world heard of *La Vie en Rose*? From Edith Piaf's 1947 original to Louis Armstrong, to Donna Summer, to Lady Gaga belting it out while dressed as a drag queen in the 2018 movie *A Star Is Born*. The decades may pass, but no appetite is lost for the power and sheer romance of the song: "Quand il me prend dans ses bras / Il me parle tout bas / Je vois la vie en rose." ("When takes me in his arms / He speaks to me softly / I see life in a rosy hue."). The version that fared best in international charts was Grace Jones' funky bossa nova take in 1977. Not that the slight increase in tempo makes the song lose any of its impact. Grace has said that she cries every time she sings it, reminded of her various French lovers. And just to let the listener know that her version was no meek lament, Grace released an accompanying video wearing barely-there gold lamé with an unapologetically exposed right nipple. Why? Because this is Grace Motherfuckin' Jones we're dealing with.

Joe le Taxi
Vanessa Paradis

Who knows what it takes for a non-English song to catch on in a place like the UK? Perhaps it's an outstanding melody. Or perhaps it's Britain's fondness for pretty French girls under the age of 16 (or has Alizée's *Moi … Lolita* now been erased from cultural memory?) Vanessa Paradis was just 14 back in 1987, when her smooth pop number about a man named Joe enjoyed success across Europe. To help its international appeal, the song mentions Joe's many musical tastes, from rhumba to "le vieux rock" to mambo, to cha-cha-cha. Vanessa later recorded a version of the song in Spanish, easily translated to *Joe el Taxi*. Not so easy to do in English though. Admittedly, *Joe the Cabbie* would lose some poetry.

Gangnam Style
PSY

You can be pretty sure you've reached international success when the leaders of the US, the UK and the UN are all talking about your song. *Gangnam Style* was to 2012 what the *Macarena* had been to 1995: a catchy, incomprehensible hit with a ludicrous dance that made otherwise-sane politicians lose their dignity in an attempt at seeming relatable. Can't you just hear Ban Ki-moon's PR team telling him it would be good for youth engagement for him to cross his wrists and pretend to ride an imaginary pony? Outside of PSY's native South Korea, the world was probably more impressed by the pony dance than the song's narrative of wannabe yuppies who claim to be from Seoul's upper-class Gangnam district. But who cares about semantics when there are imaginary lassoes to be thrown?

ER WAR EIN VIRTUOSE, WAR EIN ROCKIDOL. UND ALLES RIEF: 'COME AND ROCK ME AMADEUS!'

— FALCO

Stars 'n' Stripes
Songs about the USA

Kids in America
Kim Wilde

Kim Wilde. Pop singer. Celebrity gardener. Iconic star of a viral video in which she treats her fellow passengers on the London Underground to a particularly drunken rendition of *Kids in America*. OK, there was slurring, but also a reminder of the brilliance of this 80s classic. The track began life back in 1980, when young Kim was still living in the family home in southern England. Her brother Ricky wrote the tune on a little keyboard, while their father (a songwriter) came up with the lyrics. Kim says that her dad had a very romantic view of America as a *Grease*-style utopia of teenagers going to the movies and sipping milkshakes. And so, the resulting song embodied that notion of the USA as a youthful land where the fun never stops: "Outside a new day is dawning / Outside suburbia's sprawling everywhere ... We're the kids in America!" Some suggest that the song's huge success came from its merging of a 70s punk sound (The Sex Pistols, The Clash) with early-80s electronic. Suddenly, pop was hip. Was Kim cool enough to lead its charge? Duh!

This Is America
Childish Gambino

For a few days back in 2018, Childish Gambino basically ruled YouTube. The video for his track *This Is America* went ridiculously viral. And if the song was a palatable presentation of the unpalatable aspects of the US, then so was the video. The clip begins with an uplifting choir of black voices, only to be shockingly interrupted by Childish shooting his black guitarist in the head. The dead body is roughly dragged off-screen, while Childish carefully places the pistol on a ceremonial red cloth, presumably as a comment on where America's priorities lie. From here, Gambino performs various dance crazes, but then stops to grab a kalashnikov and gun down his entire choir. Throughout the track, the rapper reminds us that "Grandma told me / Get your money, Black man". The suggestion of both song and video seem to be that to be black in America means to perform, to entertain, to scrape a living together.

And that all this distracts from the brutality of American society, often directed at African Americans. Apple pie and picket fences, it ain't.

Letter from America
The Proclaimers

Nothing says USA quite like two Edinburgh brothers yelling out a folk number in the broadest Scottish accent known to commercial music: "When you go will you send back / A letter from America? / Take a look up the railtrack / From Miami to Canada" (if you're attempting to sing that in your head, you may wish to replace "look" with *lewk*). *Letter from America* (1987) may have a stomping guitar melody vigorous enough to keep the neighbours awake, but the lyrics tell a much sadder tale. From the Scottish coast, the singer looks out to the Atlantic and mourns his countrymen who have had to leave. In naming some of Scotland's abandoned regions ("Lochaber no more / Sutherland no more ... Bathgate no more / Linwood no more") the song links old to current. The former are Highland areas from which, centuries ago, rich landlords drove the natives away; the latter are industrial towns which suffered greatly in the recession of the 1980s. The verses point out how, yes, America is the Land of Opportunity, but to a people who have had to leave everything behind. *Och*, there'll be *nary* a dry eye in the *hoose* (said no Scottish person, ever).

Born in the USA
Bruce Springsteen

What could be more patriotic of the *Land of the Free* than Bruce Springsteen in T-shirt and jeans, rocking out to the rapturous chorus of *Born in the USA*? Well, certainly not the track's lyrics. While the blast of the chorus may sound like an ecstatic ode to Uncle Sam, the verses tell quite a different story. Bruce wrote the song in the early 80s, just a few years after the end of the Vietnam war. In fact, the song's original working title was *Vietnam*. The lyrics describe the plight of a working-class man who was sent to war: "... they put a rifle in my hand / Sent me off to a foreign land / To go and kill the yellow man". Our narrator goes on to describe his raw deal: returning to the USA to unemployment, abandonment, grief and desperation. Each bitter verse is interspersed with a sarcastic claim of delight at having been "born in the USA". For obvious reasons, the song is often misinterpreted as being strongly nationalistic. Even Ronald Reagan, who had cut funding to war veterans, wanted to use the anthem as his campaign song. Bruce politely declined.

THEY PUT A RIFLE IN MY HAND. SENT ME OFF TO A FOREIGN LAND.

— BRUCE SPRINGSTEEN

Detroit Calling
Big Motown Hits

Dancing in the Street
Martha & The Vandellas

When a teenage Martha Reeves went to audition at Motown Records, she was surprised to find an ordinary house with a hand-drawn sign out front. Grandly nicknamed Hitsville USA, the studio was actually just the suburban Detroit home of Motown founder Berry Gordon. Martha walked in to find a business in chaos, and instead of auditioning, started answering phones. She was soon on the payroll as secretary. Some time later, she also started singing for the label. One day in 1964, resident singer-songwriter Marvin Gaye caught lovesick Martha "ogling" him (that's her own choice of words, by the way). Marvin asked her if she would try out a new song he'd co-written called *Dancing in the Street*. The result would become one of Motown's most successful tunes. Marvin and his co-writers had been inspired to write the song after seeing kids playing in the spray of a fire hydrant on a hot day in Detroit: "Summer's here / And the time is right / For dancing in the street." The song lists various US cities, and many listeners were quick to notice that all had major black populations ("Chicago ... New Orleans ... Baltimore and D.C. now"). This led to the song being adopted by many Civil Rights activists as an anthem for protests, including the inner-city riots of the 1960s. Who knew that "dancing" could be such a loose term?

Ain't No Mountain High Enough
Marvin Gaye and Tammi Terrell

Throughout the mid-1960s, Marvin Gaye started to become established as one of Motown's leading singers. In 1967, the label paired him with another of their rising stars, Tammi Terrell, to make an album of duets. The opening track was an uplifting number: "Ain't no mountain high enough / Ain't no valley low enough ... To keep me from getting to you, babe." Apparently, Marvin and Tammi were great friends, and strictly platonic. Despite her young age, Tammi had seen her share of nasty boyfriends (James Brown had been abusive; fellow Motowner David Ruffin of The Temptations had proposed marriage, forgetting to mention he already had a wife, kids and another girlfriend!) Soon after the release of *Ain't No Mountain ...*, Marvin and Tammi were performing in concert when she collapsed into Marvin's arms. She was rushed to hospital, where doctors diagnosed a brain tumour. After a period of illness, Tammi passed away in 1970, aged just 24. Her grieving mother banned all Motown people from attending the funeral, except for Marvin, who she regarded as Tammi's best friend. Suddenly, the song's tale of unfailing companionship took on a far sadder tinge.

I Heard It Through the Grapevine
Marvin Gaye

Motown often had various different artists record variations on the same track. *I Heard It Through the Grapevine* was first released in 1967 as an uptempo number by the label's new signing, Gladys Knight & the Pips. Apparently, the fast-paced composition was an attempt to emulate the recent success of Aretha Franklin's *Respect*, and Motown producers wanted to "out-funk" Aretha (let us pause at this moment to digest the mere suggestion). If time has proven anything, it is that Aretha is not to be out-funked, but Gladys's danceable track nonetheless fared well in the chart. A few months beforehand, however, Marvin Gaye had recorded his own version of ... *Grapevine*. His was a much slower affair, with an atmospheric quality and vocals that cut to the bone: "Losing you would end my life you see / Because you mean that much to me". After he included it on his 1968 album *Special Occasion*, radio DJs picked up on it and listeners soon demanded it be released as a single. When Motown obliged, Marvin's song outsold the Gladys version and became the more legendary track. Apparently, Gladys was livid. Pipped to the post, as it were.

The Tears of a Clown
Smokey Robinson and the Miracles

Of course, Marvin Gaye didn't entirely run the show at Motown. Smokey Robinson was another hugely successful singer-songwriter, eventually rising to the position of Vice President of the label. Smokey was perfect for Motown: a great ear, a great voice, a Detroit native (by pure coincidence, he had grown up just a few houses away from Aretha!) He wrote songs for other artists (e.g. *My Girl* for The Temptations), as well as hits which he performed with his own band, The Miracles (e.g. *The Tracks of My Tears*). Some time in the late 1960s,

Smokey was at the company Christmas party and got talking to labelmate Stevie Wonder. Stevie had written the instrumental for a new track but couldn't come up with any lyrics. Smokey listened to the recording and thought the melody sounded like circus music. Inspiration struck. Smokey was a fan of the Italian opera *Pagliacci*, in which a clown discovers that his wife has been unfaithful, but must hide the despair behind his smiling, painted face. And so, Smokey's lyrics took shape: "Now there's some sad things known to man / But ain't too much sadder than / The tears of a clown / When there's no one around." Motown allowed Smokey and his band to record the song as an album track. In 1970, it was finally released as a single and became a worldwide smash.

Papa Was a Rollin' Stone
The Temptations

By the early 70s, Motown had outgrown its humble beginnings in Berry Gordon's suburban home and was about to move wholesale to L.A. Before the move, the Hitsville, USA studio played host to one final great recording. *Papa Was a Rollin' Stone* (1972) was co-written by Motown songwriter Norman Whitfield. By now, the label was wading into more experimental territory and Whitfield chose The Temptations to record the epic psychedelic soul number in the minimalistic style of tracks featuring in the Blaxploitation movies of the era. Also, lyrically, the song was far from bubblegum pop, kicking off with the iconic lines: "It was the third of September / That day I'll always remember, yes I will / 'Cause that was the day, that my daddy died." The rest of the track, each verse sung by a different Temptations member, tells a sad tale of a philandering father who never made time for his kids and who has now passed away. Legend has it that Whitfield purposely annoyed The Temptations to make sure that they sounded thoroughly pissed off in tone: he made them record the verses time and time again; he even reportedly wrote the song's opening line as an oblique reference to the singer's own father, who had died on the third of October. Tough tactics, but does the end justify the means? The song went to number one, won various Grammys and became one of Motown's most legendary hits.

Memphis in the House
Best Stax Records Songs

Green Onions
Booker T. & The M.G.'s

As Motown was the uptempo soul sound of Detroit that went global, Stax was the rhythm and blues sound of Memphis that took the world by storm. There were various factors that contributed to the Stax label's distinctive musical style, such as having just one recording studio, just one small team of songwriters, and just one select group of regular musicians. That house band was known as Booker T. & The M.G.'s. While their work mainly involved playing the backing music for the label's star singers, they also released several instrumental records under their own name. Their biggest hit came in 1962, with a funky-bluesy number that would go on to become possibly the most famous instrumental track of modern music. As a groove, *Green Onions* is almost impossibly slick. OK, it may be based on a church-like electric organ sound, but one that's far from inspiring reverence. Quite the opposite, in fact. Listening to the track kind of makes you feel like robbing a bank, or turning around to your nagging boss and saying something like, "You know what, Deborah? Why don't you shove your spreadsheets where the sun don't shine?" Such is the power of funk.

Hold on, I'm Comin'
Sam and Dave

Another factor that contributed to the distinctive Stax sound was the fact that the studio was based in an old cinema. The seats had been taken out, leaving a big sloped floor. This created unique acoustics, resulting in records with a sound that was full, echoey and raw. This is apparent on the label's 1966 smash *Hold on, I'm Comin'*, in which Sam and Dave break it down like it's nobody's business. The duo sing to their respective ladies, telling those lucky gals that their every need is about to be satisfied. When it was first released, some radio stations refused to play a song with such a suggestive title. Stax bosses solved this pickle by re-releasing the song as the fully revamped, totally unrecognisable *Hold on, I'm-a-Comin'*. And it worked! The track stormed the charts and remains a funk-soul classic to this day.

Knock on Wood
Eddie Floyd

Eddie Floyd began at Stax as a member of their small team of songwriters. In 1966, he co-wrote *Knock on Wood* as a potential track for the Stax superstar Otis Redding. Eddie recorded a demo and played it to the label's bosses, who figured the song was great as it was. Their hunch paid off, the single became a hit and Eddie's singing career took off. The idea behind the song is a simple one, with the singer hoping that his love will hang around: "It's like thunder, lightning / The way you love me is frightening / I'd better knock on wood". Eddie's co-writer on the track was Steve Cropper, a white guitarist from Booker T. & The M.G.'s. Stax was a progressive company for its time, shunning the racial segregation which was the general policy of 1960s Tennessee. Eddie and Steve wrote the song at the Lorraine Hotel in Memphis, where Stax employees would often hang out. In a tragic sign of the darkness that surrounded the Stax beacon, the same hotel was the location of Martin Luther King's assassination just two years later. Today, it is the National Civil Rights Museum.

(Sittin' on) The Dock of the Bay
Otis Redding

In December 1967, Stax suffered a huge blow when Otis Redding and several of the label's musicians died when their plane crashed into a lake in Wisconsin. Otis had been the biggest star at Stax, having scored hits with songs like *Try a Little Tenderness*. Just a month before his death, he met up with Steve Cropper to co-write and record *The Dock of the Bay*. Otis had come up with the first verse of the song the previous summer when he was staying in a houseboat near San Francisco: "Sittin' in the mornin' sun / I'll be sittin' when the evenin' come / Watching the ships roll in …" Cropper then wrote the subsequent verses about a man who can't seem to escape his malaise. The duo met again just three days before the tragic crash to re-record the track. They had planned on developing it further, most notably by replacing the final whistled verse with actual lyrics, but they would never get the chance. After the plane crash, Cropper followed up on an idea that Otis had requested, adding in the sound of waves and seagulls. Stax released the song in January 1968 and it became Otis's first number one – sadly, posthumously.

Don't Matter If You're Black or White
Songs about Racial Discrimination

Blowin' in the Wind
Bob Dylan

In 1963, a young Bob Dylan was gobsmacked when he was told that he was going to get a cheque for five thousand dollars. *Blowin' in the Wind* was blowin' up. The song had been covered by Peter, Paul and Mary and was selling like hot cakes. Little did he know that his simple composition, written in a café in ten minutes, would become one of the most famous songs of all time. He based the track on an old folk tune called *No More Auction Block*, sung by former slaves rejoicing their new-found freedom. To the same melody, Bob penned lyrics as a series of rhetorical questions: "... how many years can some people exist / Before they're allowed to be free? / Yes, and how many times can a man turn his head / And pretend that he just doesn't see?" While Bob has never wanted to pinpoint the meaning of the song, those particular lines surely refer to the oppression of African Americans, though they may also be influenced by Bob's Jewish ancestry. After its release, the song became an anthem at many Civil Rights protests during the 60s. The song concludes that the answer to all the world's problems is blowin' in the wind, perhaps suggesting that us humans have the power to save ourselves if we can just look outwards and read the signs. Jeez, Bob. You may as well have called it "We're all screwed".

A Change Is Gonna Come
Sam Cooke

By 1963, Sam Cooke was already an established hitmaker. One day, he heard Bob Dylan's *Blowin' in the Wind* for the first time, and he couldn't quite believe his ears, reacting "A white boy writing a song like that?" Deeply moved, Sam set about writing his own take on the state of the world. And he came up with something equally iconic, kicking off: "I was born by the river in a little tent / And just like the river I've been running ever since / It's been a long time coming / But I know a change is gonna come." Backed by sumptuous strings, Sam sang his heart out about a life of struggle. That opening line is really a merging of personal and shared experience. Sam was born in Mississippi ("by the river"), but moved to Chicago as a child as part of the mass northward migration of African Americans to escape the repressive laws of the south ("running ever since"). Sadly, Sam died in a shooting incident just two weeks before the track was to be released. The song went on to become a radio hit, but more importantly, another anthem of the Civil Rights movement. In 2008, when Obama was voted in as the first black president of the U.S., his acceptance speech included the eternal line: "It's been a long time coming, but tonight ... change has come."

IT'S BEEN A LONG TIME COMING. BUT I KNOW A CHANGE IS GONNA COME.

— SAM COOKE

Deathless
Ibeyi ft. Kamasi Washington

When Ibeyi's Lisa-Kaindé Diaz was just 16, she got arrested. In her native Paris, a policeman approached her and started aggressively asking questions. Did she smoke? Did she drink? He grabbed her bag and threw the contents on the ground. Lisa recalls how he froze when what fell out was a book of Chopin scores, as if he suddenly feared that she might actually be intelligent. Lisa is of Cuban-Venezuelan heritage, and sadly realised that she had just been racially profiled. In 2017, she wrote *Deathless*: "He said, he said / 'Do you smoke? What's your name? Do you know why I'm here?'" Each verse recounts her run-in with the officer, each chorus coming back to a defiant chant: "We are deathless!" The accompanying video hammers home the point. Lisa and her bandmate-slash-sister Naomi repeatedly give birth to each other (don't worry, they keep it tasteful). Oppressive forces might wish for these ladies to disappear, but they just keep coming back stronger.

Your Racist Friend
They Might Be Giants

Note to millennials: Taylor Swift did not invent geeky pop. She may have pushed internet cats further into the limelight (which, we can all agree, is where they belong), but she cannot claim to be the originator of odd lyrics that sound like an overheard conversation. That accolade must surely go to They Might Be Giants, keeping things quirky since the early 80s. In *Your Racist Friend* (1990), the Giants tackle the issue of discrimination with a story about a night out: "This is where the party ends / I can't stand here listening to you / And your racist friend ... I feel like a hypocrite talking to you / And your racist friend." Apart from its combination of merry accordion with snaps of heavy metal guitar, the track is also interesting for its take on prejudice. It's not just calling out the racist, but also the friend who allows ignorant comments to fly by unchallenged. By the end of the song, the racist is attempting to blame his insensitivity on the booze, the singer is storming out in a huff and the friend – we assume – is left wondering if failing to act can be an act in itself.

Clandestino
Manu Chao

In the year 2000, the chilled-out vibe of Manu Chao's *Clandestino* made it a firm favourite of beach bars around the world. Because nothing says *Vaycayyyy* quite like sipping on a piña colada while listening to a tale of harrowing injustice. Despite the cheerful reggae-like strumming, the track's Spanish lyrics tell the sad story of an African migrant who has crossed the Med in search of a better life in Europe. Far from living the dream, the undocumented migrant now feels condemned to a life of hiding: "Para una ciudad del norte / Yo me fui a trabajar / Mi vida la dejé / Entre Ceuta y Gibraltar." ("To a city in the north / I went to work / My life, I left behind / Between Ceuta and Gibraltar."). In many of Manu Chao's songs, the French-Spanish singer makes himself the voice of the voiceless. Never one to shy away from an uncomfortable truth, he once pointed out to an interviewer: "Look around – maybe 30% of the people in this street are *clandestino*." Maybe even the friendly waiter who served your piña colada.

Alright
Kendrick Lamar

Tormented, combative Kendrick Lamar was not the most obvious person to become the voice of serenity for a generation. But with the 2015 release of *Alright*, it was immediately apparent that the rapper was rising above. In the same year, the Black Lives Matter movement was gaining ever more support across the US, as people vented their anger at story after story of racially motivated police killings. Kendrick took the cue to remind black communities to remain steadfast: "Wouldn't you know / We been hurt, been down before ... and we hate po-po / Wanna kill us dead in the street fo sho' ... But we gon' be alright." Apart from society's ills, the track also deals with the rapper's battles with depression and dealings with the devil (a character who he names Lucy, short for Lucifer). Grim as it all may seem, Kendrick keeps coming back to the mantra that things are "gon' be alright", both personally and as a community.

The track struck a chord and became adopted as a chant by protestors at BLM rallies. For many, *Alright* is the 21st century's *We Shall Overcome*: a fist-in-the-air cry of hope, despite it all. And yes, that's Pharrell rapping on the chorus, who presumably took a moment out from his busy schedule of writing songs about Minions.

WANNA KILL US DEAD IN THE STREET FO SHO' ... BUT WE GON' BE ALRIGHT.

— KENDRICK LAMAR

People, Rise up
Protest Songs

People Have the Power
Patti Smith

When Patti released this song in 1988, it didn't set the charts alight. Decades later, its lyrics echo through protest marches around the world. And what lyrics they are: "... the people have the power / To redeem the work of fools / Upon the meek the graces shower / It's decreed – the people rule". The singer allows herself to dream of a world united, where people grasp control from the ruling idiots. Patti acknowledges a certain sadness related to the track. While she was the one behind the optimistic lyrics, the music and concept came from her late husband, who never got to see its true impact. She says that he introduced the idea by bursting into the kitchen and announcing that they were going to make a song called *People Have the Power*. Patti was disgruntedly peeling potatoes at the time. She admits that her initial thought was how she wished she had the power to make him peel those damn potatoes. Relatable.

Fight the Power
Public Enemy

Packed with cultural references, jammed with dozens of samples, the core message of *Fight the Power* is simple. It's all in the title really. The 1989 track was commissioned by Spike Lee for his movie *Do the Right Thing*, telling Public Enemy that he wanted something "defiant". And that is certainly what he got. Amid reworkings of the words of speakers like Malcolm X and Martin Luther King, rapper Chuck D laid down just what it was like to be black in the USA at the end of the Decade of Decadence: "'People, people we are the same' / No we're not the same / Cause we don't know the game". Anger at inequality builds to accusations of unfiltered racism, calling out cultural icons: "Elvis was a hero to most / But he never meant shit to me you see ... Mother fuck him and John Wayne". Chuck D would later tone down his criticisms of Elvis, but never found the need to do so for John Wayne. John had, after all, given an interview to *Playboy* (yes, *Playboy*) in which he bluntly stated "I believe in white supremacy". Oh, shut up, John. If only *The Quiet Man* had lived up to his name.

Working Class Hero
John Lennon

One has to wonder what exactly had pissed off John Lennon on the day he wrote *Working Class Hero* (1970). Some memory of bullies from his youth? Some posh git at a restaurant demanding an autograph? Sneering and bitter, the song's verses follow the life of a working-class person, from bleak early childhood to tormented schooldays to soul-crushing working life. And at every turn, the powers-that-be are there, breathing down your neck, forcing you to submit and conform. For John, it's all part of a bigger system, designed to keep the Little Man little: "Keep you doped with religion and sex and TV / And you think you're so clever and classless and free / But you're still fucking peasants as far as I can see ..." While we may feel that things have evolved since the Dark Ages, to the rulers of this world, we're still all just toothless wenches who smell of onions (which, let's be honest, is not an entirely inaccurate description for most of us). John rounds off each verse with a sarcastic scoff to anybody claiming how great it is to start out from zero: "A working-class hero is something to be ..." What is such a hero? Is it the working-class bloke who's clawed his way up the ladder? And if so, at what cost? What pieces of your soul must you sell to rise to the top? A decade into his role as global superstar, it sounds like John had some thinking to do.

Let's Impeach the President
Neil Young

2006 was not a good year for left-leaning Americans. *Dubya* was in his second term in office, the invasion of Iraq was raging, the controversial government response to Hurricane Katrina had laid divisions bare. Having already fulfilled his role as the voice of a generation, Neil says that by the mid-2000s, he was waiting for some younger voice to do the protesting. But it just wasn't happening. And so, the Canadian superstar got to work on a heartfelt album about the state of affairs in his adopted homeland, including this track: "Let's impeach the president for hijacking / Our religion and using it to get elected / Dividing our country into colours / And still leaving black people neglected". The singer describes the song as nonpartisan, implying that Bush was such an epic failure that impeaching him would actually have been a positive thing for the Republican party. Could that mean that Neil is a closet Republican? Probably not.

Redemption Song
Bob Marley

Of Bob's many contributions to the genre of protest songs, perhaps the most powerful was his last. *Redemption Song* (1980) was the final track on his final album, recorded when the singer was aware of his cancer and contemplating his own mortality. The true impact of the song is how it describes subordination, but instead of voicing anger and shouting at the guards, it lets us know how to get out of jail. Kind of like the file hidden inside in the cake. Bob asks us to forget the evil overlords, the slave traders and warmongers, and to focus on our wider purpose: "Emancipate yourselves from mental slavery / None but ourselves can free our minds!" Calm and resolute, the song's chorus seems like Bob's parting wish. He wants us to carry on the only message that he has ever given: "Won't you help to sing / These songs of freedom? / Cause all I ever have / Redemption songs ..."

WON'T YOU HELP TO SING. THESE SONGS OF FREEDOM?

— BOB MARLEY

Heading into Combat
Songs about War

Sunday Bloody Sunday
U2

Right from the military-style rat-a-tat drumbeat that opens U2's 1983 classic, you know that Bono and co are seriously pissed off. Bloody Sunday is the name given to an infamous incident in Northern Ireland, in which British soldiers killed 14 unarmed civilians. The song is U2's cry for reason to people everywhere who opt for violence, as Bono wonders, "How long must we sing this song?" (course-of-humanity spoiler alert: very long). The track kicks off with the singer in a state of shock, reflecting, "I can't believe the news today". This opening line had originally been the much more overtly political "Don't talk to me about the rights of the IRA, UDA" (both were terrorist groups on each side of the Northern Irish divide). Aside from the bizarre fact that the more controversial line seems to contain *way* too many syllables to fit the music, the band also feared that it could put them in serious danger, and so they rewrote it. Incidentally, the violin strings on the track came about when some Dublin guy called Steve saw U2 guitarist The Edge at a bus stop one morning, as you do. He asked if U2 had any need for a violinist and soon found himself in the studio, recording some of rock's most iconic fiddling. It never hurts to ask.

Buffalo Soldier
Bob Marley

While it is tempting to imagine that Bob Marley's classic is actually a song about a grenade-lobbing buffalo in a tight, sweaty vest, a closer analysis of the lyrics suggests that this is not the case. Bob recorded *Buffalo Soldier* shortly before his death in 1981. The song is basically a brief history lesson of a type which textbooks might shy away from. In the American Indian Wars of the late 19th century, many African Americans fought for the US in all-black regiments. They battled

against Native Americans, who gave the black recruits the nickname Buffalo Soldiers. Bob seems to despair at the thought of the white oppressor using black soldiers to do the dirty work: "And he was taken from Africa, brought to America / Fighting on arrival, fighting for survival". Adding insult to injury, the white rulers seem far from grateful for the sacrifice. They treat the song's black protagonist with derision, asking him "who the 'eck" does he think he is when he asks for equal treatment. Interestingly, the song seems far from angry in tone, the black soldier singing his famous "Woy-yoy-yoy" chant as he roams the land. Rather than recriminate, it seemed like Bob was simply in the mood to set the record straight.

A Hard Rain's A-Gonna Fall
Bob Dylan

No, Dylan's 1963 classic is not a warning to wear sensible, closed-toe footwear. It is, rather, a slightly more sombre announcement about, oh, you know, our own impending doom. When the record first came out, the sleeve notes quoted Dylan as saying the song was about the Cuban Missile Crisis of 1962. However, Bob later corrected this, saying that the lyrics were more generally about an approaching finale, nuclear or otherwise. The singer was clearly quite convinced that the end was nigh, with the song reflecting on wars and other hardships, both personal and collective: "I've stumbled on the side of twelve misty mountains ... I heard the roar of a wave that could drown the whole world". Dylan wanted each line of the song to sound like the opening line to a completely new track, telling *Rolling Stone*, "I thought I wouldn't have enough time alive to write all those songs so I put all I could into this one." By the final verse, Bob seems to have decided that his role in all this is simply to keep singing, so that everybody will get the message about the terrible path we're on. He must be getting a bit hoarse by now.

AND WE WERE SO GUNG HO TO LAY DOWN OUR LIVES.

— BILLY JOEL

Goodnight Saigon
Billy Joel

From the opening rumble of approaching helicopters, it's clear that *Goodnight Saigon* is going to be an epic affair. Written for his friends who had served in Vietnam, Billy paints a picture of everyday youngsters, quickly transformed: "We met as soul mates on Parris Island / We left as inmates from an asylum / And we were sharp, as sharp as knives / And we were so gung ho to lay down our lives." The kids bond instantly at Parris Island (a base for Marines in South Carolina), but finish their training almost brainwashed. The song goes on to describe the horrors they would face in the war, each chorus coming back to the soldiers' bittersweet chant of camaraderie: "And we would all go down together." The line seems falsely heroic, perhaps a sarcastic dig at American society for abandoning these same soldiers upon their return. Indeed, Billy has stated how, whether or not people agreed with the war, the returning soldiers were at least entitled to be welcomed home. In an effort to right some wrongs, Billy often brings veterans onto the stage as he performs this song in concert.

Shipbuilding
Elvis Costello and The Attractions

At the start of the 80s, things were far from rosy in the UK, particularly up north. As industries died off, unemployment reigned. In April 1982, the UK went to war. Argentina had invaded the Falkland Islands and it was time, as *Newsweek* famously put it, for the empire to strike back. For shipping communities such as those in Liverpool and Glasgow, this unexpected war brought a conundrum. Suddenly, their abandoned shipyards were in high demand to refit vessels for the war. But at what cost? In *Shipbuilding* (1983), Elvis Costello lets us in on some small-town gossip: "It's just a rumour that was spread around town ... Soon we'll be shipbuilding / Well, I ask you / The boy said, 'Dad, they're going to take me to task / But I'll be home by Christmas.'" The town's fathers rejoice that work and money are on the way, but the ships they build will ultimately carry the same town's sons to war. With sparse piano and a trumpet solo by Chet Baker that just might – literally – break your heart, Elvis reflects on what it's all about. He wonders why we need to dive into the waters looking for survivors of torpedoed ships "when we could be diving for pearls". Given the choice between beauty or ugliness, humans so often seem to go for the latter. Hence the popularity of *Crocs* sandals.

DON'T IT ALWAYS SEEM TO GO / THAT YOU DON'T KNOW WHAT YOU'VE GOT TIL IT'S GONE?

— JONI MITCHELL

They Paved Paradise
Songs about Environmental Matters

Big Yellow Taxi
Joni Mitchell

Big Yellow Taxi (1970) is possibly the most famous song about that cute, uniquely human, tendency to destroy the very planet that sustains us. "They paved paradise, put up a parking lot" is more than just catchy alliteration. Joni says the sentence came from a real-life observation. On the first morning of a trip to Hawaii, she drew back the curtains to see the island's gorgeous mountains, only to be struck by a hideous parking lot stretching out before her. The song goes on to lament deforestation, the commercialisation of our lands, toxic pesticides on the food we eat. In the final verse, Joni sings that "A big yellow taxi took away my old man". In hippie slang, might her "old man" be her boyfriend? In which case it seems like he's packed his things and caught the nearest cab. Joni ties together her two stories about joy left to slip away: "Don't it always seem to go / That you don't know what you've got til it's gone?" It seems like Joni is telling us that matters of the planet are just like matters of the heart: backpedalling will get you nowhere.

Virtual Insanity
Jamiroquai

Genetic engineering was big news in July, 1996. Dolly the Sheep had just become the first mammal to be cloned, opening the doors to the cloning of other animals, and the possibility of one day cloning humans. Just a month later, Jamiroquai released *Virtual Insanity*, a song about dubious science and what it might mean for humans and the future of the planet. And the timing couldn't have been more perfect: "Future's made of virtual insanity / Now always seem to be governed by this love we have / For useless, twisting, our new technology ..." The inspiration for the song didn't actually come from Dolly, however. Singer Jay Kay was first inspired when the band were in Sapporo, Japan, and went to see an underground town. It clearly scared him silly, offering a glimpse of some dystopian future when the Earth's surface would no longer be inhabitable. Don't worry, Jay Kay, that scenario is still at least a year or two away. By the way, did you know that Dolly the Sheep was named after none other than Dolly Parton herself? One of the (male) biotechnicians responsible stated, "Dolly is derived from a mammary gland cell and we couldn't think of a more impressive pair of glands than Dolly Parton's." Crass! But who wouldn't want to be named after the Queen of Nashville?

4 Degrees
Anohni

Climate change can lead to lot of finger-pointing. In this 2016 song, Anohni points right at herself, noting her complicity in the destruction of the planet. She adopts the attitude of an untroubled bystander, the kind who might roll their eyes at the mention of something like a carbon footprint. She repeats her mantra "It's only four degrees". Of course, this is a temperature increase on a scale which experts warn us would bring catastrophic consequences. Over building synths, Anohni equates her complacency with the mindset of a psychopath: "... all those lemurs and all those tiny creatures / I wanna see them burn, it's only four degrees". In real life, you get the feeling that Anohni probably isn't driving around in an SUV, windows down with the A/C on full, ten children in the back munching on some red meat. And yet, when discussing the track, the singer has reflected on her role in the planet's demise "as a taxpayer, as a consumer, as a passive participant". The climate crisis is complex. And it's a tough one to explain to a lemur.

Sweet Harmony
The Beloved

It seems that the mid-90s was something of a boom time for songs about climate change. Perhaps it was the moment when people started thinking how we really do need to get this thing sorted out. No problems on that front! The chorus of *Sweet Harmony* (1993) is basically a rally call: "Let's come together / Right now / Oh yeah / In sweet harmony". Many people thought that the song was about sex, presumably due to the singer's sultry voice, the repeated instruction to *come together* and a video which featured him completely in the nip and surrounded by equally unclothed female models. But no. Lyrically, this is as family-friendly as you can get (except for the underlying message that we're all essentially going to burn to death due to our reliance on single-use plastics): "Make the world your priority / Try to live your life ecologically / Play a part in a greater scheme / Try to live the dream on a wider scene." Simple as that. So, why the nudity? Well, in an era when Naomi was starkers on billboards claiming she'd rather go naked than wear fur, perhaps The Beloved figured they'd have a go at saving the planet via similar means.

Praying for Time
George Michael

If you're searching for solace, George was certainly not dealing it out when he wrote *Praying for Time* (1990): "It's hard to love, there's so much to hate / Hanging on to hope / When there is no hope to speak of / And the wounded skies above say it's much, much too late / Well maybe we should all be praying for time." The song offers a pretty harsh glance at human selfishness and how it both distracts us from, and hurries us towards, our impending annihilation. Perhaps this was George's musical equivalent of *Game of Thrones*: everybody bickering and trying to outmanoeuvre each other, ignoring the inevitable existential threat that "Winter Is Coming" (Cersei Lannister would never have been a George Michael fan). In an interview with the *New York Times* to promote the song, George expressed his despair that, in a world with finite resources, "We're taught that you have to grab what you can before it's gone." You have to wonder what George used to make of the Black Friday sales.

According to the Scriptures
Songs with Biblical References

1 Corinthians 15:55
Johnny Cash

It shouldn't come as too much of a surprise that bible-related songs can get a bit, well, morbid. The world didn't get to hear Johnny's *1 Corinthians 15:55* until several years after his own death in 2003, when it appeared on his posthumous *American VI* album (2010). In fact, the song may well have been the last that Johnny ever wrote, appearing as the only self-penned track on the album. For such a big task, Johnny chose his theme carefully. He had always identified as a Christian, albeit one who described himself as "the biggest sinner of them all". (Lest we forget, Johnny used to be quite the wild child. He was arrested numerous times, once for drunkenly picking flowers from somebody's garden at 2 a.m. When police threw him in a cell for the night, he reacted by kicking the door so hard that he broke his toe!) OK, so Johnny's relationship with God was complex. Several years before his death, he recorded an audio-reading of the New King James version of the New Testament. And it was from there that he chose the passage, 1 Corinthians 15:55, that would become the central idea of his final track: "Oh Death, where is thy sting? / Oh Grave, where is thy victory?" The famous lines appear in the bible as St. Paul's assertion that life can be eternal, that death is not a defeat. Johnny elaborates, imagining himself on a ship, sailing towards a "harbour of lights". A bit funereal? Definitely, but he *was* the man in black.

Lazarus
David Bowie

Lazarus (2015) was the final single of David Bowie's life. And what better Biblical character for David to choose for his swan song? Lazarus was basically the man who triumphed in the face of death, the believer who died of an incurable illness and who Jesus then raised from the dead. Bowie clearly had mortality in mind when he wrote the track. He was undergoing cancer treatment in New York and seems to have had a good idea that his time was running out. The song makes it clear from the outset that this is David's farewell to the world: "Look up here, I'm in heaven / I've got scars that can't be seen / I've got drama, can't be stolen / Everybody knows me now." The public had been generally unaware of Bowie's illness, only finding out about it when his death made headlines. Could this secrecy around his health explain why David sings about scars that we can't see? The whole thing may sound a bit depressing, but – as in the parable of Lazarus – the idea of immortality is certainly also present in the song, almost as if David is singing to us from beyond the grave. The single was released in December, and its accompanying video in January 2016, just three days before Bowie's death. And what a video it is, David being dragged skywards from his hospital bed, frantically scribbling his thoughts on paper, before finally, quietly, shuffling away.

Doo Wop (That Thing)
Lauryn Hill

"Talking out your neck, sayin' you're a Christian / A Muslim, sleeping with the jinn / Now that was the sin that did Jezebel in ... Showing off your ass 'cause you're thinking it's a trend, girlfriend ..." Lauryn Hill must have made quite a few enemies for herself back in 1998. The queens of hip-hop (Lil' Kim, Foxy Brown) showed as much skin as they damn well pleased while rapping about their sexual prowess. And then along came Lauryn, issuing a Godly warning. *Doo Wop (That Thing)* tells ladies that dressing like a stripper, or giving it up too easy (in Islam, "the jinn" is a potentially evil spirit), just serves to attract the no-good playboys. Not that Jezebel was actually a stripper. In the Old Testament, she was the rouge-wearing seductress who used her womanly wiles to persuade King Ahab to abandon God. For her sins, she got thrown out a window, her corpse then eaten by stray dogs. Now, clearly Ms. Hill would never suggest that donning your most fabulously slutty halter-neck will get you devoured by rabid hounds (or would she?), but we get the idea. And in the interest of balance, the second half of the song turns its attention to men, particularly the type of fellow who's obsessed with "his rims and his Timbs" (referring to fancy hubcaps and Timberland boots). The overall message seems to be that if men want women for just one thing (*that* thing), well, ladies are just after one thing too: a big, bulging wallet. And the Good Book would certainly not approve.

Hallelujah
Jeff Buckley

When Leonard Cohen wrote *Hallelujah* in 1984, he could never have known that it would become a type of blank canvas. The song has seen many cover versions, each interpretation bringing a certain mood, altered lyrics, a new intention (even if that intention is just to cash in, as exemplified by *X-Factor UK*'s Alexandra Burke). Cohen described his own recording of the song as "joyous"; Jeff Buckley described his 1994 cover as "a hallelujah to the orgasm". Though, that's not to say Buckley's version is all fun and tickles. The song begins with David, the gifted young harpist who would grow up to be king, trying to compose a number called *Hallelujah*. But David's lady friend isn't much of a music fan, so she's not really impressed (she'd probably be more into that Alexandra Burke version). From there, the song stays with biblical references to tell a tale of a man broken by love. The lady becomes Bathsheba ("You saw her bathing on the roof"), a married woman who King David claimed as his lover, with disastrous consequences. Next, the lady is Delilah, the seductress who brought down Samson ("She broke your throne and she cut your hair / And from your lips she drew the Hallelujah ...") Throughout Buckley's version, the cries of "Hallelujah" are somewhere between pleasure and pain, as his lover treats him mean and eventually abandons him, leaving him with just the memories of a passion that once was. Jeff submitted himself to lust, and it's left him very sore indeed. A nice narrative to bear in mind the next time you hear *Hallelujah* being sung by your local children's church choir.

AND FROM YOUR LIPS SHE DREW THE HALLELUJAH ...

— JEFF BUCKLEY

The Father and the Son *Songs about God and Jesus*

Jesus He Knows Me
Genesis

There's a moment in the video for this song where we see a placard that reads *Genesis 3:25*. Before audibly gasping and/or splurting out the sip of tea you've just taken, rest assured that *The Book of Genesis* still has only 24 verses. The placard is an in-joke, referring to the three members of the band and the number of years they had been in operation by the time of the 1992 video. And if the placard isn't really about God, neither exactly is the song itself. Rather, it's a track about a man who plays God. With televangelist programmes filling US television schedules at the time, Phil Collins decided to take a pop at the unscrupulous hosts promising miracles for cash: "I'll get you everything you wanted / I'll get you everything you need / You don't need to believe in hereafter / Just believe in me". Of course, our song's narrator offers hypocrisy of the highest degree, preaching traditional family values but failing to mention his mistress "... or the man I met last night". If you're tempted to argue that the satire could be more subtle, spare a thought for the many internet forum posters who mention their guileless religion teachers of the 1990s, getting pupils to bop along to the cheerful sounds of "Jesus he knows me"!

Stairway to Heaven
Led Zeppelin

Is *Stairway* really about God? Well, with lyrics dense enough to confuse even the most devout fans of prog-rock, you could argue that it's not NOT about God. While people will forever disagree about the ideas behind the world's most famous rock song, there is at least some consensus that the 1971 anthem has something to do with a spiritual journey. The first verse introduces us to a woman who thinks she can pay her way into heaven ("There's a lady who's sure / All that glitters is gold / And she's buying a stairway to heaven"). From there, the track seems to move from reflection to building realisation, and to ultimate enlightenment. That final point is the climax of the song, right after the epic guitar solo, when Robert Plant's hitherto soothing voice changes into rock music's most memorable shriek: "And as we wind on down the road / Our shadows taller than our soul / There walks a lady we all know / Who shines white light and wants to show ..." Such an ending might suggest a oneness, all of us walking together into the setting sun to meet a benevolent being. Or it might not. Given the number of conspiracy theorists who claim that the song contains a satanic message when played backwards ("Here's to my sweet Satan", in case you don't want to ruin your stereo), it seems that it's up to each listener to decide on *Stairway*'s true level of Godliness.

Laughing With
Regina Spektor

"No one laughs at God in a hospital / No one laughs at God in a war / No one's laughing at God / When they're starving or freezing or so very poor ..." Let's face it: in the 21st century, God could do with a decent PR team. These days, describing yourself as a loyal disciple of Jesus is definitely not going to help your street cred, and there is no upcoming Whoopi Goldberg blockbuster that's going to change that. In *Laughing With* (2009), Regina Spektor reflects on that tendency to look down our noses at religion. Yes, we make God jokes. Until times get tough, that is. There's something about an unexpected health scare, or a 3 a.m. knock on the front door, that quietens our jest. Perhaps it's humility. Not that Regina is telling us to get on our knees in pious devotion. Rather, she seems to be asking us to keep an open mind. For her, what's truly funny is when people see God as some sort of turbo-powered Santa Claus. Even more hilarious is when the bible bashers tell us God hates us for some reason or other. Regina finds that very funny indeed. And she thinks God would laugh along too. Guess that explains the song's title.

God's Song
Randy Newman

When Randy Newman performs *God's Song* (1972) at concerts, he often introduces it with a veiled warning: "This is a song in which God is going to speak to all of you through me. I know it's a surprise, you'd have thought he would've chosen Paul McCartney or Phil Collins." Goodness knows what opinions Macca or Phil hold on the Almighty, but legendary songwriter Randy is clearly not up for joining any flock of the faithful. True to his introduction, Randy delivers the track in the voice of God himself. But the message seems far from divine. Randy's God is, essentially, a sadist: "I burn down your cities, how blind you must be / I take from you your children and you say, 'How blessed are we?' / You all must be crazy to put your faith in me / That's why I love mankind ..." It's all a bit dark really, a mood aided by the morose, gospel-like piano melody. And, wait, there's more. Not only is Randy's God callous and sneering, but also calculating. As the Lord scoffs at humanity's intense stupidity, he concludes that he can do so without fearing any loss of devotion: "... You really need me / That's why I love mankind." It seems that God can dish out the most excruciating torment, safe in the knowledge that his followers will remain unquestioningly loyal. Apparently, this is also the mentality behind musical releases by The Black-Eyed Peas.

AND AS WE WIND ON DOWN THE ROAD / OUR SHADOWS TALLER THAN OUR SOUL ...

— LED ZEPPELIN

When You're Chewing on Life's Gristle … *Monty Python Songs*

Penis Song (Not the Noël Coward Song)

Where better a place to start a list on Monty Python songs than with a frisky little number about dicks? The track first appeared in the group's 1983 film *The Meaning of Life* in a scene which features Eric Idle playing the role of lounge singer, à la Noël Coward (hence the clarification in the song's subtitle). As some very posh folks dine, their charming entertainer sits at the piano and launches into a song as exquisite as the Beaujolais: "Good evening, ladies and gentlemen / Here's a little number I tossed off recently in the Caribbean … Isn't it awfully nice to have a penis? / Isn't it frightfully good to have a dong?" By the end of it all, as the diners nod and applaud, we're left in deep reflection about which penis term said it best ("your piece of pork", perhaps?)

The Silly Walk Song

It is, apparently, a source of bemusement to the Pythons that one of the sketches they are best remembered for is *The Ministry of Silly Walks*. Nothing highbrow here; the group admit that the sketch is just pure silliness. It first appeared in 1970, as part of their TV series *The Flying Circus*. John Cleese plays a British civil servant – complete with bowler hat – whose job it is to develop silly walks for a government ministry. The walks range from absurd tiny two-steps to outlandish, circular leg sweeps. All for no particular reason. When Monty Python reformed for a series of live performances in 2014, John Cleese made it clear that his silly-walk days were behind him. And so, the group wrote a song and hired some lithe young dancers to perform it. *The Silly Walk Song* directs its ridicule at the preposterousness of modern life itself: "Morning Jim, morning Fred / Work all day until you're dead / Money is the root of evil / Money is the fruit of sin …" The perfect track for your morning commute.

The Lumberjack Song

Another *Flying Circus* fan-favourite is *The Lumberjack Song*, which originally appeared on British TV screens in 1969. In the accompanying sketch, a man sings about his dream to become a lumberjack. Suddenly, a choir of Canadian Mounties pop up, echoing his verses: "He's a lumberjack and he's OK / He sleeps all night and works all day." It's all a very rugged tale, with tree-cutting and manly bravado. That is, until our protagonist begins to elaborate, revealing his penchant for high heels, a bra and suspenders. The choir, at first on board, grow increasingly uncomfortable with their echo chorus and their gender-ambiguous lead. Was it PC? Goodness, no. Even back in the late 1960s, the Pythons seemed to be aware that the whole thing was a little risqué. Immediately after the sketch, a matronly lady is heard objecting "All this sex on the television! I keep falling off!"

Every Sperm Is Sacred

Of course, Monty Python have never been far from controversy. In few of their songs is this more the case than in *Every Sperm Is Sacred*, again from 1983's *The Meaning of Life*. The accompanying sketch begins with a Catholic father singing to his 63 children about the reason the family is so large: "Every sperm is sacred / Every sperm is great / If a sperm is wasted / God gets quite irate." With such a catchy chorus, the children can't help but sing along gleefully. For the second verse, a particularly wide-eyed little girl takes the lead, singing about the heathens who "spill theirs" all over the place, without so much as a thought for God's wishes. By the end of the song, the whole Catholic neighbourhood has joined in, cartwheeling and high-kicking while bellowing about the sanctity of semen. The Protestant neighbours look on, finally commenting that they have just two children, which is the exact number of times that they have had sex. At least the satire was dealt out to one and all.

Always Look on the Bright Side of Life

From Monty Python's vast back catalogue, there's one work that will always stand out. *Always Look on the Bright Side of Life* was the song from the very end of their 1979 film *Life of Brian*. In a closing scene to (again) make the Catholics wince, our protagonist Brian is crucified, as a cheeky Cockney hanging on the cross next to him breaks into song. Modelled on the sugary feel-good numbers from old Disney musicals (such as Pinocchio's *Give a Whistle*), the song reminds Brian that being crucified isn't really all that bad: "When you're chewing on life's gristle / Don't grumble, give a whistle / And this'll help things turn out for the best / And, always look on the bright side of life ..." Soon, a whole bunch of condemned men are joining in on the song's chorus, swaying and whistling as they dangle from their crosses. Despite the controversy (or perhaps because of it), the song is deeply beloved. Since 2014, it has been the most popular funeral song in the UK, proving the fact that nobody appreciates slapstick irreverence quite like the Brits.

Where Everybody Knows Your Name

Iconic Theme Tunes of TV Series

How Soon Is Now?
The Smiths

As a TV series, *Charmed* was many things. But, edgy? Surprising, then, that producers chose a Smiths song about crippling social rejection as the theme tune: "I am human and I need to be loved / Just like everybody else does". Or perhaps the choice wasn't so out-there. After all, *Charmed* was a tale of three sisters who were witches, a demographic who might know a few things about social side-lining. And just to keep it Hollywood, the series eschewed The Smiths in favour of a cover version which had already featured on the soundtrack to the hit movie *The Craft*. Anyway, The Smiths can rest assured that their original track does not go underappreciated. Case in point: the composer of the theme tune for *The X-Files* has stated that its famous whistle sound was inspired by the guitar riff of The Smiths' *How Soon Is Now?* And, of course, there was the subsequent 2002 cover version by pop act t.A.T.u. When Smiths singer Morrissey was told about this version, it was pointed out to him that "They're the teenage Russian lesbians", to which Morrissey famously replied "Well, aren't we all?" Profound.

Falling
Julee Cruise

May, 2017. After a hiatus of 26 years, *Twin Peaks* is back. The TV series that changed television has returned for one final season and fans have worked themselves into a frenzy. The ad break finishes, the studio name pops up, the TV screen fades to black. Suddenly, a misty forest; a flash of that iconic old photo of a prom queen, long dead. And then, a hauntingly familiar tune: *dun ... dun-dun*. To say that many fans shed a tear would be an understatement. A lot changes in 26 years, and here was an aural journey to the past, to a simpler time. And it sounded every bit as good. The theme tune to *Twin*

Peaks was composed in the late 80s by regular David Lynch collaborator Angelo Badalamenti. The composer admits that he never imagined his instrumental would feature on the opening sequence of the show. But once David Lynch heard it, he just knew, telling Badalamenti, "This is the identity of *Twin Peaks*". And that it was: eerie, warm, blissful, menacing, all at the same time. Lynch added in lyrics, performed by another regular collaborator, Julee Cruise. The legendary chorus is about as simple as it gets ("Falling / Falling / Are we falling / In love?") It all sounds sickly sweet. Until you begin to wonder whether the song is supposed to be heard as the ethereal, ghostly voice of Laura Palmer, the prom queen from that photo who reveals her story from beyond the grave.

FALLING, FALLING, ARE WE FALLING IN LOVE?

— **JULEE CRUISE**

Where Everybody Knows Your Name
Gary Portnoy

"Making your way in the world today takes everything you've got / Taking a break from all your worries sure would help a lot." The opening lines of the *Cheers* theme tune sound more suited to some gritty drama about a tough-nosed cop who's about ready to go postal. But the song soon launches into a heart-lifting chorus that reminds us that no matter how tough life gets, *Cheers* bar will always be there, offering companionship and sweet, annihilating liquor. Since the TV series ended in 1993, the song has shown remarkable staying power and topped many polls as people's favourite theme tune of all time. Let us never underestimate the public's fondness for getting smashed. Interesting fact about the TV series: apparently, Kelsey Grammar was often intentionally given unfunny lines by writers, just to see how he'd spin them into something hilarious.

Suicide Is Painless
The Mash

The TV series M*A*S*H ran from 1972 to 1983. As a comedy series about US army doctors, viewers may have been struck by its surprisingly moving theme tune: "Suicide is painless / It brings on many changes / And I can take or leave it if I please." So, where did the song come from? Originally, it appeared in the movie MASH in 1970, when a character (a dentist whose nickname is Painless) announces that he is going to commit suicide. The scene is farcical, and there's never any real suggestion that the suicide will happen. To accompany the absurd narrative, director Robert Altman said that he wanted "the stupidest song ever written" and so, enlisted his 14-year-old son to write the lyrics in a matter of minutes. Whether or not the son achieved his father's wishes is a matter of debate. Many find great depth to the song and it went on to be a hit in various countries. Years after the movie, Altman pointed out that while he had only made $70,000 from directing it, his son had made over a million from the song.

Bet You Think This Song Is About You

Songs Inspired by Actors or Actresses

Bette Davis Eyes
Kim Carnes

In Kim Carnes's 1981 anthem, it's not just Bette Davis who gets a mention. The song describes a captivating femme fatale, who lures men with both the looks and the affectations of various screen sirens. The opening line focuses on the physical: "Her hair is Harlow gold / Her lips sweet surprise". The Harlow in question is, of course, the original Blonde Bombshell Jean Harlow. But why stop at just one icon? This seductress knows her Hollywood history: "She got Greta Garbo stand-off sighs / She's got Bette Davis eyes." Bette was known for her gorgeous big eyes. But rather than playing the blinking damsel, Bette usually portrayed characters who were a little off-kilter, even untrustworthy. And that's exactly the case for the lady in the song, the maneater who looks like butter wouldn't melt. The chorus had originally contained the line "And she knows just what it takes to make a crow blush ..." Apparently, this expression means to be adept at all sorts of sordid behaviour. Kim Carnes didn't understand the slang, and changed "crow" to "pro". Most listeners assumed "pro" referred to a prostitute, so it seems the original meaning remained intact.

You're So Vain
Carly Simon

"You're so vain / You probably think this song is about you ..." So, who was the narcissist who believed (apparently justifiably) that he was the subject of one of the biggest hits of the 1970s? For many years, Carly Simon was not telling. *You're So Vain* (1972) became almost as famous for its intrigue as for its catchy chorus. Rumours circulated that the song might have been about Hollywood heartthrob Warren Beatty. In a 1983 interview, Carly remained as coy as her song, claiming that the legendary actor "certainly thought it was about him" (wink, wink). After decades of playing up the mystique, Carly finally came clean in 2015. The singer confirmed that the second verse of the song is about Beatty. That's the part where she sings about a handsome commitment-phobe: "You had me several years ago / When I was still quite naïve / Well, you said that we made such a pretty pair / And that you would never leave ..." As for the other verses, Carly has said that they refer to two other people. But guess what? She's not saying who (you may, at this moment, allow yourself an eyeroll of appropriate scale). One contender could be Mick Jagger. If you listen carefully, that's actually him singing uncredited backing vocals during the second half of the track. Anyway, whoever those other vain suitors might be, the song has undoubtedly gained the status of an all-time classic. And to think that Carly had originally written it as a sappy love song called *Bless You, Ben*. Hard to imagine that lyric would have sparked quite as much gossip.

Barbra Streisand
Duck Sauce

What does Duck Sauce's 2010 worldwide smash actually have to do with Barbra Streisand? Not much; the group just thought it would be a fun name to repeat throughout the track. Then again, there are various nods to the diva herself. The disco-house style of the track sounds kind of like an updated version of Barbra's own dancefloor classics, like *No More Tears (Enough Is Enough)*. Duck Sauce can't take full credit for that 70s vibe though, having based their track largely on a sample from the 1979 Boney M hit *Gotta Go Home*. And then there's the whole New Yorkness of the fast-paced beat and the buoyant vocal ("Woo-ooh-ooh-oooooh ...") In fact, both the video and the album version of the track begin with a brief recording of Babs describing NYC as the best place in the world to follow your dreams. Indeed, she would know. Barbra grew up in a poor, single-parent family in Brooklyn and left school at 16 to try to get into showbiz. A 1963 newspaper review of one of her early performances read "When Streisand cries you a river, you got a river ... and she will be around 50 years from now ..." Can we say the same about Duck Sauce?

Man on the Moon
R.E.M.

"Now, Andy, did you hear about this one? / Tell me, are you locked in the punch? / Andy, are you goofing on Elvis? 'Hey, baby' ..." Andy Kaufmann was an American comedy actor who, throughout the 70s, became enormously famous thanks to TV shows such as Saturday Night Live. With a style somewhere between comedy and performance art, Andy would provoke audiences by always committing to the gag (some suggest that the song line "locked in the punch" refers to this). Amid Elvis covers and brawls with wrestlers, it was never quite clear when – if ever – Andy was being serious. When it was announced that Andy had died of cancer in 1984, aged just 35, many people wondered if it was all another hoax. Some still have their doubts. In R.E.M.'s 1992 classic, Michael Stipe looks back on his own childhood and his memories of Andy. He starts to question everything: the moon landing, science, religion. He imagines Andy standing at a truck stop rather than at the gates of heaven. Is Andy alive? What's real? What's fake? Can fake be real? Can ambiguous lyrics bring on a seizure? (That latter question may not be directly posed by the song.)

That Don't Impress Me Much
Shania Twain

The year was 1999, the country-pop genre was in overdrive and some batshit chick in head-to-toe leopard print was hitchhiking her way across the Mojave Desert. That lady was Shania, in the video for her country crossover classic *That Don't Impress Me Much*. Why the animal print? Well, Shania does seem like the kind of legend who might describe leopard as her favourite colour. What was the song about? Oh, where to begin? Shania meets a series of men who are all very keen (a fact possibly related to the leopard-print bra). The first is a mansplainer, the second is a narcissist, the third has a fancy car. But guess what? Shania is not impressed, at least not much. As for the actor reference, the song contains the famous nonplussed line "Okay, so you're Brad Pitt ..." In 2017, Shania revealed that Brad had actually been the inspiration behind the whole track. "*What?!*", you ask, "Shania had a thing with *Brad*??" No. Apparently, she saw some naked photos of him in *Playgirl* and figured he wasn't all that. We could go into more detail, but a significant percentage of readers have no doubt put down this book by now to engage in a frantic Google Images search.

The Silver Screen
Songs about Films

Mrs. Robinson
Simon & Garfunkel

Ah, Mrs. Robinson, pop culture's original cougar. In the movie *The Graduate* (1967), she was the older lady who got involved with 21-year-old Benjamin (Dustin Hoffman). Nothing too shocking there, we might think, until Benjamin starts dating Mrs. Robinson's daughter and the cougar bares her claws. At the time of filming, director Mike Nichols was a huge fan of Simon & Garfunkel. When he asked them to contribute to the soundtrack, they put forward a song they had previously written titled *Mrs. Roosevelt*. Nichols loved it and, a quick tweaking of syllables later, the film had a lead track. Apart from the new title, though, the song seems much more suited to the struggles of former First Lady, Eleanor. President Roosevelt was famously unfaithful and the track's lyrics seem to tell the tale of a woman whose husband's indiscretions have led her to the psychiatrist's couch: "We'd like to know a little bit about you for our files

/ We'd like to help you learn to help yourself ..." So, was it a case of lyrical laziness by Simon & Garfunkel? Not quite. *The Graduate* is basically about the shifting morals of the late 1960s. And in outlaying the story of the wronged Mrs. Roosevelt, the song laments the morally upstanding heroes of the past: "Where have you gone, Joe DiMaggio? / A nation turns its lonely eyes to you ..." In coming years, will Simon & Garfunkel be tempted to pen a track in a similar vein titled *Ms. Melania*? Time will tell.

Don't Cry for Me, Argentina
Julie Covington

Ok, slightly cheating here. Julie Covington's turn as *Evita* was as part of the 1978 West End musical that started it all. *Evita* the film only came out in 1996, and of course starred Madonna in the title role. How and ever, after a somewhat heated discussion with this book's editorial department, we have opted for the Covington version of the song. And that's just fine. It's fine. No really, it's fine. *Don't Cry for Me, Argentina* is the core of *Evita*, the story of Evita Perón and her incongruous relationship with Argentina's working classes. A girl from a humble background who goes on to marry a dictator, it is up to the viewer to decide whether Evita abandoned her people in favour of the high life, or whether she naïvely tried to effect change from within: "And as for fortune and as for fame / I never invited them in / Though it seemed to the world / They were all I desired." Back in the 1970s, the song's writers had initially been reluctant to make the word "Argentina" so central to the song, fearing it would damage sales of a potential single. Ridiculous as that thought may now seem, their fears were confirmed a few years later, when the song was banned from the BBC during the 1982 Falklands war.

Barefoot in the Park
James Blake ft. Rosalía

Perhaps James Blake is not the most obvious musician to write a song about a romcom. His brooding electropop seems a bit more suited to some sort of arty flick involving Timothée Chalamet, woolly jumpers, pensive gazing, tea. But the movie *Barefoot in the Park*, from 1967, is most definitely, unashamedly a romcom. Starring Jane Fonda and Robert Redford, the classic film is basically a tale of the odd couple. Corie is a fun-loving free spirit; her husband Paul is a reserved young lawyer. As the plot unfolds, we learn that carefree Corie is a fan of wandering barefoot in the park near their tiny New York apartment. Prudent Paul, set in his ways, cannot be convinced to join her. But this is a romcom, so you can probably guess where the story is headed (albeit with a few surprises). Over 50 years later (in 2019), along comes James Blake with an idea for how to turn the tale into a song. Teaming up with the newly crowned queen of flamenco pop, Rosalía, the duo came up with a surprisingly moving number about falling in love and picking up some good habits: "I call off the chase / Who needs balance? I'll see you every day / Barefoot in the park / You start rubbing off on me ..." Yes, it's the old tale of opposites attract and being undone by love. Yes, it's the basic narrative of almost all pop songs. But rarely has it sounded this good.

Debaser
Pixies

It seems like a teenage rite of passage to rock out to *Debaser* (1997). It's really got it all: a manic bassline, demented screaming, a catchy hook. And then, those twisted lyrics: "Got me a movie, I want you to know, / Slicing up eyeballs, I want you to know … I am un *Chien Andalusia*!" Teens the world over pat themselves on the back for having paid enough attention in French class to identify one of the words in that chorus. But, "Andalusia"? Isn't that Spanish? Pixies lead man, Frank Black, has pointed out that the track's muddled linguistics were no accident. He based the song on the 1929 short film *Un Chien Andalou*, the brainchild of Salvador Dalí and director Luis Buñuel. The black-and-white short features a barrage of surrealist scenes, most famously the gag-inducing sequence of an eyeball being slashed open with a razor blade. Frank Black admired the movie's intention to corrupt viewers, to debase their morals and ideas of art. And so, he set about writing a jolting, rocking noise-fest with the same goal. Of course, writing a rock song about an old arthouse film could come across as somewhat pretentious. Just to avoid any highbrow airs, Frank made sure to name-drop the film title incorrectly. Here's to more examples of vocabulary confusion in popular culture – like the time that boxer Mike Tyson expressed his concern that he might "fade to Bolivian" (apparently, he had meant to say "oblivion").

GOT ME A MOVIE, I WANT YOU TO KNOW, SLICING UP EYEBALLS, I WANT YOU TO KNOW…

— PIXIES

The Making Of Timeless Music Documentaries

Amy (song: *Tears Dry on Their Own*)
Amy Winehouse

Amy begins with a grainy video of four London kids chatting and laughing on the night of their friend's 14th birthday. In unison, they begin to sing *Happy Birthday* but the other voices quickly dissipate as an impossibly fresh-faced Amy takes the lead, delivering the song in a warble worthy of Etta James. This 2015 documentary went on to win an Oscar, a Grammy, and about every other award under the sun. The film's footage ranges from the hilarious (Amy's horror-stricken reaction when a journalist compares her to Dido) to the deeply sad (the inebriated singer on stage in Belgrade, at what would become her final performance). Upon its release, Amy's father denounced the documentary. Most strikingly, the film includes a video of Amy enjoying a trip to St. Lucia in an effort to escape the frenzy and addictions of her life back in London. Just as the star is beginning to look relaxed and healthy, her father shows up with a reality TV crew. Apart from the tragic storyline of Amy's private life, the truly fascinating part of the film is, of course, the wonderful music that lives on.

Standing in the Shadows of Motown (song: *Nowhere to Run*)
Martha & The Vandellas

Behind every great man is a great woman. And behind every music legend is a masterly session drummer (or bassist, keyboardist, etc.) Motown was the record label that changed everything, with a sound so distinct that its name has become synonymous with an entire genre of uptempo soul music. It's the unsung heroes behind this sound who feature in *Standing in the Shadows of Motown* (2002). While history remembers big names like Stevie Wonder or Diana Ross, the documentary argues that the sound of Motown was largely influenced by a group of 13 or so session musicians who came to be known as The Funk Brothers. They broke all the rules. For example, on Marvin Gaye's *I Heard It Through the Grapevine*, they used three drummers; on *Nowhere to Run* by Martha & The Vandellas, they used snow chains to create the distinct clinking sound. So, the next time you're listening to your John Legend collection (if you are so inclined) and pondering how he owes so much to Stevie, spare a thought for The Funk Brothers, who might be due at least as much credit.

The Devil and Daniel Johnston (song: True Love Will Find You in the End)

Daniel Johnston

In 1990, Daniel Johnston was returning from a performance in a two-seater plane which his dad was flying. In a manic episode, he started to believe that he was *Casper, The Friendly Ghost*, snatched the plane's key from the ignition and threw it out the window. His father managed to crash-land in a forest. Both passengers escaped with only minor injuries, but the extent of Daniel's mental problems was suddenly undeniable. Soon after, he was committed for a stint to a psychiatric hospital. In *The Devil and Daniel Johnston* (2005), we get to know the genius and the inner demons of Daniel, the famed singer and visual artist. From childhood, he taped much of his life and thoughts on a small cassette recorder, allowing the film-makers a huge amount of material to piece together his life story. And what a story it is. International success, comparisons to Bob Dylan, Kurt Cobain as his biggest fan, all while battling the voices of his schizophrenia and bipolar disorder. The documentary is proof of Daniel's fascinating power to wear his heart – and his mind – on his sleeve.

Lomax, The Songhunter (song: Johnny B. Goode)

Chuck Berry

Believe it or not, music was not invented by Cher. Alan Lomax dedicated his life to recording traditional folk music from around the world. In this way, he created a digital catalogue before such types of music get wiped out by globalisation. *Lomax, The Songhunter* (2004) was filmed in the final years of Alan's life and travels the world, from America's Deep South to rural Spain, to interview the singers and musicians (or their relatives) who Alan had recorded as part of his research earlier in his life. As an expert on world music, Lomax also worked on the *Voyager Golden Record*. This is a vinyl record which was sent into space with the Voyager spacecraft in 1977. The aim of the disc was to provide a selection of recordings from planet Earth, which could ultimately be discovered by extraterrestrial life forms. Lomax fought fiercely to have the disc include ethnic music, such as Azerbaijani bagpiping, rather than the more obvious choice to just go for classical compositions. The disc also featured more contemporary songs, like Chuck Berry's *Johnny B. Goode*. Despite the disc's late-70s launch date, Gary Glitter sadly didn't make the final cut.

Stop Making Sense (song: *Burning Down the House*)
Talking Heads

Ok, granted, *Stop Making Sense* is not exactly a documentary. No fly-on-the-wall footage and heartfelt interviews. It is simply a video of a concert. But not just any concert. This was Talking Heads at the height of their powers in late 1983, leaving a visual record for all music acts which will ever exist of *how it is done* (take note, jaded rockstars of the 21st century). The film begins with singer David Byrne taking to the bare stage for a solo performance of *Psycho Killer*. For the second song, bassist Tina joins him; for each successive song another member of the band joins in, and the audience's hysteria builds. By the time the set reaches the funky, high-energy *Burning Down the House*, the full line-up is finally present, and it seems as though something – or someone – might actually explode from the sheer delirium of it all. Later, David appears in his iconic, oversized business suit. Why? Apparently, he wanted his head to look small. Then again, we should know better than to ask questions of a group so determined in their mission to stop making sense.

Clowns to the Left of Me
Songs Featured in Tarantino Films

Stuck in the Middle with You
Stealers Wheel
(movie: *Reservoir Dogs*)

What could be more Tarantino than a smartly suited psychopath, gruesome torture and groovy, retro rock 'n' roll? The psycho was Mr. Blonde (Michael Madsen), the torture included severing the ear of a kidnapped policeman, while the soundtrack was provided by Scottish rockers Stealers Wheel. Their 70s hit is about a night out at a fancy London restaurant for a record-label event, full of pretentious types and a gloating CEO, both of which cause the singer to despair: "Clowns to the left of me / Jokers to the right / Here I am / Stuck in the middle with you". Although the lyrics mention nothing about jewellery heists or razor blades, the fun track provided the perfect, juxtaposed accompaniment to the bloody scene. As the singer mocks the industry minions kissing up to their boss and saying "Please! Please!", the viewer can only imagine the same words going through the mind of the helpless policeman.

Girl, You'll Be a Woman Soon
Urge Overkill
(movie: *Pulp Fiction*)

In this day and age, can you imagine some heartthrob like Nick Jonas penning a love ballad to his teenage fans centred around the lines: "Girl, you'll be a woman soon / Soon, you'll need a man"? Eww. Well, in 1967, a 26-year-old Neil Diamond did just that. Somehow the lyrics seem a little less creepy when applied to the charmingly odd bond between *Pulp Fiction*'s Vince (John Travolta) and Mia (Una Thurman). Tarantino chose a 1992 cover by Chicago rockers Urge Overkill to set the mood for one of the movie's most famous scenes. Vince is playing escort for the night to Mia, the wife of his mobster boss. With rising sexual tension between the two, Vince takes a trip to the bathroom to cool off, knowing that he really needs to resist temptation. The power dynamic is an interesting one: which of the two is the song's seductive predator? Meanwhile, Mia snorts a large line of what turns out to be heroin, and she immediately OD's. As the song fades, Mia's eyes roll back and it's clear that Vince's woes have just gotten a hell of a lot more complicated.

Across 110th Street
Bobby Womack
(movie: *Jackie Brown*)

Jackie Brown is a woman with a mission. Working as a flight attendant, she bumps up her small salary by smuggling money for an illegal gun trader. In the 1997 movie's opening sequence, we see uniformed Jackie (Pam Grier) steadfastly walking towards the airport gate with a heavy bag draped over her shoulder. Black, strong and unflinching, what better song to accompany our heroine than Womack's soul classic? *Across 110th Street* is a soaring tale of doing what it takes to make it out of the ghetto (110th Street is in South Harlem): "You don't know what you'll do until you're put under pressure / 'Cross 110th Street is a hell of a tester". When the song hits its chorus and refers to the ghetto's pimps "trying to catch a woman that's weak", Jackie's determined face tells viewers that this woman is anything but.

Bang Bang
Nancy Sinatra
(movie: *Kill Bill Vol. 1*)

"Bill, it's your baby", the pregnant bride (Uma Thurman) utters to Bill just before he shoots her in the head in the opening sequence of the movie. This was supposed to be her wedding day, cut short by Bill and his group of assassins. The heart-stopping scene cuts to the opening credits and to Nancy's 1966 version of *Bang Bang*. Not that Sonny Bono intended the song about lost love to be taken quite so literally when he wrote it: "Music played, and people sang / Just for me the church bells rang ... Bang bang. He shot me down / Bang bang. I hit the ground ..." It's almost as if the scene was written around the song. In true Tarantino style, our female protagonist rises from the ashes: the bride awakes from a coma. By the closing chords of the song, her epic mission is about to begin: to find, and to kill, Bill.

Cat People
David Bowie
(movie: *Inglourious Basterds*)

When Tarantino was a young movie buff working at a video store, he watched the 1982 erotic horror *Cat People.* What struck him most was that its classic theme song, written by David Bowie, had been relegated to the closing credits. He vowed that if he ever got the chance, he would right the wrong. Fast forward almost three decades, Quentin Tarantino is *Quentin fucking Tarantino* and is working on a World War II movie called *Inglourious Basterds*. Central to its plot is a character named Shosanna, who lost her Jewish family to the Nazis as a child and who now lives under a false name in Paris and runs a cinema. When news arrives that Hitler and the entire Nazi leadership are to hold a movie premiere at her cinema, Shosanna mulls it over. As we see her pensively gazing out the eye-shaped window of the projector room, Bowie's voice comes in: "See these eyes so green / I can stare for a thousand years". Could this be Shosanna's chance to avenge a lifetime of anguish? The song builds to its central line, Bowie shouting "putting out fire with gasoline!" And we instantly suspect that whatever resolution Shosanna is contemplating, it might just involve giving the Nazis a dose of their own fiery medicine.

The Wild Child
Songs Featured in Pedro Almodóvar's Films

Encadenados
Lucho Gatica
(movie: *Entre Tinieblas / Dark Habits*, 1983)

Almodóvar, the *enfant terrible*. At the start of the 80s, who else would have made a movie about a lesbian nun with a heroin habit? And in Catholic Spain! *Entre Tinieblas* first introduces us to Yolanda, a drug-taking cabaret singer on the run from the law. She's given refuge at a local convent, home to a group of eccentric Sisters of Mercy. The Mother Superior is immediately smitten with sultry, provocative Yolanda, so the two are soon flirting wildly. And what better soundtrack to a story of tangled passions than the slow-tempo melodrama of a Latin-American *bolero*? *Encadenados*, recorded in 1958 by Chilean crooner Lucho Gatica, is the perfect accompaniment to the smouldering scene where Yolanda and the reverend mother recognise a spark. The two ladies sing along to the song's verses, telling a tale of a liaison best avoided: "Tal vez sería mejor que no volvieras / Quizas fuera mejor que me olvidaras / Volver es empezar a atormentarnos ..." ("Perhaps it would be better if you didn't come back / Perhaps it would be better if you forgot me / Coming back is to begin to torment each other ..."). Both Yolanda and the Mother Superior fall into a raucous relationship of coke and heroin sessions. It's only when Yolanda decides to go clean that the Mother Superior will truly understand what those anguished *bolero* lyrics were truly all about.

Un Año de Amor
Luz Casal
(movie: *Tacones Lejanos / High Heels*, 1991)

What could be more Almodóvar than a sassy, soaring ballad, lip-synched by a gorgeous drag queen? Especially while the other characters in the room exchange sideways glances that suggest love triangles, love rectangles, love pentagons ... you get the idea. The queen in question is named Letal and is performing *Un Año de Amor*, an early hit by famous singer Becky del Páramo. But guess what? Becky is in the audience with her daughter Rebeca and son-in-law Manuel. And as for those glances, they just might be related to the fact that Becky and Manuel used to be lovers. The song, actually sung by legendary Spanish performer Luz Casal, mirrors the story of a past passion that continues to smoulder: "Recordarás, nuestros días felices / Recordarás, el sabor de mis besos / Y entenderás, en un solo momento / Que significa un año de amor." ("You'll recall our happy days / You'll recall the taste of my kisses / And you'll understand, right then / The meaning of a year of love."). As the song builds to its climax, emotions stir for all our characters. Will Becky and her son-in-law give into temptation? And what will daughter Rebeca do when she helps Letal out of his dress after the performance, only to be confronted by his gobsmackingly enticing package?!

RECORDARAS, NUESTROS DIAS FELICES / RECORDARAS, EL SABOR DE MIS BESOS ...

— LUZ CASAL

Cucurrucucú Paloma
Caetano Veloso (movie: *Hable con Ella / Talk to Her*, 2002)

While Almodóvar films are beloved for their glorious ridiculousness, that's not to say they don't pack an emotional punch. In few scenes is this more evident than in the early stages of *Hable con Ella*, when wedding guests gather to watch Caetano Veloso perform the old Mexican folk song *Cucurrucucú Paloma*. On a balmy summer night, the crowd sits in silence as the singer softly delivers a tale about a man whose soul turns into a mourning dove after the loss of his loved one. The lonesome dove returns to the house he used to share with his love, cooing his heartbreak to the empty building: "Cucurrucucú, paloma / Cucurrucucú, no llores / Las piedras jamas, paloma / ¡Que van a saber de amores!" ("Coo-coo, mourning dove / Coo-coo, don't cry / The stones will never, mourning dove, / Understand anything about love!"). The scene's protagonist, Marco, is overwhelmed with grief as he listens to the song, reminded of a past love. He is comforted by his new girlfriend, Lydia. Sadly for Marco, the song will prove to be more fitting to his story than he could ever have imagined.

Volver
Estrella Morente (movie: *Volver*, 2006)

When Raimunda (Penelope Cruz) sits down to sing *Volver*, she tells her audience that she hasn't sung in a very long time. Tonight, she has chosen a number taught to her by her mother, who passed away three years previously. Raimunda launches into a passionate flamenco ballad (thanks to the voice of Granadan *cantaora* Estrella Morente, rather than Penelope) which speaks of an unresolved past: "Tengo miedo del encuentro / Con el pasado que vuelve / A enfrentarse con mi vida ..." ("I'm afraid of the encounter / With the past which has returned / To confront my life ..."). As Raimunda sings about the past coming back to haunt her, she begins to tear up. And she's not the only one. Watching from a nearby parked car is none other than the ghost of her mother. Raimunda may not know it yet, but mom is back in town for a showdown with the daughter who resents her so much. The song builds to a bittersweet insistence on making amends: "Volver / Con la frente marchita ... Sentir / Que es un soplo la vida / Que veinte años no es nada ..." ("Returning / With a wrinkled brow ... Feeling / That life passes like a gust of wind / That 20 years is nothing ..."). As the scene concludes, ghost mom is sobbing uncontrollably. Might it be time for her to make an appearance?

We Exist!
Songs about Gender Identity

Get Back
The Beatles

Was the mainstream music industry capable of depicting transgender people in a respectful way as far back as 1969? Let's not get carried away. But the idea of gender as a construct was at least present. The tune for *Get Back* started off as a jam session, with nonsensical lyrics thrown in. And then a vague story began to form: "Sweet Loretta Martin thought she was a woman / But she was another man / All the girls around her say she's got it coming / But she gets it while she can". The Beatles never really explained their surprising verse, and many fans suggest that it was written in haste as a last-minute replacement. Paul McCartney admitted that he had originally written the song as a parody of anti-immigrant British MP Enoch Powell, in which the instruction to "Get back to where you once belonged" was directed at foreigners in the UK. The group thought better of their ironic version, and instead went for their cryptic tale about Loretta, which to be honest still sounds a tad objectionable. Should we give Paul the benefit of the doubt and assume he was still in parody mode?

Walk on the Wild Side
Lou Reed

In 2017, a students' association at an Ontario university issued a public apology for having included *Walk on the Wild Side* in a playlist at a campus event. They expressed regret for having played a song that was hurtful to the trans community. Lou Reed's friends were having none of it. They pointed out that the late Lou was an ally of all the marginalised, and that he had written the 1972 track as a love song to trans idols like Holly Woodlawn and Candy Darling: "Holly came from Miami, FLA / Hitchhiked her way across the USA / Plucked her eyebrows on the way / Shaved her legs and then he was a she". Ok, so these days Lou would probably be more sensitive about his pronouns, but the singer was clearly in awe of the wild,

gender-bending characters of the Warhol-led New York underground scene. As many of his fans point out, it wasn't just a coincidence that … *Wild Side* came from an album called *Transformer*.

HOLLY CAME FROM MIAMI, FLA / HITCHHIKED HER WAY ACROSS THE USA …

— LOU REED

We Exist
Arcade Fire

Lead singer of Arcade Fire, Win Butler, says that he originally wrote *We Exist* (2013) as a story of a gay kid coming out to his father. The song tells a tale which is sadly familiar to most members of the LGBTQ community, of a world which would rather deny than accept: "They're down on their knees / Begging us please / Praying that we don't exist … But we exist!" What caught the attention of the trans community in particular was the accompanying video. It features actor Andrew Garfield as a trans woman in the early stages of her coming-out process. In a storyline that shifts from harrowing to euphoric, the video's protagonist endures a horrific beating, only to emerge transformed as a superstar goddess. As is often the case, many viewers wondered why a story about a trans woman hadn't been filmed using a trans actress. Were cis folk just jumping on the trans bandwagon? Butler says the decision was to do with exposure. Andrew Garfield had been keen to do the role and Win liked the idea of kids around the world seeing their hero Spiderman playing a trans role. You have to admit, it's a good argument.

Nancy Boy
Placebo

On the UK music scene, 1997 was the era of Oasis. It was a time when lads were lads and ladies were ... also lads (though some preferred the term *ladettes*). And then along came Placebo: three guys playing thrashy punk, wearing tight dresses and exquisite make-up, serving gender-fluid *realness*! Their first major hit, *Nancy Boy* was an ambiguous tale of sex 'n' drugs, with an undoubtedly flexible take on sexuality and gender. The song's exact subject matter is a point of much discussion. Is it about gay sex ("Lose my clothes, lose my lube")? Is our protagonist a rent boy ("Fifty pounds press my button going down")? Or perhaps a drag queen ("Does his makeup in his room / Douse himself with cheap perfume")? Whatever the message of the song, it was something far more leftfield than would ever be offered by those anorak-wearing Gallagher brothers.

For Today I Am a Boy
Antony and the Johnsons

Back in 2005, fans of Antony and the Johnson's were intrigued by the group's new album, *I Am a Bird Now*. The cover featured trans icon Candy Darling, fabulously coiffed and made-up, staring down the lens. But far from a joyous shot, Candy is laying in the hospital bed where she would soon pass away. It's a powerful photo, and fans wondered why Antony might have chosen it. Of the album's many great songs, perhaps the one which stood out most was the deeply moving *For Today I Am a Boy*. Antony, who would later transition to Anohni, seemed to be getting right to the point: "One day I'll grow up, I'll be a beautiful woman / One day I'll grow up, I'll be a beautiful girl / But for today I am a child, for today I am a boy". It's interesting that Anohni doesn't seem to be angry or revulsed at being mislabelled as male. It's almost as if she sees it as a growing stage on her path to being perceived as a woman. Would the butterfly feel annoyed at having once been seen as a caterpillar? Can butterflies even get pissed off? Oh whatever. Surely, Candy Darling would have been very proud.

What's in a Name?
Songs Based on Women's Names

Martha
Tom Waits

If you ever happen to find yourself in a contest of first-one-to-cry-buys-the-next-drink, do try to steer clear of Tom Waits' *Martha* (1973). One listen and you're doomed. What could be sadder than an elderly gentleman, phoning up the former girlfriend from 40 years ago who he's never managed to truly let go? In the track, Tom Waits assumes a character named Tom Frost. Now in the autumn of his years, Tom phones Martha to tell her about his fond memories of their time together: "Those were the days of roses, of poetry and prose / And Martha, all I had was you and all you had was me." We find out that both characters went on to marry other people, and that Martha (at least) still seems to be wed. As the piano and strings stir emotions, old Tom gets braver and bolder, finally blurting it out: "Martha, Martha / I love you can't you see?"

The Wind Cries Mary
The Jimi Hendrix Experience

Insight for today: if the wind is speaking to you, this may be pointing to some unresolved issue in your life. In Jimi's 1967 hit, it seems he's got it bad. To the melody of *that* iconic strumming, Jimi tells us that he "can hear happiness staggering on down the street", presumably leaving him to indulge in a good ol' wallow. Most commentators agree that Jimi wrote *The Wind Cries Mary* about an argument that he'd had with his girlfriend. The verses suggest a tempestuous relationship, of the kind where plates get smashed. And now, "Somewhere a queen is weeping / Somewhere a king has no wife." Kind of a lose-lose, really. Interestingly, the song is more of a lament than an apology. It doesn't seem like Jimi was in the mood for fawning, especially when you consider that his girlfriend's real name was Kathy. Apparently, Mary was her second name, and she hated it. Shady tactics, Jimi.

Angie
The Rolling Stones

"Angie, Angie / When will those clouds all disappear?" In the Stones' 1973 classic, it looks like the rain is setting in on a relationship. In fact, perhaps the moment has come for a poignant goodbye. No anger or recrimination here, Mick Jagger keeps things simple and sweet. It's time for him and Angie to face some hard truths: "With no loving in our soul / And no money in our coats / You can't say we're satisfied." It's really all quite adult of Mick, just a heartfelt acknowledgement that a relationship has run its course. Stones enthusiasts point out that if you listen carefully to the track, you can hear Jagger's vocal guide in the background (that's a previous recording of the song which he sang along to in the studio). Angela Merkel enthusiasts (no, really) point out that the song was used as part of her 2005 election campaign, when she first got voted in as German Chancellor. Of course, it would be ridiculous to claim that Mick Jagger established the path of European politics for most of the early 21st century. Wouldn't it?

ANGIE, WHEN WILL THOSE CLOUDS ALL DISAPPEAR?

— THE ROLLING STONES

Matilda
alt-J

Natalie Portman, responsible for incarnating the most badass 12-year-old that cinema has ever seen. The movie *Léon* was released in 1994. It tells the story of a girl named Mathilda, played by a very young Portman, whose family get murdered by a corrupt cop. Mathilda escapes the killers by taking refuge in the apartment of her neighbour, Léon, who happens to be a hitman. Léon and Mathilda strike up a friendship: he trains her in weapons, she teaches him how to read. alt-J's *Matilda* (sic), from 2012, is an ode to the pre-teen renegade herself. The song is delivered in the voice of her loyal friend Léon: "Put the grenade pin in your hand, so you understand who's boss ... Oh, this is from / This is from / This is from Matilda." There's really no way of explaining the track without some major spoilers, so you may want to stop reading now. Fans of the movie will recall its climactic scene, when a wounded and dying Léon hands something to that corrupt cop, uttering the classic line "This is ... from ... Mathilda." It's a grenade pin. Boom!

Black Betty
Ram Jam

In the late 1970s, the world rocked out to the pounding, repeated sound of "Whoa, Black Betty (bam-ba-lam)". For a brief few weeks, it seemed like New York rockers Ram Jam were taking over the world. What few radio listeners may have realised is that *Black Betty* was no recently-penned composition. Rather, it originated as an African-American work song dating back to the early 1900s, often credited to the black folk singer Lead Belly. These days, the whole thing would lead to yells of cultural appropriation. But it was the 70s, Twitter didn't exist, and Ram Jam were free to commercialise whoever's history they pleased. Fans argue that the song is a simple appreciation of a beautiful black woman named Betty. Others suggest that a Black Betty is a musket rifle, hence the "bam-ba-lam", or even a whip which was used on slaves. Such ambiguity pushed civil rights groups to call for a boycott of the song when it was released. Ram Jam never quite took off and soon disbanded.

Valerie
Amy Winehouse

When British indie rockers The Zutons first released *Valerie* in 2006, the track climbed to number nine in the UK charts and then disappeared soon after. It was hardly the trajectory of a radio classic. But the song had found a famous fan: queen of big hair and modern soul, Amy Winehouse. Perhaps it was those jailbird lyrics: "Did you have to go to jail? / Put your house on up for sale / Did you get a good lawyer?" The lead singer of The Zutons says the Valerie in question was an American friend who had fallen into trouble with the law and who he now missed. A year later, Winehouse was considering which song to contribute to an album of covers that her producer friend Mark Ronson was putting together. When Amy suggested *Valerie*, Ronson was surprised. Amy had previously stated that she didn't listen to anything written after 1967 and had no interest in white music. And yet, she wanted to have a go at this modern indie track. Mark Ronson took her vocal and set it to the beat of *Town Called Malice* by The Jam. Et voilà. A true classic was born. The Zutons must be a bit peeved, though.

You Can Choose Your Friends ...
Songs about Parents

Down by the Water
PJ Harvey

Probably not the ideal background music for a pleasant family meal, *Down by the Water* (1995) tells the story of a creepy mother who drowns her own daughter. Once the evil deed has been told, the song advances into the iconic, eerie whispering of indie music's most demented mother: "Little fish, big fish, swimming in the water / Come back here, man, gimme my daughter". Harvey has publicly despaired at the idea of people taking her lyrics literally, claiming that some critics "believe I have actually given birth to a child and drowned her". Oh, humanity! By that logic, The Sex Pistols literally wanted God to save the Queen (doubtful) and Michael Jackson really was bad (ok, this latter argument is more problematic). Anyway, let us allow PJ her poetry. Could the daughter in question be the singer's younger self? That's for PJ to know, and for fans to get into arguments about on Reddit.

A Boy Named Sue
Johnny Cash

In February 1969, Johnny Cash performed to a captive audience. Literally. The King of Country held a concert for inmates at San Quentin State Prison, California. And what better song to include on the setlist than a jaunty number about an angry hick and his no-good Paw? *A Boy Named Sue* tells the tale of a young lad whose father named him Sue and then skipped town. The name makes the boy an easy target for bullies, making him resolve as an adult to get his revenge on "the dirty, mangy dog that named me Sue". When the boy grows up and finally tracks down dad, father and son engage in a rootin'-tootin' bar-brawl, until Sue emerges victorious. Defeated, dad looks the son in the eye and lets it all out: "Son, this world is rough / And if a man's gonna make it, he's gotta be tough … So I give you that name and I said goodbye / I knew you'd have to get tough or die …" Plot-twist level: Expert! Those San Quentin prisoners didn't know what hit them, erupting into cheers. Johnny knew a classic recording when he heard one and released the track as a single a few months later. It went on to become his biggest ever chart hit.

> *LITTLE FISH, BIG FISH, SWIMMING IN THE WATER. COME BACK HERE, MAN, GIMME MY DAUGHTER.*
>
> — PJ HARVEY

Ode to My Family
The Cranberries

"My mother, my mother she'd hold me / Did she hold me, when I was out there / My father, my father, he liked me / Oh he liked me …" The lyrics of The Cranberries' *Ode* (1994) have led to many discussions over the years. Some question whether the word "like" is too mild to describe a father-daughter bond. But The Cranberries grew up in rural Ireland in the 80s; perhaps love was just one of those cringey things Americans spoke about on TV. All things considered, the song seems to be a bittersweet ballad contrasting the singer's unhappiness as an adult with her relatively content upbringing ("... we were raised / To see life as fun and take it if we can"). Singer Dolores clarified the debate in a 2002 interview: "You know who really gets that song? People who've lost their parents ... 'cos they go, 'Why didn't I tell them when they were alive?'" When her own father passed away in 2011, Dolores was unable to perform the song for a while. After Dolores' own death in London in 2018, she was flown back to Limerick and buried next to dad. Now if *that* doesn't make you well up while listening to the track, then you are 100%, certified, one cold-hearted bitch (that includes male readers).

I'm My Own Grandpa
Willie Nelson

Ever married your own cousin? If so, buckle up, you may have a new favourite song. *I'm My Own Grandpa* was first recorded in the 1940s and covered by Willie in 2001. Ok, it's not quite about cousins marrying, but close enough. The song describes the life of a man who finds himself in a somewhat unique situation: through a series of ludicrous (but weirdly possible) marriages and births, the man realises that he is now his own grandfather. It all begins when the singer marries a woman who has an adult daughter. The singer's father then marries this adult daughter, and thus the mind-boggling proceeds: "This made my dad my son-in-law / And really changed my life. / Now my daughter was my mother / 'Cause she was my father's wife". Both couples then go on to have children, adding further links to the complex chain of events. The song must surely be praised for touching on the rare theme of family as a sordid, tangled web. On an entirely unrelated note, the track was originally recorded by country duo Lonzo and Oscar, who hail from Alabama and Kentucky (respectively). Just saying.

Sisters (and Brothers) in Arms
Songs about Siblings

You Are My Sister
Antony and the Johnsons ft. Boy George

When it comes to siblings, it can really go either way. For every Beyoncé and Solange (i.e. "Got your back, girl!"), there's a Noel and Liam (i.e. "Shut yer cake 'ole!"). In *You Are My Sister* (2005), Anonhi (who at the time was known as Antony) wears her heart on her sleeve. It seems she's lucked out, honoured since birth to have a loyal kindred spirit: "You are my sister / And I love you / May all of your dreams come true." The song could easily be a loving tribute to a friend, though various references to shared childhood memories might suggest that this relationship is genuinely genetic. The verses really couldn't be more simple, Anonhi wishing nothing but the best for her beloved sis. Anonhi's later gender transition added an extra layer to the song, allowing it to be interpreted as a love-song to the sisterhood of the entire trans community. Funny how songs can take on new meanings.

The Mother We Share
Chvrches

Euphoric synths, tear-inducing harmonies, heartfelt lyrics about … about … siblings?? "Come in misery, where you can seem as old as your omens / And the mother we share / Will never keep your proud head from falling …" Chvrches' 2013 electropop anthem does present itself as a very likely candidate to be a song about brothers or sisters, but upon closer inspection it seems like "mother" is a loose term. Singer Lauren once claimed: "I would say it's not literally about families and siblings, but I don't know … I suppose it's what kind of experiences people are having at that time." So, the track is what you make it to be. Could the "mother" in question be an experience? Or is it the past? Or is it (curveball alert!) Mother Nature? However we choose to understand the song, it clearly contains a strong element of siblinghood. What's not so clear is who, or what, the sibling is.

DANIEL, MY BROTHER, YOU ARE OLDER THAN ME.

— ELTON JOHN

Daniel
Elton John

"Daniel my brother, you are older than me / Do you still feel the pain of the scars that won't heal? / Your eyes have died, but you see more than I." Elton John's lyricist (Bernie Taupin) sure knows how to tell a good story. He says that the lyrics for *Daniel* (1973) were inspired by an article that he once read about a US soldier who had returned home from the Vietnam war. As with many returnees, the man was finding it difficult to adapt to life back home. The song imagines that the soldier (Daniel) goes to Spain to start a new life, his departure described to the listener by his tearful younger brother. Why have Daniel's eyes "died"? Was he blinded during the war? Or does he have a blank stare of PTSD? And why Spain? That's an easier answer: because "Spain" rhymes with "plane", according to Taupin. Deep, man. Reportedly, Donatella Versace named her son after this song. Because nothing says "good luck in life" quite like being named after an imaginary, traumatised war vet.

Little Sister
Ry Cooder

No, Ry Cooder's 1979 hit is not an ode to the sweet wee lass who he grew up with. Not in the conventional sense, anyway. The song is a cover of an old Elvis track and it is most certainly not directed at the singer's own sibling. Rather, the lyrics are addressed to the little sister of Ry's ex-girlfriend. It seems the singer has a soft spot for this particular family, begging: "Little sister don't you kiss me once and twice / Say it's very nice and then you run / Little sister don't you do what your big sister done". Paranoia, much? Creepy-older-guy, much? While the song's rockin' vibe and soulful backing vocals will never go out of style, lyrically, the track may not have stood the test of time so well. This sense is certainly not helped by a later verse where Ry notices that the little sister "been a growing ... from your head down to your toes". Now, surely the latter part of that line is unnecessary.

LITTLE SISTER DON'T YOU KISS ME ONCE AND TWICE.

— RY COODER

It's My Desire! Songs Involving Jack White

Seven Nation Army
The White Stripes

Jack White. Hellraiser. Taxidermy enthusiast. Most prolific man in rock. While Jack has many musical formations under his belt, he is best known for his namesake group, The White Stripes. Actually, the name White originally came from his wife, Meg. He adopted her surname when the two married in 1996 (his original was Gillis, which is so much less cool). The duo formed The White Stripes in 1997 and quickly caught people's attention with banging tracks and their trademark red, white and black aesthetic. It also helped that they thoroughly bamboozled the public by letting on that they were siblings. The marriage ended in 2000, though not on bad terms, and the group continued until 2011. *Seven Nation Army* is their 2002 classic, a tale of telling the haters (and the gossip mongers) to back off: "I'm gonna fight 'em off / A seven nation army couldn't hold me back." Incidentally, "seven nation army" is the name that a very young Jack used to call *Salvation Army* charity stores. With its fightin' talk and mind-blowing riff, the track became a huge international hit. It also provided a new chant of choice for sports fans (and Jeremy Corbyn supporters) around the world.

Steady, As She Goes
The Raconteurs

Reaching worldwide success would be an excuse for many a rocker to rest on their laurels, head to the Bahamas, sit on gold-plated toilets and such. But not Jack. In 2005, amidst various other musical projects, Jack wrote a song with his friend Brendan Benson. The result was *Steady, As She Goes*, a storming rock hit about settling down, finding a wife and ... regretting it at leisure: "Well here we go again / You've found yourself a friend that knows you well / But no matter what you do / You'll always feel as though you tripped and fell." The song convinced both Jack and Brendan of their creative compatibility. Soon after, they drafted in a bassist and a

I'M GONNA FIGHT 'EM OFF / A SEVEN NATION ARMY COULDN'T HOLD ME BACK.

— JACK WHITE

drummer (both from a group called The Greenehornes) and began work on an album. The following years would see a tour with Bob Dylan, another album, an eight-year hiatus and an eventual return to the scene in 2018. All that stopping and starting. Jack's CV must be a fucking mess.

SOME PEOPLE DIE JUST A LITTLE. SOMETIMES YOU DIE BY THE DROP.
— JACK WHITE

Die by the Drop
The Dead Weather

Right, so it may be sinking in by now that Jack White is really quite a busy man. In 2009, perhaps unsurprisingly, he lost his voice while touring with The Raconteurs. As a solution, they asked Alison Mosshart (from the group The Kills) to fill in for Jack on certain songs. He clearly admired the job she did because soon the two were in the recording studio. They drafted in a guitarist and a bassist from other groups and Jack decided that this time, he would be drummer. Yes sir, Jack is the pony of many tricks, including drumming. Several albums and tours later, The Dead Weather are still going strong. *Die by the Drop* is a track from 2009, in which Jack thumps his way through a familiar theme of a life not fully lived: "Some people die just a little / Sometimes you die by the drop".

Over and Over and Over
Jack White (solo)

More versatile than a tub of Vaseline, in 2012, Jack decided to try his hand as a solo artist. And, shock, it all worked out pretty well for him. Industrious as ever, *Over and Over and Over* comes from his third album (2018). To write it, Jack claims to have been influenced by rappers from the 80s and 90s.

Apparently, the track had been in his head for a while: he had initially considered it as a track for The White Stripes, then The Raconteurs, then as a possible collaboration with Jay-Z. In the end, he kept it for himself. And the hip-hop references come across loud and clear, the track sounding more Beastie Boys than White Stripes. Jack sings about his angst, comparing himself to Sisyphus, the mythological king condemned to pushing a boulder up a hill for all eternity: "Anxiety and I rolling down a mountain / (Over and over) / My shoulder holds the weight of the world." Maybe the most prolific man in rock could do with a holiday?

Danger! High voltage!
Electric Six

And so, to conclude this list firmly on the leftfield, we turn to the inimitable Electric Six. Ok, so Jack wasn't actually ever a member of the band. But legend has it that he is responsible for the delirious, shrieking voice on the group's stomping party duet *Danger! High voltage!* (2002). Officially, the vocals are credited to a certain "John S. O'Leary", who the group claim was a mechanic that had won a competition to feature on the track. Hmm. Those shrieks sure are quite Jack-like though, as is the mildly twisted nature of lyrics about a lust that can't be quenched: "Don't you want to know how we keep starting fires? / (It's my desire!) It's my desire, *it's my desire!*" The song is equally remembered for its video. It featured the group's singer Dick Valentine (yes, that's his name) performing the duet with a somewhat older lady, interspersed with scenes of the two kissing aggressively while their private parts light up in the frenzy. Perhaps as a nod to Jack's infatuation with taxidermy, the video also features a rather aroused-looking stuffed moose.

Spinnin' a Yarn
Songs that Are Short Stories

Hurricane
Bob Dylan

Few musicians fit the bill as master storyteller more than Bob Dylan. After all, how many other singers can claim a Nobel Prize for Literature? (Although, time will tell if Mr. President will ever receive proper recognition for mid-90s anthem *Coco Jambo.*) At over eight minutes long, *Hurricane* (1975) is pretty much a condensed novel set to music. But sadly, this is no work of fiction. The song tells the tale of the African-American boxer Rubin "Hurricane" Carter, who was convicted of a triple murder which occurred in 1966. He was sent to jail, where he wrote his autobiography to protest his innocence. That was the book that inspired Dylan to write his classic song, outlining the rotten, racist system that had led to Carter's conviction: "Here comes the story of the Hurricane / The man the authorities came to blame / For something that he never done ..." The song's success drew public attention to Carter's case, as did the two benefit concerts for the ex-boxer that Dylan performed. In 1985, after 18 years in prison, a judge ruled that Carter was innocent and released him. Such is the power of a well-told story. Especially when it's true.

Roland the Headless Thompson Gunner
Warren Zevon

In the mood for a war song or a ghost story? Get yourself a man who can do both! Warren Zevon's 1978 classic is a song that straddles genres, even down to its musical style which is somewhere between bluesy piano and Irish drinking ballad. And then there's the tale itself. Roland is a Norwegian mercenary who heads to Africa to fight in wars there during the 60s. He is considered to be the best in the world with a Thompson submachine gun, a fact that draws too much attention: "So the CIA decided / They wanted Roland dead / That son-of-a-bitch Van Owen / Blew off Roland's head".

The rest of the song sees Roland's headless ghost roaming the continent to have his revenge on Van Owen, the man who betrayed him. While Warren Zevon was never a singer to fill stadiums, he did have a cult following and often teamed up with R.E.M. He was also a regular guest on *The Late Show*, and host David Letterman begged him to play *Roland …* at a recording of the show in 2003. Warren happily obliged. It turned out to be his final public performance before he passed away later that year.

SO THE CIA DECIDED / THEY WANTED ROLAND DEAD.

— WARREN ZEVON

Don't You Want Me?
The Human League

Who knew that The Human League's 80s pop classic was actually inspired by the movie *A Star Is Born*? Lots of people, apparently. Lead singer Philip Oakey has often spoken about how he got the idea for the track after seeing the classic film (that's the 1976 version with Barbara Streisand and Kris Kristofferson, rather than the more recent Gaga remake). The basic movie plot is about a male singer whose career is on the decline while his girlfriend's singing career takes off. And it was a story that would lend itself surprisingly well to one of pop's most memorable duets. In the song, Oakey's character is caustic about the star he helped create: "... don't forget, it's me who put you where you are now / And I can put you back down too". Meanwhile, his ex-lady has other ideas: "But now I think it's time I live my life on my own / I guess it's just what I must do ..." These days, the characters' creepy dynamic seems weirdly prescient of the #metoo movement, with the man threatening career destruction for the woman who leaves him. That air of menace is even stronger in the song's video, where the song's protagonists are workers on the set of a murder mystery which turns out to be less fictional than it may first appear.

Carolina Drama
The Raconteurs

Ladies and gentleman, pull up a chair and get comfortable. Jack White is in a storytelling kind of mood. In The Raconteurs' track from 2008, we find their oddball frontman at his bluesy, gothic best. And the saga begins: "It was a junk house in South Carolina / Held a boy the age of ten / Along with his older brother Billy / And their mother and her boyfriend ..." The song basically follows the trajectory of a particularly gripping Hollywood thriller, from a calm beginning, to building tension, to a fiery climax, to an epilogue that will make you want to replay the whole thing and piece it all together. From the outset, we find out that mom's boyfriend is an asshole with a temper. When a preacher shows up at the house one day, all hell breaks loose, for various reasons and for everybody involved (as suggested by the title of the track). In the interest of not giving too much away, let's just say that things get bloody. Like, *Dexter*-style bloody, involving – among other things – a milk bottle. As the frenzy of the song slows to an ending, it leaves us with a riddle. To understand the full story, we must "Go and ask the milkman." Who is the milkman? Is it Billy? Is it his younger brother? Is it the mother's secret lover? Or someone else? Time to phone up Jessica Fletcher.

As the Miller Told His Tale
Songs Inspired by Legends

A Whiter Shade of Pale
Procol Harum

Ah, the 60s. The decade of blissful melodies, romantic liaisons and cryptic lyrics that hippies pretended to understand. *A Whiter Shade of Pale* became the international hit that defined 1967's *Summer of Love*. It was certainly blissful, its tune a twist on one of Bach's most famous compositions. And it certainly dealt with love, the singer clearly singing to some special lady. As for the cryptic message, well, that involves some delving: "And so it was that later / As the miller told his tale / That her face, at first just ghostly / Turned a whiter shade of pale". Those timeless lines are presumably a reference to Chaucer's *The Miller's Tale*, a 14th-century fable about a man whose wife cheats on him with a student lodger (not sure how good your Middle English is but apparently, it all begins when the lodger grabs the willing wife "by the *queynte*", and it all ends when the lodger receives a red-hot poker "amidst the *ers*"). Anyway, in the song, might the lady's pallid expression be due to her cheating being rumbled? In later verses, the singer mentions "vestal virgins". These were priestesses of Ancient Rome who were generally revered, but if it was discovered that a priestess had broken her vow of chastity, she would be buried alive. We find out that the "virgin" of the song is about to skip town. Again, because she's been unfaithful? The Summer of Love must have been a confusing time.

Corpus Christi Carol
Jeff Buckley

While we're on the subject of Middle English, *Corpus Christi Carol* is a hymn that's thought to date back to the early 1500s. No *queyntes* in earshot here, this song is dealing with matters of a more pious nature. The meaning of the lyrics has been discussed, literally, for centuries. Is the song a hymn to Christ? Or is it more a legend, sort of guest-starring Jesus as one of those background characters who helps move the action along? (A biblical Heather Locklear, if you will.) After Jeff Buckley included his own version of the carol on his album *Grace* (1994), he explained his own understanding in an interview: "The 'Carol' is a fairy-tale about a falcon who takes the beloved of the singer to an orchard. The singer goes looking for her and arrives at a chamber where his beloved lies next to a bleeding knight and a tomb with Christ's body in it." Whatever your interpretation of the song, it's impossible not to be moved by Jeff's mighty falsetto, pining for the love he's lost: "Lu li lu lay lu li lu lay / The falcon hath bourne my mate away."

IT SEEMS YEARS SINCE YOU HELD THE BABY / WHILE I WRECKED THE BEDROOM …

— SINÉAD O'CONNOR

The Emperor's New Clothes
Sinéad O'Connor

When you think of Hans Christian Andersen, it's usually cute fairies that spring to mind, rather than the bald-headed fury of Sinéad O'Connor. But, man, what a combo. From the opening line, you know that Sinéad has not come to play around: "It seems years since you held the baby / While I wrecked the bedroom ..." Woah, back up. Time for a background briefing. 1987 was quite a year for the singer. Aged just 21, she got pregnant and got married, all while her first album climbed the charts around the world. Three years later, *The Emperor's New Clothes* appeared, and that iconic opening was addressed to her (by now) ex-husband. From that line, the track then turns into a bangin' tune about defiance. The singer invokes Andersen's legend of the deluded emperor to lambaste the people who surrounded her younger self, preaching to her about how to manage her career, her pregnancy, her marriage. They may snigger at Sinéad's life choices, but to her, they are no better than the brainwashed townsfolk of the fairy tale: "Everyone can see what's going on / They laugh 'cause they know they're untouchable / Not because what I said was wrong". Weirdly, the lines seem equally fitting to where Sinéad's life would lead just two years later, when she essentially killed her career by ripping up a photo of the pope on US television in protest at the child abuse scandals of the church.

Avalon
Roxy Music

In the legends of King Arthur, Avalon was a place of dreams. It was an island of abundant fruit, an almost heavenly place which provided all that its visitors could ever wish for. It's not surprising that Roxy Music had idyllic isles in mind, given that they recorded the song (and album) *Avalon* in the Bahamas back in 1982. And the track's sparse sound and faint strumming certainly bring to mind soft Caribbean breezes. As for the reason why Bryan Ferry had dreamy utopia in mind, the lyrics might suggest that he's lucked out at the end of the night: "Now the party's over / I'm so tired / Then I see you coming / Out of nowhere ... Avalon". The song doesn't get into the nitty gritty of where the night leads, just the floaty magic of delectable slow dancing with an intriguing stranger in the wee hours. Swoon!

Heathcliff, it's Me, it's Cathy! Songs Inspired by Novels

Wuthering Heights
Kate Bush

Early on in Emily Brontë's 19th-century novel, a visitor to the creepy country manor called *Wuthering Heights* is awoken by a noise at the window. He opens it and is gripped by an icy hand. The hand is of a young lady, saying her name is Cathy and exclaiming "I'm come home: I'd lost my way on the moor!" We soon discover that this is the ghost of Cathy, the deceased former young lady of the house who had fallen in love with her adopted brother, Heathcliff. Passions ran deep, but their love was doomed from the outset. Kate Bush says she wrote her classic song in 1977, aged just 18, after watching a BBC adaptation of the famous book. The song inserts various quotes from the original text, like in its soaring chorus: "Heathcliff, it's me, Cathy / Come home, I'm so cold / Let me in-a-your window". As with the novel, the song has become an all-time favourite in the UK and beyond. Bush later discovered that she has the same birthday as Brontë. Kind of spooky, but not as spooky as a restless ghost wailing her sorrows across the moors.

Paranoid Android
Radiohead

In writing this song, Radiohead admit being strongly influenced by *Bohemian Rhapsody*. And like all multi-part rock-opera anthems, *Paranoid Android* (1997) is far from simple. Parts of the lyrics may seem baffling, unless – of course – you happen to be a fan of *The Hitchhikers Guide to the Galaxy*. The track contains more than a few references to the series of novels by Douglas Adams, specifically to the character of *Marvin the Paranoid Android*. Marvin has an enormous brain, but he rarely gets to use it and is treated cruelly by the humans. And so, Marvin is deeply sad, surrounded by idiocy. Now, Thom Yorke is not trying to tell us that he has a huge brain and that most people are imbeciles. But he kind of is. But it's a joke (keep up!) In the song, Thom assumes a Marvin-like character. He writes about a real-life event that happened to him in an LA bar, when he found himself surrounded by a bunch of coked-up yuppies. A friend of his spilled a drink on a lady's jacket and she lost it: "Ambition makes you look pretty ugly / Kicking, squealing, Gucci little piggy". Thom-slash-Marvin looks at all those blockheads around him and feels rage, depression, maybe a type of acceptance. In an interview, Thom summed up the song in the best way possible: "*Paranoid Android* is about the dullest fucking people on Earth."

AMBITION MAKES YOU LOOK PRETTY UGLY.

— **RADIOHEAD**

White Rabbit
Jefferson Airplane ft. Grace Slick

Is there any song that better defines hippie culture than *White Rabbit*'s jangling guitars, echoey vocals and trippy feel? And let's not forget that barely-masked message of drug-enabled mind expansion and freeing oneself from society's shackles. Far out, man. The 1967 track may contain a whole load of allusions to drugs, but always under the guise of references to Lewis Carroll's *Alice's Adventures in Wonderland* stories. The song's opening line "One pill makes you larger / And one pill makes you small" is clearly a 60s twist on Alice ingesting a potion to shrink her and then a cake to turn her into a giant. From there, the song takes the listener down the rabbit hole into an exciting new world of talking animals, newfound freedom and limitless learning. On that latter point, the track's most iconic moment is the singer's final, repeated cry to "Feed your head! / Feed your head!" Or as they say these days, get woke.

The Ghost of Tom Joad
Bruce Springsteen

Readers of *The Grapes of Wrath* will recall Tom Joad as the protagonist of John Steinbeck's iconic novel. Tom is a son of the Joad family who are forced to leave their farm in 1930s Oklahoma and head on an epic journey out west in search of work. When California doesn't prove to be the promised land that they had dreamed of, Tom fights for justice, but as a result needs to leave his family (basically, he needs to abandon them for their own safety). And so, we imagine, Tom must continue his wandering alone. Springsteen's 1995 ballad picks up the story in modern times. The Great Depression may have ended, but it seems the more things change, the more they stay the same: "Shelter line stretching around the corner / Welcome to the new world order / Families sleeping in the cars in the southwest / No home, no job, no peace, no rest". The song's narrator is one of those homeless down-and-outs. He camps under a bridge, waiting for someone like old Tom Joad to come and fight the good fight. For a while, Springsteen stopped performing this song at concerts. In 2018, he reintroduced it, amid Trump's controversial treatment of migrant families.

Scentless Apprentice
Nirvana

"Like most babies smell like butter / His smell smelled like no other ..." Not exactly mood music for tea and biscuits, *Scentless Apprentice* (1993) is a spiral into truly dark corners of Kurt Cobain's mind. It's also based on the book *Perfume*, by Patrick Süskind. The novel begins with the birth of a baby who has an astoundingly keen sense of smell, but who has no scent of his own. Shunned by society, the orphan grows up to become an apprentice perfume maker, but always with a poisonous obsession to find the perfect smell. Before long, he turns to distilling scents which can only be achieved by murder, and the gorefest begins. Kurt said that *Perfume* was his favourite novel. From his own troubled childhood and teenage years, perhaps Kurt felt some affinity to the abandoned boy. Like the novel, Nirvana's track is no walk in the park. At the end, it includes the line, "You can't fire me because I quit!" It's a reference to the apprentice's rejection by various employers but took on new meaning after Kurt's suicide. Drummer Dave Grohl said, "If there's one line in any song that gives me the chills, it's that one."

Star-Cross'd Lovers (and Haterz)
Songs with Shakespearean References

The Gypsy Faerie Queen
Marianne Faithfull ft. Nick Cave

Shakespeare's *A Midsummer Night's Dream* has inspired a wealth of works. In Marianne's 2018 song, she uses two of the play's characters to offer a bittersweet glimpse into her own life. The track is told from the perspective of Puck, a mischievous fairy of the forest, loyal to his fairy queen. In the song, Puck follows his ruler all across the land: "She bears a blackthorn staff / To help her in her walking / I only listen to her sing / But I never hear her talking / Anymore". It's difficult not to think that the fairy queen might refer to Marianne herself. Back in the 60s, Marianne famously partied harder than any of her rock 'n' roll boyfriends (she was once caught in a drug-bust at Keith Richards' house, where police apparently found Marianne wearing only a fur rug and clutching a Mars bar). Could it be that the former wild child is feeling that she has entered her twilight years? Indeed, on the song's related album cover, Marianne does indeed bear a staff: she appears regally seated with her walking stick centre-frame. Ageing she may be, but the track also points to the unending devotion of a loyal follower. Her fans? A partner? Or perhaps just a good friend, like Nick Cave who contributes piano and backing vocals.

Romeo and Juliet
Dire Straits

The most obvious presence of Shakespeare in pop must surely be in this Dire Straits' 1981 classic. The bard's tale of star-cross'd lovers was given a twist by Mark Knopfler, in that Juliet fails to declare her eternal devotion. In fact, she makes up her mind to leave her Romeo, and he's really not too happy about it: "You promised me everything, you promised me thick and thin / Now you just say, 'Oh Romeo, yeah, you know I used to have a scene with him.'" The lyrics are apparently directed towards Mark's ex-girlfriend who he felt had used him so that she could get famous. And so, Mark seems bitter and sad, but perhaps with an element of forgiveness for the lady who's broken his heart: "*There's a Place for Us*, you know the movie song? / When you gonna realize it was just that the time was wrong, Juliet?" That former line is a reference to the romantic song *Somewhere (There's a Place for Us)* from the movie *West Side Story*, itself a retelling of the same Shakespearean play. As for the latter, it seems like lovelorn Mark is willing to put the whole sorry story down to a case of bad timing.

I Am the Walrus
The Beatles

Thank you, John Lennon, for getting demented on acid and returning to this shared universal plane to let humankind know *the truth*. John was very open about the fact that he had written parts of *I Am the Walrus* (1967) while on LSD. No shit: "I am the egg man / They are the egg men / I am the walrus / Goo goo g'joob". He also admitted that the lyrics to the track were intentionally confusing. His motivation came from a letter which he received from a schoolboy, in which the pupil informed him that Beatles lyrics were now being studied in English classes. John found this funny and, after writing *Walrus*, reportedly exclaimed, "Let the fuckers work that one out." As for the Shakespearean reference, the song includes grainy extracts from *King Lear*, most notably at the end of the track. This came about while editing the song, when John started fiddling with a radio dial and stumbled across a BBC recording of the

play. He liked the resulting combo, and decided to leave it in. Of course, Beatle maniacs question whether the song has some deeper meaning, particularly the Shakespearean character's exclamation of "O, untimely death!" as the song fades. Fate or randomness? It probably depends on how much acid you've consumed today.

OH ROMEO, YEAH, YOU KNOW I USED TO HAVE A SCENE WITH HIM.
— DIRE STRAITS

Exit Music for a Film
Radiohead

OK, back to *Romeo and Juliet*, the Shakespeare play of choice for mind-blowing rock songs. Radiohead wrote this track at the request of Baz Luhrmann for his 1996 movie based on the classic play. And Thom Yorke et al certainly did their homework. Musically, *Exit Music for a Film* follows the formula of a Baroque lament, moving from melancholic descending bass to harmonic crescendo. Lyrically, Thom Yorke embraced the raw emotion of the Shakespearean tragedy, beginning with a description of the teenage lovers planning their escape: "Pack and get dressed / Before your father hears us / Before all hell breaks loose". While this escape could refer to the pair's suicide, some fans argue that Thom has reimagined the plot to a story where Romeo and Juliet run away and avoid their doomed fate. The song's most famous line is its repeated closing mantra: "We hope that you choke / That you choke". This seems to be aimed at the teenagers' families, too pigheaded and rule-obeying to allow young love to blossom. So, what better curse for the naysayers than to wish upon them an untimely death by choking? After the song's release, "We hope that you choke" became a sort of slogan for many Radiohead fans, a protest cry against oppressors the world over. It also makes for a cool T-shirt print.

Isn't it Good, Norwegian Wood? *Songs Featuring in Haruki Murakami's Novels*

Norwegian Wood
The Beatles
(novel: *Norwegian Wood*, 1987)

"I once had a girl / Or should I say, she once had me? / She showed me her room / 'Isn't it good, Norwegian wood?'" Although John Lennon was married in the mid-60s, he admitted that this song was about one of the many nights when he would end up in the home of another woman. The lady seems very keen to show off her home décor, not least the Norwegian wood panelling. On the night in question, she turns down sex with John, saying that she has to be up early for work. When John awakes alone the following morning, he gets his revenge by setting her precious wood alight (because what lady can resist a sex pest *and* an arsonist?) The original Japanese title of Murakami's breakout novel is *Noruwei no Mori*. The word *Mori* translates as "forest", rather than "wood" as a material. And it is the Beatles' classic song that starts the story off. Toru, the book's male protagonist, hears it playing and is taken back to the 60s, when – as in the song – he had felt torn between two women. One of these women is very troubled and needs to spend some time at a sanatorium located in the midst of the snowy forest. As the novel takes a turn to darker places, we realise that Murakami's *Norwegian Wood* is a much more tragic tale than John Lennon's ode to his own wandering trouser snake.

South of the Border
Sam Cooke
(novel: *South of the Border, West of the Sun*, 1992)

Apart from his exceptional talent as a writer, Murakami's obsession with Western songs and culture is another reason behind his international appeal. His novel *South of the Border ...*, tells the story of Hajime and Shimamoto. It's a tale as old as time: Hajime is a lonely young boy; Shimamoto is the girl who's a little different from the rest. The two are inseparable, spending long afternoons listening to Nat King Cole and enjoying a meeting of souls. But when the time comes to go to high school, their intense friendship is forced to a close. Fast forward a few decades and Hajime is married with kids, but in the midst of a midlife. When who should turn up? (There is literally only one person who could turn up.) The song *South of the Border* is a true classic, having been covered by countless jazz and country artists. In Murakami's book, the track is attributed to Nat King Cole, but it seems Nat never really did record a version. Hajime runs a jazz bar, so perhaps it was Sam Cooke's smooth, mariachi-influenced version that the author had in mind. And what better song to set the tone for a tale of yearning for a past love never realised? "Then she sighed as she whispered, '*mañana*' / Never dreaming that we were parting / And I lied as a whispered *mañana* / 'Cause our tomorrow never came." As the track closes out, Sam Cooke trills a pained, Mexican-style sigh: "Ay, ay, ay, ayyy". Bewildered, torn Hajime must be feeling just the same way.

How to Disappear Completely
Radiohead
(novel: *Kafka on the Shore*, 2002)

In his novels, Murakami treats music almost like a movie soundtrack. As a soundtrack sets the mood for certain scenes, Murakami evokes a particular feel by telling us the songs and compositions that his characters are listening to. In *Kafka on the Shore*, the protagonist is a 15-year-old boy named Kafka who runs away from home in a quest to find his absent mother and sister. He also wants to escape his cruel father, who has told Kafka that the teenager bears an Oedipal curse to kill his father and have sex with his mother. Once away from his father's house, Kafka is left with no sense of belonging and is unable to turn off the voice in his head about the deadly curse. He is listening to Radiohead's *Kid A* album on repeat. While no specific track is mentioned, a clear contender is *How to Disappear Completely*. Thom Yorke wrote the song about a time in his life when the manic life of concerts and fame got too much for him. In the song, Thom imagines that he is able to vanish, float through the walls. The song's chorus is a mantra passed on to Thom by his friend Michael Stipe: "I'm not here / This isn't happening / I'm not here /

I'm not here". Lonesome Kafka is also on a mission to disappear, but how is it always the case that the past has a way of following us around?

Sinfonietta: 1
Leoš Janáček
(novel: *1Q84*, 2009)

Murakami's fans are so dedicated that the music he includes in novels can sometimes boost sales of certain tracks. Kind of like some soppy ballad that hits the Top Ten a week after it's appeared on *Grey's Anatomy*. But, you know, less cheesy. In the week following the release of *1Q84*, Japan saw a surge in sales of *Sinfonietta*, an orchestral piece composed in 1926 by Czech composer Leoš Janáček. The composition is quite a rampageous affair, with a huge brass section and a dizzying melody. The whole thing is thought to be an expression of human courage, but when Murakami first heard it, he admits finding the piece "Strange. Very strange ..." And so, it seemed like the perfect piece to open the weird story of *1Q84*. The book begins with a situation we can all relate to: lead character Aomame is on her way to murder somebody but she gets stuck in traffic. And her stress levels are not being helped by the fact that her taxi driver is listening to the really quite unnerving *Sinfonietta*. The driver suggests that she could get out of the car and climb down an emergency escape, but with the slight caveat that doing so may lead her into an alternative reality. Long story short, Aomame soon finds herself in some sort of parallel universe called 1Q84, and all sorts of stuff goes down, including a religious cult, badass ladies bent on revenge, a bit of telekinesis. And all this while *Sinfonietta* keeps following Aomame around. Never let it be said that a Murakami novel lacks ambition.

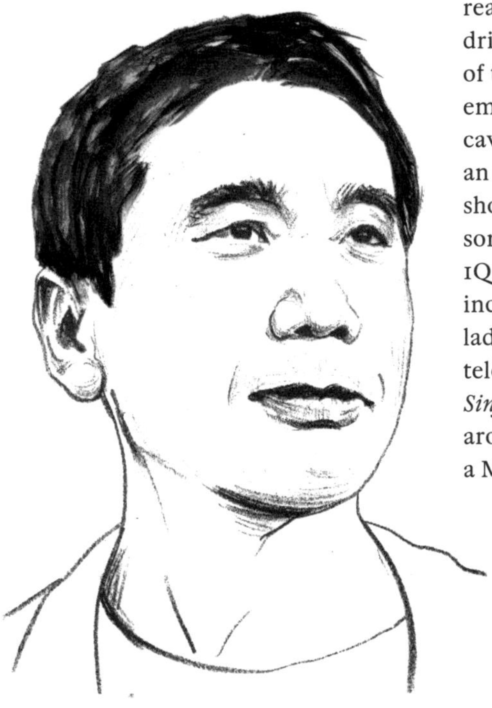

The Unreliable Narrator
Songs that We Can't Quite Believe

Love and Marriage
Frank Sinatra

It's not only literature that concerns itself with plot devices. The key to many an intriguing song is that it tells a story from a perspective that we're not sure we can believe. A prime example: Frank Sinatra's 1955 classic, *Love and Marriage*. To the playful melody of brass and strings, Frank tells us that love and marriage are – without a doubt, totally inarguably – one and the same thing: "... Love and marriage / It's an institute you can't disparage / Ask the local gentry and they will say it's elementary." We imagine that Frank is telling us this as the devoted husband, only to discover that our narrator is in fact, of much younger years: "Dad was told by mother / You can't have one without the other". Hmm. We get the feeling that Dad gets lectured quite frequently on the virtues of marriage. Of course, the wry nature of the song was made even clearer when it became the theme tune to the 90s sitcom *Married ... with Children*. The show revolved around the marital bliss (or lack thereof) of dim-witted Al Bundy and his lazy wife Peggy. The Bundys could be described as many things, but hardly as the toast of the local gentry.

I Hold No Grudge
Nina Simone

"I hold no grudge / And I'll forgive you your mistake / But forgive me if I take it all to heart". Nina's factual, flat tone lets the listener know that when she says she holds no grudge, we can be damn sure the lady holds a grudge. Less an unreliable narrator than a bitterly sarcastic one, the singer is clearly not in the mood for niceties. And who could blame her? She co-wrote this song around 1966 (incidentally, with *Twin Peaks* composer Angelo Badalamenti), amid the storm of the Civil Rights movement. Nina was an activist who was acutely aware of issues such as the recent murders of African Americans, as well as segregation laws which continued to exist until 1965. Nina may tell her white audience that she can "extend the laurel leaf", but her sharpness suggests that the only forgiveness she's capable of is in words alone. Her heart's just not in it.

I'm Not in Love
10cc

If you're going to tell a straight-out lie, you may as well make it sound breath-taking. *I'm Not in Love* (1975) is 10cc's dreamy love song that claims to be anything but: "I'm not in love / So don't forget it / It's just a silly phase I'm going through ..." Singer Eric Stewart says he was inspired to write the lyrics after his wife pointed out that he hardly ever told her he loved her. A schmaltzy ballad didn't appeal to him, so instead, Eric came up with lyrics about a man in denial. It was an interesting twist, so now 10cc just needed to come up with the music. They first tried bossa nova, but drummer Kevin Godley thought it sounded "crap". He had another idea, though, saying, "... the only way that song is gonna work is if we totally fuck it up". And so, the group decided to record the track with waves and waves of their own voices. This was the mid-70s, so that involved metres of tape loops and weeks of studio time. But it paid off; the result was a euphoric, harmonic wall of sound. In the end, Godley still felt it was lacking something. They came up with an idea to include a hushed vocal saying "Big boys don't cry". But who to do it? At that moment, the group's secretary popped her head into the studio to tell Eric that he had a phonecall. Her husky tones and posh enunciation made people's ears prick up. And thus was born pop's most pornographic whisper. The track became a worldwide smash.

IT'S THE RETURN OF THE 'AH, WAIT, NO WAY, YOU'RE KIDDING / HE DIDN'T JUST SAY WHAT I THINK HE DID, DID HE?'

— EMINEM

Billie Jean
Michael Jackson

Michael sure does go to great lengths to remind us that "the kid is not my son". Could it be the case that our narrator doth protest too much? Apparently, *Billie Jean* (1983) was inspired by groupies who Michael used to run into when he was part of the Jackson 5. He suggested that these girls used to basically get down 'n' dirty with band members, like his brothers, and then later claim that their babies had come about as a result. The audacity of claiming child support! The imaginary Billie Jean is one such lady, walkin' round town saying that Michael is the father of her son. Michael denies it. Slightly confusing, however, that the song builds towards an allusion that Michael did – in fact – give into temptation: "She came and stood right by me / Then the smell of sweet perfume / This happened much too soon / She called me to her room / Hey hey!" Woah! Could that final "Hey hey!" be used as incriminating testimony? Oh, who needs tiptoeing around words when you can afford a good lawyer?

The Real Slim Shady
Eminem

"It's the return of the 'Ah, wait, no way, you're kidding / He didn't just say what I think he did, did he?'" In the genre of unreliable narrators, few artists can lay more claim to the title than Eminem. The rapper is the master of the alter ego, ranging from his real name Marshall Mathers to rap superstar Eminem, via cartoonish hellraiser Slim Shady. In *The Real Slim Shady* (2000), it's clear from the outset that Slim is at the helm on this one. That means listeners need to brace for impact, and to take the manic diatribe with more than a pinch of salt. Like a spotty teen after far too many Red Bulls, Slim informs us that he has murdered Dr. Dre, that feminists love Eminem (unlikely), that he is soon to retire to a nursing home with a large stash of Viagra. Unfortunately, we're never quite sure where the joke ends, hence the justified accusations of homophobic and misogynist lyrics. Not that feckless Slim cares. He's too busy being the OG punk of hip hop, as demonstrated in those immortal lines, "Will Smith don't gotta cuss in his raps to sell records / Well, I do, so *fuck* him and *fuck* you too!" Classic.

Putting it on Paper
Books by Musicians

Things the Grandchildren Should Know (song: Things the Grandchildren Should Know *by Eels*)

In life, some people get a smooth ride; others get a rollercoaster. Eels frontman Mark Oliver Everett is more in the latter camp. As a musician, his group have enjoyed worldwide success. But his 2008 autobiography let fans in on a personal background that establishes beyond any doubt that fact can be so much stranger – and darker – than fiction. We learn that Mark's father was Hugh Everett III, the famed American physicist who came up with the *Many Worlds Theory* (basically, the idea that everything that could possibly have happened in the past has indeed happened in some other universe). As a father, Hugh was emotionally distant, leaving a young Mark and his sister to run wild. Teenage Mark was finally getting closer to his dad until one day, Hugh died of heart failure and Mark found the body. The following decades also brought tragedy: Mark's sister committed suicide; his mother died of cancer. His cousin lost her life on September 11th when she was travelling on the plane that hit The Pentagon. The plane crashed into the side of the building where Mark's dad used to work, leaving Mark to wonder whether it had actually struck his father's old office. It all sounds very grim, but Mark somehow recounts his life with zero indulgence. The tone echoes the 2005 song *Things the Grandchildren Should Know*, the Eels track which gave the book its title. Like the book, the song's lyrics are straightforward and sad, but also accepting. About his dad, he sings: "… I never really understood / What it must have been like for him / Living inside his head / I feel like he's here with me now / Even though he's dead." Despite it all, you get the sense that Mark has made his peace.

JESUS DIED FOR SOMEBODY'S SINS / BUT NOT MINE ...

— PATTI SMITH

Just Kids (song: *Gloria: In Excelsis Deo* by Patti Smith)

When Robert Mapplethorpe was laying on his deathbed, Patti Smith made a promise to him. She told him that one day, she would write the story of their relationship. Robert died in 1989; a lifetime later, in 2010, Patti finally made their story public. In *Just Kids*, the original Queen of Punk talks about how Robert and she met. The two recent arrivals to New York got talking in a bookshop and realised they had a lot in common: both were 20 years old, both were unspeakably broke, both had a ravenous appetite to create. Soon, they were sharing a tiny apartment in Brooklyn, romantically involved, Patti working odd jobs to support them. They were kindred spirits in most things, except in their ambition. Patti's love was poetry, her goal was to be part of a community of writers; Robert discovered a skill for photography, and he wanted the world. As opportunities began to arise for the two, Patti recalls, "We were both praying for Robert's soul, he to sell it and I to save it." Things got complicated. Robert discovered that he was gay, though Patti was less upset by this than by his newfound fondness for the moneyed in-crowd. Of course, Robert would go on to become the avant-garde, legendary photographer, and sadly die of AIDS. But interestingly, it was unassuming Patti whose career took off first. She started putting her poems to music and soon released the album, *Horses* (1975), which would become an instant punk classic. The record began with an all-out reworking of Van Morrison's *Gloria*, changing the lyrics for one of Patti's poems. The opening verse was a memorably bold statement: "Jesus died for somebody's sins / But not mine ... My sins my own, they belong to me / *Me*". At the very start of her career, Patti was telling the world exactly how she lives her life: her own way.

Mo' Meta Blues The World According to Questlove (song: You Got Me **by The Roots ft. Erykah Badu & Eve**)

Ahmir "Questlove" Thompson. Talented drummer of The Roots, recognisable face of *The Tonight Show Starring Jimmy Fallon*, walking encyclopaedia of all things music, Tweeter extraordinaire. And also, apparently, a gifted writer. In his 2013 memoir, Questlove begins by describing the depths of his musical geekiness. His childhood was spent touring around with his singer parents who had their own doo-wop band. By the age of seven, he was already playing drums at some of the shows. This showbiz upbringing, as well as his later success with The Roots and as a producer, gives Questlove a whole lot of stories to tell and names to drop. For example, the book describes one night when Questlove got an odd phone message inviting him to a roller-skating party with Prince. He made his way to an eerily quiet suburban rink to find just about a dozen people, minus Prince but plus Eddie Murphy. At about 2 a.m., The Purple One finally arrived bearing a large briefcase, opened it and took out some clear skates that shot out multicoloured laser sparks. Prince got on the rink, and as Questlove puts it, His Royal Badness "could skate like he could sing." Apart from artists of Godlike status, the book is also fascinating for the smaller names. Or better said, names that used to be small. Questlove writes about his mid-90s jam sessions with fellow Philly performers, as yet unknown, such as Eve and Jill Scott. Both artists would later be involved (Eve as rapper, Jill as writer) in The Roots' 1998 hit *You Got Me*. If ever there was a need to prove that geek is chic, Questlove seems like the right man for the job.

How Music Works (song: Once in a Lifetime by Talking Heads)

If anybody is qualified to write an all-encompassing manual on music, it's David Byrne. In his 2012 book, the legendary frontman of Talking Heads basically asks readers to gather round for a fascinating session of *this much I know*. Obsessed with music in all its forms, David has had decades to learn the many ins and outs. That gives the book a vast scope, ranging from how technology alters music to how to a musician can turn a profit, to how music changes according to time and context. He also comments on the tendency to divide art into "high" and "low", so that city councils might fund the local orchestra, but sneer at "lesser" forms of music like pop, punk, bongo playing. For David, it's all valid. In fact, he points out how the original fans of opera in Germany or Italy were the in-your-face punk rockers of their time. David comes across as the type of man who sees the same authenticity in an Ariana Grande track as in one by Bob Dylan. The book's arguments are brought to life by David's retelling of his own experiences with Talking Heads. For example, he reveals how the group's megahit *Once in a Lifetime* (1981) was inspired by a recording of a Southern preacher. David turned that into a funky tale about a man who lives his life on autopilot: "... And you may find yourself in a beautiful house, with a beautiful wife / And you may ask yourself, 'Well... how did I get here?'" The book gives the impression that, unlike that fellow from the song, David Byrne is anything but unthinking.

Tell Me about it
Spoken-Word Songs

Little Fluffy Clouds
The Orb

Every few years, a spoken-word track goes mainstream. In the early 90s, that track was *Little Fluffy Clouds* (1990), a trippy house number featuring a lady who gives a lavish description of the Arizona desert skies that she used to see as a child: "The sunsets were purple and red and yellow and on fire / And the clouds would catch the colours ..." The dreamy monologue is all set to ambient synths and a mid-tempo beat, sort of having the same effect on the listener as a mildly hallucinogenic cactus. The voice recording was taken from an interview with American singer Rickie Lee Jones, who says she was battling a heavy cold while speaking (who needs electronic voice distortion when a simple cold virus can do the trick?) Orb producer Martin Glover first came across Rickie's interview when a fan posted him a cassette which had the voice recording on one side and a song on the other. Martin found them both interesting and took samples from each. A few more samples, such as some harmonica from an Ennio Morricone track, and *Little Fluffy Clouds* was brought into existence. A sunset has never sounded so awesome.

The Revolution Will Not Be Televised
Gil Scott-Heron

"The revolution will not be brought to you by Xerox / In four parts without commercial interruption / The revolution will not show you pictures of Nixon / Blowing a bugle ... The revolution will not be televised." When Gil Scott Heron first released his defiant poem back in 1970, you have to wonder if he knew that its basic message would still be getting written on protest placards decades later. The slogan that gave the track its title originated in the Black Power movement of the 60s, but it was Gil who popularised it and expanded on the breadth of its meaning. And what a timeless point he makes: we all know that the media is run by corporations, oppressive leaders and filthy-rich overlords, so let's not forget that it will never encourage any challenge to their authority. If oppressed people (such as African Americans) want to fight for equality, they needn't expect to see it on the 9 o'clock news. Not that Gil was encouraging literal fighting. He always argued that the revolution that he spoke of was one of the mind, a change in people's way of thinking. And angry as the sentiment may be, the poem also has humour in certain lines: "The revolution will not make you look five pounds thinner." A killer line, reminding us to aspire to more than what we're sold by the Murdochs (and Zuckerbergs?) of this world.

The Raven
Lou Reed

In 2003, Lou Reed released an album of Edgar Allan Poe's works set to music. Reed's rendition of *The Raven* is simple, narrating the verses over quiet violins. His voice is theatrical, drawing the listener into Poe's creepy tale of a man nodding off to sleep when suddenly, he hears a knock at the door: "While I nodded, nearly napping / Suddenly there came a tapping / As of someone gently rapping / Rapping at my chamber door ..." Could it be a visitor? Or could it be the ghost of his lost love, Lenore? Spoiler alert: it's neither. Further knocking prompts him to open the window, at which point a raven flies in and perches in the room. Our protagonist proceeds to ask various questions of the bird, to which the raven unwaveringly replies, "Nevermore". A limited script for the bird character, but satisfyingly eerie.

Everybody's Free (to Wear Sunscreen)
Baz Luhrmann ft. Quindon Tarver

The year was 1997 and radio stations around the world were playing a university graduation speech set to uplifting music. It caught the ears of the public with snippets of advice like "get to know your parents", "remember the compliments you receive", and "in 20 years you'll look back at photos of yourself and recall ... how fabulous you really looked". The narrator acknowledges that all advice is subjective, that we tend to offer a rose-tinted version of the past. But there's one thing he can say with confidence: you really should wear sunscreen. Baz Luhrmann first read the speech in an email. In fact, this being the mid-90s, the text was one of the first chain emails to go viral. And in typical chain-email fashion, the origins were all a bit hazy. The speech had supposedly been delivered by author Kurt Vonnegut to graduating students at MIT. A quick search on Google (or some horrendous 90s equivalent like *Ask Jeeves*) revealed this not to be the case. The piece had actually been written as a newspaper column for the *Chicago Tribune* by a journalist called Mary Schmich. Baz's people contacted her to secure copyright, got an actor to narrate the text and set it to a remix of the song *Everybody's Free*. And soon, the whole world was hooked. Soon after, some clever-clogs invented the Spam Folder, ensuring that Baz's track will possibly forever remain the only hit to be based on a chain email.

Everything Is Everything
Bootsy Collins

Norman Cook: former Housemartin, Mr. Freak Power, the Drunk Soul Brother. You may also know him as Fatboy Slim. The most monikered man in music must sometimes look in the mirror and wonder, "Who am I today?" In October 2007, Norman was most certainly Fatboy Slim as he took the reins to curate a compilation album called *Late Night Tales*. The final track was a simple spoken poem which had been written by fellow Housemartin Paul Heaton (perhaps better known as the lead singer of The Beautiful South). The poem is narrated by American grandmaster of funk, Bootsy Collins, in his trademark sing-song style. But don't be fooled by that light-hearted delivery. The poem begins as a critique on the superficial, plastic nature of the music industry: "When hip-hop is selling perfume and boybands are selling grief ... Jazz has come to nothing but transparent handkerchief". From there, it goes on to look at society as a whole: "With Easter eggs in January and Christmas lights in June / Anything that's barely over's coming back real soon ..." It seems that writer Paul has had about enough, maybe suggesting that a 21st-century attitude of anything goes can bring with it a certain loss of specialness. Everything is everything indeed. Or, as Paul himself told a newspaper, "I just started listing the things that annoyed me, and it wouldn't stop."

Are You Lonesome Tonight?
Elvis

While not entirely a spoken-word track, the most outstanding feature of this Elvis megahit is undoubtedly that iconic lengthy spoken bridge. The song begins with Elvis crooning as only he could, from reverberating baritone to near whisper, wondering aloud if his ex-girl is missing him. As the first verse draws to a close, listeners begin to wonder if they just might swoon off their chairs, when suddenly, The King is ... he's speaking! In slow, dramatic monologue, Elvis lets it all out: "Honey, you lied when you said you loved me ... But I'd rather go on hearing your lies / Than to go on living without you." As you might have guessed from the song's sparse, moody ambience, Elvis recorded the song in the wee hours of the morning, completely in the dark.

After several takes, he reportedly told the producers to scrap the recording, saying that he just couldn't do the song justice. Luckily, they ignored his request. Sharp-eared listeners have pointed out a quiet clicking sound at the very end of the song, which some suggest was the sound of a stapler as the producer prepared Elvis's contract. Even a superstar's gotta get paid.

HONEY, YOU LIED WHEN YOU SAID YOU LOVED ME ...

— ELVIS

Getting the Creeps
Songs to Unsettle

I Fink U Freeky
Die Antwoord

Some songs move us to tears or laughter, while others are designed to disturb. Deeply. Die Antwoord have always been open about their fondness for shock factor. The group base their style on the *zef* culture of their native South Africa, which is basically all about screwing the norm. *Zef* was originally a derogatory term akin to the US idea of trailer trash. More recently, however, it's come to be worn as a badge of pride by youngsters who might not have much money, but who ooze attitude and rock a style that's more than a little rough around the edges. In *I Fink U Freeky* (2012), Die Antwoord's Yo-Landi kicks off with a stonking chorus, her childlike vocals and the hard techno beat instantly letting us know that this love song is anything but soppy: "I fink you freaky and I like you a lot" (repeat ad infinitum). And if you remain unstirred by the frantic ride of the song's English-Afrikaans rapping mixed with blaring synths, there's always the mindfuck of its accompanying video, featuring crawling vermin, demon eyes and all sorts of political incorrectness. Oh, with cool dancing too.

They're Coming to Take Me Away, Ha-Haaa!
Napoleon XIV

In 1966, radio listeners probably didn't know quite what to make of the mad ramblings of Napoleon XIV. The novelty single had been created by a sound engineer called Jerry Samuels, who went by the name of an imaginary French emperor because, well, why not? The resulting track was a pretty freaky monologue, delivered in a seesaw style that sort of weirdly resembled iambic pentameter, all set over a stomping beat and wailing sirens. The tale was of a man driven round the bend after his love walks out on him (we later discover that the deserter in question is his dog). The whole affair has left him so unhinged that the folks in white coats are about to arrive: "They're coming to take me away ha-haaa / They're coming to take me away ho ho hee hee ha haaa / To the funny farm". Listening to the

track these days, it's hard to decide whether to be more bothered by the chipmunk voice or by the lack of sensitivity around mental health. In fact, even back then, the song's major success was cut short when it was dropped from many station playlists because of complaints from doctors. Napoleon remained undeterred, going on to create similarly screwball tracks such as *Photogenic, Schizophrenic You* and *Bats in My Belfry*.

Somebody's Watching Me
Rockwell

If you had to pick a year to release a song about crushing paranoia, 1984 seems like a good bet. Rockwell's pop smash may not be exactly unsettling, but its minor keys and spooky church-organ give at least an air of sinister. And then there's the anxiety-laden lyrics: "I always feel like somebody's watching me / And I have no privacy". Might that voice on the chorus sound familiar? He may not have been credited, but of course it was Michael Jackson. So, how did the unknown Rockwell get the world's biggest popstar onboard? Well, the story may seem like the plotline of some feelgood 80s sitcom, but it's true. Rockwell's real name is Kennedy Gordy and his father was the CEO of Motown Records. As a teenager, Kennedy played his father a demo of *Somebody's Watching Me*, but was met with a less-than-enthusiastic reaction. He then played the track for his good friend, Michael Jackson, who loved it so much that he wanted to be involved. The two recorded another demo and Kennedy submitted it to Motown, this time under the alias Rockwell. He was so eager to hide his identity that he even performed his parts of the track in a very dubious attempt at a British accent. Anyway, the label loved it and signed him immediately. It was only later that the CEO realised that the label's hot new signing was actually his son. The song became a global hit.

I Scare Myself
Thomas Dolby

Thomas Dolby's song from 1984 isn't exactly pee-your-pants scary; its genre of fear is more of the creeping, sinister type. Musically, the track is lovely to listen to, with smooth jazz, chilled strumming and playful backing vocals bringing to mind all those blissful

Sade singles from the same era. The whole thing is so seductive. Hypnotic, even. And therein lies the unease. What tale do those lyrics tell? "I scare myself just thinking about you / I scare myself when I'm without you / I scare myself the moment that you're gone / I scare myself and I let my thoughts run ..." Is Thomas just a man who can't enjoy his own company? A hopeless extrovert who should really consider yoga? Hmm. As the song advances, we start to think that perhaps the singer's anxiety is less to do with FOMO and more to do with a fixation: "'Cause the stars already crossed our paths forever / And the sooner that we realise it the better ..." As the verses go by, we get more of an image of our narrator as the type of fellow who might just be standing outside your window in the rain. In a trench coat. Just watching. Fun fact: after Thomas Dolby enjoyed some chart success in the early 80s, he set up a Silicon Valley "sound" company. The technology he developed was used to write the Nokia tune, that omnipresent ringtone from the first major wave of mobile phones. So we may not have known it, but the sound of the 90s really was Thomas Dolby.

What's He Building?
Tom Waits

OK, enough of the mildly disturbing. If you're the kind of person who gets excited by the prospect of sleepless nights, look no further than Tom Waits's snarling spoken-word piece from 1999. Here, Waits plays the role of nosy neighbour, peeking out the window at the new arrival to the neighbourhood. Over creepy industrial sounds and background

static, Waits paints a picture of a man who is not to be trusted: "He has no children of his own, you see / He has no dog / And he has no friends and his lawn is dying". Waits hears noises coming from the house, leading him to bring each thought back to the line "What's he building in there?" (emphasis on the *building*, giving the impression that Waits is not granting his neighbour the benefit of any doubt). As the track progresses, we realise the depth of Tom's obsession, his curtain-twitching habits feeding his paranoia. Who is truly the bad guy here? The reclusive neighbour or the snooping one? Waits says the track was inspired by the infamous Unabomber: the frantic, deluded idea that anybody – or perhaps everybody – could be out to get you.

The Black Dog Runs at Night **Thought Gang, David Lynch, Angelo Badalamenti**

If you happen to be in the mood to truly have the living bejesus scared out of you, it should come as no surprise that David Lynch is the one to provide a suitable track. *The Black Dog Runs at Night* appeared in *Fire Walk with Me*, Lynch's prequel movie to the *Twin Peaks* series. It accompanied a scene in which the character Leland Palmer pays a visit to a prostitute. The sense of foreboding is heavy, not least because of the warped background music. Over an ominous bassline and distant shrieking, a distorted voice (performed by David himself) simply repeats the line which gives the track its title. So, what's it all about? Many folk tales and novels refer to a black dog who appears at night as some sort of demon or symbol of death, most famously in *The Hound of the Baskervilles*. In fact, the track even features a howling wind that could equally belong on the moors of northern England as much as in the mountain forests of *Twin Peaks*. As the synths build and the voice gets ever deeper, you might begin to wonder whether this is the most skin-crawling track ever recorded. And then you remember Geri Halliwell's solo career.

I FINK YOU FREAKY AND I LIKE YOU A LOT.

— DIE ANTWOORD

The Blank Canvas
Songs Inspired by Paintings

Mona Lisa
Nat King Cole

If you're going to write a pop song about a painting, go big or go home. Nat's chart-topper from 1950 drew inspiration from the world's most famous artwork, *La Gioconda* herself. Judging by those perfectly-crooned lines, it would appear the song's narrator has met a very special lady who reminds him of the enigmatic, smiling face from the Renaissance portrait: "Do you smile to tempt a lover, Mona Lisa? / Or is this your way to hide a broken heart? ... Are you warm, are you real, Mona Lisa? / Or just a cold and lonely lovely work of art?" From those lyrics, we can garner that the lady in question is either (a) flirtatious, (b) heartbroken, (c) the real deal, or (d) just hot with zero personality. These days, a quick stalk on social media would solve the puzzle in five minutes or so. But back in the 50s, it was more the done thing to write a gorgeously romantic song about the whole affair. No wonder Nat described the track as one of his favourites.

Vincent (Starry Starry Night)
Don McLean

"Starry, starry night / Paint your palette blue and grey / Look out on a summer's day / With eyes that know the darkness in my soul ..."

Don McLean's teary classic is an ode to various paintings by Vincent Van Gogh, but always coming back to the artist's swirling masterpiece *The Starry Night*. McLean says that he wrote the song after reading a biography about the tragic artist, from the infamous ear severing to his time in an asylum to his eventual suicide. The song could be thought of as Don's attempt to view Van Gogh with the compassion that was denied to the artist during his short life: "Now I understand / What you tried to say to me / And how you suffered for your sanity ..." For McLean, to mislabel Van Gogh as "crazy" is a great injustice; he was simply ill and misunderstood, his true talent only recognised after his death. Since 1972, the song has proved itself as the tearjerker that listeners never seem to tire of.

Even the late, great Tupac Shakur was a huge fan, and apparently the rapper had the song played to him at his hospital bed in his final moments.

Ballad of a Runaway Horse
Emmylou Harris

They say a picture is worth a thousand words. But then again, the average Leonard Cohen song probably *is* a thousand words, so go figure. Leonard wrote and recorded *Ballad of the Absent Mare* back in 1979 as an epic tale about a cowboy and his missing horse. In 1993, Emmylou released her own version, retelling the story from the standpoint of a cowgirl whose stallion has bolted. And what an emotional kick the gender-reversal has, as we follow our desperate heroine in her quest to regain her dear companion: "Say a prayer for the cowgirl, her horse ran away / She'll walk til she finds him, her darling, her stray ... And the crickets are breaking her heart with their song / As the day caves in and the night is all wrong." As you may have guessed, this stallion might be a little more human than equine. Or maybe not.

Leonard Cohen wrote the song based on a series of simple paintings (and accompanying poems) called *Ten Bulls*, from the ancient Zen tradition. So perhaps the song is more about inner enlightenment, the horse a metaphor for matters of the soul. Either way, it might just have you bawling after 30 seconds.

All the Rowboats
Regina Spektor

Regina Spektor doesn't seem like the kind of lady who you'd bump into at the IKEA bargain bin, on a quest to find the perfect mass-produced cityscape for her downstairs toilet. Don't tell Regina that a painting is décor; for her, an artwork lives and breathes. *All the Rowboats* (2012) finds the singer in a gallery looking at paintings of sailing scenes, mourning their fate: "They'll keep hanging in their gold frames / For forever, forever and a day / All the rowboats in oil paintings / They keep trying to row away, row away." For Regina, a gallery is a prison where the inmates are paintings, sculptures, artefacts. Their crime? Timeless beauty. It might all sound a bit uppity (is Regina really asking the dreaded "What *is* Art?"), but the track's dizzying piano solos and Regina's wounded voice give the impression that these verses are right from the heart. The thing that crushes her most is the gallery's exhibited violins: "In glass coffins they keep coughing / They've forgotten, forgotten how to sing ..." Is Regina reflecting on the nature of her own art – her music – which exists in a space of public scrutiny? Do the trappings of fame make her feel like one of those dusty old violins? Is she commenting on the nature of recording, of trying to freeze beauty and emotion? Or are the lyrics really just about an unsatisfying trip to the gallery? Like an oil painting itself, this is one song that has layers.

THEY'LL KEEP HANGING IN THEIR GOLD FRAMES.

— REGINA SPEKTOR

Shades of Meaning
Songs about Colours

Pink
Aerosmith

The colour pink has many connotations. And in their 1997 hit, Aerosmith would like us to explore a few. Steven Tyler begins by proclaiming "Pink, it's my new obsession". Oh, interesting, what might your latest infatuation involve, Steven? Vivid sunsets? "Pink on the lips of your lover". Hmm, where is this headed? "Pink, as the bing on your cherry". Right, gotcha. Vaginas. This is a song about vaginas. "I want to wrap you in rubber". Oh, well it wouldn't be entirely common to – "'cause pink, it's my favorite crayon, yeah". Wait; game changer. Dicks. You are now singing a song to a penis. Your own, to be precise. Admittedly, this could all be just a misinterpretation of innocently themed lyrics about cotton candy and Crayola shades. Although considering *Pink* came from the album that gave us the hit *Falling in Love (Is Hard on the Knees)*, some listener discretion is surely allowed.

Blue (Da Ba Dee)
Eiffel 65

As soon as *Blue* hit the airwaves back in 1998, theories started to circulate about the song's ambiguous "I'm blue, da-ba-dee-da-ba-dai". Was it a hidden threat of suicide ("I'm blue, I will bleed, I will die")? Was it a secret gay love song ("I'm blue, I'm in need of a guy")? Was it an unsettling premonition about a murderous Scot ("I'm blue, in Aberdeen I will die")? Ok, time to take off the tin foil hat. Eiffel 65 say that the track is simply about a man who sees everything in the colour blue. We can only assume that this is a metaphor for depression, despite (or because of?) the Eurodance beat: "And all day and all night and everything he sees is just blue / Like him inside and outside ..." The group began in Turin, Italy, where they used to work together at a record label. One day, keyboardist Maurizio started playing a new piano hook that drew the others into the room in amazement. A bit of brainstorming later, *Blue* was born. The track was a total flop when they first released it. But then it got picked up by a radio station, became a hit in Italy and soon, the rest of the stratosphere was declaring, "Yo, listen up, here's a story ..."

Black
Pearl Jam

With a title like *Black*, Pearl Jam's classic was never going to be about rainbows and unicorns. In fact, the band refused to ever release it as a single, with lead singer Eddie Vedder claiming the track was too personal to get the MTV treatment. Label executives undoubtedly gritted their teeth at the thought of not cashing in on the group's biggest anthem, but they complied.

Most fans agree that the song is Eddie's mourning for a relationship: "And now my bitter hands cradle broken glass / Of what was everything / All the pictures have all been washed in black / Tattooed everything."

As the verses move towards a conclusion, Eddie acknowledges that his ex-girl will have a happy life, but he wonders why it can't be with him.

Regardless of the band's attempts to keep the song low-key, it still became a fan favourite. One night, years after it first appeared as an album track, Eddie was sitting by the sea mulling over the recent death of a friend. From a hill behind him, he heard a group of hikers belting out the track. Their karaoke was cut short when out of the nearby bushes walked *the* Eddie Vedder, asking them to please put a sock in it!

Golden Brown
The Stranglers

"Golden brown, texture like sun / Lays me down, with my mind she runs … Never a frown with golden brown." Gee, The Stranglers sure were fans of an amber hue. When their song first hit the airwaves in 1982, it quickly became beloved by wildly different demographics. Grannies loved it for its soothing melody and harpsichord; punks loved it because they got the reference. *Golden Brown*, as we all know by now, is largely about heroin. It took a few decades for lead singer Hugh Cornwell to talk about the true inspiration behind the song. He did clarify, however, that the lyrics are not an all-out ode to the greatness of smack. In the second verse, he describes himself as being "tied to the mast", presumably in a self-imposed effort to resist the siren calls of a nice, bubbly spoonful of mellow yellow. Back in the early 80s, Hugh probably knew that one day he'd be able to talk openly about the meaning of the song. What he couldn't have imagined is that his native UK would end up with a Prime Minister called Gordon Brown, leading to a raft of spoof versions of his hit.

Yellow
Ken Nordine

No list of colour-themed songs would be complete without Ken Nordine. Ok, he was no mega-famous rockstar, but his voice is instantly recognisable as the deep baritone behind countless movie trailers and ads. In the early 60s, he was approached by a paint company to do a series of radio commercials, each one based on a particular colour of paint. Rather than just catchy slogans, Ken got creative and came up with timeless tales for each shade. In *Yellow*, we hear a story of deep envy, in which jealous Green is devising a plan to get rid of the sunniest colour of them all. That is, until Blue and Yellow get together to show Green that maybe he's not as indispensable as he thinks. The drama! The commercial began with the profound instruction: "The Fuller Paint Company invites you to stare with your ears at Yellow." Apparently, the jazz-style background music was completely improvised, with musicians simply reacting to each line of Ken's tale. Radio listeners were instantly hooked, and kept phoning up the stations to ask them to replay the ad spots! Not one to deny his fans, Ken soon released an album of his creations, simply titled *Colors*.

The Years, They Do Pass By
Songs about Getting Older

When We Were Young
Adele

"Let me photograph you in this light / In case it is the last time that we might / Be exactly like we were ..." Adele has described this song as her favourite that she's ever written. Oozing all the elements of a true soul classic – pained vocals, sombre piano, soaring choir – *When We Were Young* (2016) is the exact track to catch you off-guard as you're washing the dishes, suddenly reducing you to pathetic snivelling. Damn you, Adele! The singer says that the setting for the song is an imagined gathering of long-time friends who are now middle-aged. Among the group, she spots an old flame and the memories of their time together come flooding back. The chorus of the song revolves around Adele's wish to freeze time, to take a photo and capture this fleeting moment of youth regained, forgetting the concerns of time which have worn them all down into haggard old husks of their former selves. Ok, forget the washing-up. Just pour yourself a gin.

A Lady of a Certain Age
The Divine Comedy

In some cultures, ageing is seen as a revered journey of spiritual awakening. For the high-flying ladies of upper-class English society, no such luck. The Divine Comedy's tongue-in-cheek track from 2006 is an elegant orchestral number about a former party girl for whom life is beginning to sag: "Scaling the dizzy heights of high society / Armed only with a cheque book and a family tree ... You chased the sun around the Côte d'Azur / Until the light of youth became obscured". As we hear about the questionable life decisions of our rich-bitch antihero, perhaps we can allow a tiny shrug of sympathy as we find her trying to chat up young men in the bar. Oh well. If she's made her bed and must lie in it, she can at least do so with some hot young thing.

Time in a Bottle
Jim Croce

"If I could save time in a bottle / The first thing that I'd like to do / Is to save every day till eternity passes away / Just to spend them with you". When the late, great Jim Croce wrote this track in 1970, the passing of time was on his mind. He was approaching his 30s, juggling jobs, trying to get his break as a singer. And his wife had just told him that she was pregnant, leading to the main sentiments in the song. In the following years, Jim got a record deal and saw his single *Bad, Bad Leroy Brown* go to number one. In 1973, however, Jim tragically died when his plane crashed just after take-off. The significance of *Time in a Bottle*, with its message of time running short, gained huge poignancy. Originally appearing as an album track in 1972, the label released it as a single after Jim's death. It became his second number one.

Landslide
Fleetwood Mac

When it rains, it pours. And when it snows, it can bury you completely. In 1973, Stevie Nicks was going through a life crisis. Still in her mid-20s, her first album with boyfriend Lindsey Buckingham had totally flopped. Things had turned sour in their relationship, Stevie was thinking about giving up her music ambitions, her dad's health wasn't the best. When Lindsey got a job playing for a different group, Stevie was left to contemplate life at a house in Aspen, Colorado. Looking out at the snowy mountains, Stevie came to a realisation that the past is best left behind: "Well, I've been afraid of changing / 'Cause I've built my life around you / But time makes you bolder, even children get older / And I'm getting older too." Was she singing to her boyfriend? Her dad? Her dreams? Whichever way, it seems that Stevie has chosen to use her landslide moment in life to do some growing up. Within a year, both Stevie and Lindsey would join Fleetwood Mac, and the rest is history. Their relationship didn't last, though. No ending is *that* happy.

> *... TIME MAKES YOU BOLDER, EVEN CHILDREN GET OLDER / AND I'M GETTING OLDER TOO.*
>
> — FLEETWOOD MAC

I Remember Sex
Loudon Wainwright III ft. Dame Edna Everage

The only thing more depressing than reading that song title and releasing a knowing sigh is if you are doing so without yet having reached old age. In his 2012 album *Older Than My Old Man Now*, Loudon Wainwright (father to Rufus and Martha) teamed up with Dame Edna for a camp duet that probably won't make it into the kids' panto. Amid tinkling piano, Loudon and Edna play the elderly couple taking a trip down memory lane: "I remember sex, I started on my own / When you and I stopped having it, I tried it on the phone". Loudon makes quite the comedy partner to Edna's matriarch. Hardly surprising, given that he was the singer who brought us such gems as *Rufus Is a Tit Man* (referring to his baby boy during breastfeeding). Poor Rufus must surely have been taunted in school, especially as it became apparent that the song's title was certainly *not* the case.

This Mortal Coil
Songs about Dying

I'm Going In
Lhasa de Sela

Life, death, the great unknown. In a just world, Lhasa de Sela would be a name as famous as Jennifer Lopez. But it's doubtful Lhasa's thought-provoking reflections would be entirely suited to romcom soundtracks and songs about big butts. After more than ten years touring the world delighting audiences, Lhasa finally passed away from cancer in 2010. Her final album had been released just months beforehand and featured the song *I'm Going In* as a frank, sad, wonder-filled examination of death and where it might lead: "I need straw for the straw fire / I need hard earth for the plow / Don't ask me to reconsider / I am ready to go now". Born in New York, Lhasa made Canada her adopted home. Fellow Montrealite Rufus Wainwright says that her music helped him to understand his own mother's death: perhaps Lhasa's beautiful voice and lyrics tell us what the dying often can't, or won't, say.

The Drugs Don't Work
The Verve

Verve singer Richard Ashcroft prefers not to get into explanations of his lyrics, saying that people are free to take whatever interpretation they please. For some, *The Drugs Don't Work* is a song about joyless addiction; for others it is musical mourning. While it's true that Ashcroft battled with drug dependency around the time of the song's recording, it's also the case that he lost his father when he was aged just 11. Many fans hear the song's chorus as a sad goodbye to a loved one who has come to the end of the road, to the point where doctors can only offer a shrug and a heavy heart: "Now the drugs don't work / They just make you worse / But I know I'll see your face again". The fact that so many see the song as a form of grieving could be influenced by the fact that it was coincidentally released the day after Princess Diana died in 1997. The UK was in a state of lament, and The Verve provided the soundtrack.

You Want it Darker
Leonard Cohen

In the final months of his life, Leonard released his final album. Throughout 2016, he had recorded it in his living room, housebound and in pain due to multiple spinal fractures. *You Want it Darker* was the title track, and many fans believe that the master troubadour saved his best for last. As a man with neither the time nor the patience to faff around, Leonard addresses his Maker directly, and he's not in the mood for fawning prayers: "Magnified, sanctified / Be thy holy name ... A million candles burning / For the love that never came / You want it darker / We kill the flame." It's thought that the line about the candles could possibly be a reference to the Holocaust. Leonard is accusing his God of being calculatingly cruel, almost coaxing humans to suffer. At the end of his life, Leonard sees the dark underside of things, and he wants out. The chorus centres around the line: "Hineni, hineni / I'm ready, my Lord" ("Hineni" is old Hebrew for "Here I am"). Depressing as it all may sound, the song is lifted by soaring backing vocals provided by a choir from Leonard's childhood synagogue back in Quebec. Having always loved their singing as a child, perhaps their presence here gives a sense of things coming full circle for Leonard: an acceptance that it is time to move on.

Death with Dignity
Sufjan Stevens

If anybody can do a sensitive ballad about death, it's Sufjan Stevens. In *Death with Dignity* (2015), he sings about the loss of his mother, who died of cancer. Sufjan's mother had been an irregular presence in his life. She suffered from mental problems and substance abuse and abandoned the family home when Sufjan was just a baby. However, Sufjan maintained a relationship with her and found it hard to come to terms with her death. In the opening verses, the singer keeps coming back to the same thought: "I don't know where to begin ..." In interviews, Sufjan has spoken about how the period after his mom's death was a dark, mind-boggling time. But it seems he managed to make sense of things, telling Pitchfork Magazine, "We blame our parents for a lot of shit, for better and for worse, but it's symbiotic. Parenthood is a profound sacrifice." This perspective comes through as the song draws to a close, when the lyrics turn from questioning to a bittersweet affirmation: "I forgive you, mother, I can hear you / And I long to be near you / But every road leads to an end ..." Sad as it all is, it seems like Sufjan is well on the way to accepting what was, what is and even what will be.

Joanne
Lady Gaga

"Every part / Of my aching heart / Needs you more / Than the angels do". Do radio pop hits usually cut to the bone quite so much? In *Joanne*, we find Lady Gaga in heartbreaking form. Her 2018 hit is a dedication to her aunt Joanne, who died over a decade before the singer was even born. She passed away from a lupus-related illness at just 19, but her name always remained an intense presence in the family home. Gaga came to feel a strong sense that her own life should be lived for both herself and her aunt, meaning to the fullest. Does that explain Gaga's stratospheric career and fondness for the wild side? The raw country track centres around the hook, "Girl, where do you think you're going?", perhaps as a question to Joanne from the perspective of Gaga's father or grandmother in younger years. In the documentary *Gaga: Five Foot Two*, there's a scene where the singer plays a recording of the track to her grandmother for the first time. As Gaga and her dad are engulfed with tears, grandma merely displays supportive interest. At the end of the song, she tells her superstar granddaughter that she likes it, but "don't become maudlin over all this". A simple reminder from an old lady that, sad as death is, there's no need for melodrama.

Back to Life
Songs for Doing CPR

Stayin' Alive
Bee Gees

Who ever said that emergency chest compressions needed to be so tedious? Experts recommend that compressions should be about five centimetres deep and administered at a rate of 100-120 per minute. How to keep count? A bangin' tune with a similar *bpm*. Such as this Bee Gees classic from 1977, which offers the bonus feature of lyrics focusing on survival: "Whether you're a brother or whether you're a mother / You're stayin' alive ..." The drumbeat on this track was actually just a recorded loop. As a joke, the Bee Gees credited it to an invented drummer, Bernard Lupe. The track's success led to many enquiries from other artists who were keen to work with this fabulously talented Mr. Lupe. The song has been used in public CPR campaigns by both the American Heart Association and the British Heart Foundation.

You Can't Hurry Love
Phil Collins

If you find yourself at death's door, let the soothing voice of Phil Collins give you the heart massage that just might save your life. Ok, we all know that Phil's version is a cover. But websites dedicated to tracking the *bpm* of songs (yes, they really do exist) rate the original version by The Supremes as being far too fast, perhaps due its more enthusiastic use of the tambourine. So Phil it is, singing about a conversation with his (improbably named) "mama", who reminds him not to worry as love will come to him in good time. Never has there been more resonance to the lines: "But when I feel that I, I can't go on / Well these precious words keep me hanging on ..."

Cecilia
Simon & Garfunkel

With a *bpm* of 103, Simon & Garfunkel's 1970 smash is another ideal candidate for warding off the Grim Reaper. In fact, it was the drumbeat that the artists built the rest of the song around. Simon & Garfunkel were at a late-night party and started banging out the rhythm on a piano seat (those poor neighbours!) They recorded it and later added the melody and lyrics about Cecilia. This song could be of particular interest if your cardiac-arrest case happens to be a Catholic. While the lyrics seem to refer to an unfaithful lover, Paul Simon has suggested that they could also refer to St. Cecilia, the patron saint of music. In this case, the transitory lover Cecilia becomes a metaphor for Paul's fleeting musical inspiration. Now that's an intriguing tidbit to coax someone back to the land of the living.

WHETHER YOU'RE A BROTHER OR WHETHER YOU'RE A MOTHER / YOU'RE STAYIN' ALIVE ...

— BEE GEES

Walk Like an Egyptian
The Bangles

Looking for a more exotic take on chest compressions? America's biggest-selling hit of 1987 has you covered. Again, the drumbeat is one of the song's main talking points. Debbi Peterson was The Bangles' drummer and, like the rest of the band, also sang vocals. In the studio, all four band members recorded lead vocals for this track. However, the producer didn't like Debbi's version, so he cut her out and left a verse each for the other members. Oh, and then he decided that the whole thing would sound better with a drum machine, relegating Debbi (by now livid) to the role of jilted backing dancer. Ouch. The song's writer said it was inspired by a time he saw people walking across a ferry deck, trying to keep their balance, in a way that reminded him of ancient Egyptian sketches. Please wait until CPR has satisfactorily terminated before engaging in the song's winning dance moves.

Short 'n' Sweet
Songs under Two Minutes

The Letter
The Box Tops

"Gimme a ticket for an aeroplane / I ain't got time to take a fast train … My baby just wrote me a letter". Songwriter Wayne Carson said that his initial inspiration for this track came from a suggestion from his father to write a song with the first line "Gimme a ticket for an airplane". To fit the rhythm, the American airplane became the British aeroplane and a groovy 60s classic began to take shape. It was short, but perfectly formed. Carson sent the demo to a studio in Memphis. The men in suits loved it, but who were they going to get to actually record it? The studio owner had recently heard of a local teenage group called The Box Tops. Yeah, they were young, but they could handle it. Couldn't they? The band's 16-year-old singer, Alex Chilton, was told to try to get his voice "a little gruff". One can only imagine the producers' wonder when the baby-faced teen came out with the rich, gravelly tone of a particularly soulful whiskey-drinker (maybe that's why Joe Cocker decided to cover the song in 1970). The end result was a number-one hit in the US, the final time to date for a song under two minutes in length.

Woo Hoo
The 5.6.7.8.'s

If seeking international appeal, it's not the worst idea to write a song featuring "Woo hoo" as its sole lyric. Originally a hit in 1959, the song enjoyed a 21st-century revival after it featured in *Kill Bill: Vol. 1*. As a brief interlude to dismemberment and bloodshed, we see the hit performed as part of a medley by Tokyo rockabilly girl group, The 5.6.7.8's. Tarantino says he first came across the group when he heard their music playing in a clothes shop in downtown Tokyo. In a scenario that must have involved at least one "Don't you know who I am?" moment, Quentin demanded that the shop assistant sell him the CD from the stereo. And what a stroke of luck for the girl group that the store worker complied. Tarantino invited them to appear in the film, and worldwide exposure followed. Clocking in at just under two minutes, the song allowed rare international success for a Japanese act.

Song 2
Blur

From one "Woo hoo" to another. Ok, so *Song 2* is slightly breaking the rules in that it is meticulously edited to run for exactly two minutes and two seconds. It also features just two verses and two choruses, predictably appears as track two on the album and – suspiciously – reached number two in the UK charts back in 1997. With an unusually heavy style for Blur, the song is thought to be a piss-take of grunge or metal tracks, high on noise and low on substance. Indeed, *Song 2*'s chorus could be seen as poking fun at the waffled nonsense of such songs: "Woo hoo! When I feel heavy metal / Woo hoo! And I'm pins and I'm needles ..." As is wont to happen, the song went on to become a huge hit in the exact market that it was supposedly parodying and remains a favourite to this day among drunk college students and drunker football fans.

Grandma's Hands
Bill Withers

One has to wonder what Bill Withers makes of the fact that his 1971 classic is these days better recognised as the sample music for Blackstreet's 1996 hit *No Diggity*. Is he angry with Blackstreet that they turned his tender homage to dear grandma into a hip-hop track about some flush ho who enjoys pushin' phat rides? Or is he just happy with the royalties? Bill's song, as the title suggests, is a tribute to the loving, protective hands of his grandma: "Grandma's hands used to hand me piece of candy / Grandma's hands picked me up each time I fell ..." Apparently, Bill's grandmother had been born into slavery and had been a strong influence during his upbringing in West Virginia. Later in the song, we learn that grandma is no longer around but what remain are the memories of her kindness, her zest, her loving lessons, all of which found expression through her hands. Short and sweet, the song also gave us what is possibly modern music's most iconic hum ("Mm – hmm – hmm").

They'll Never Play That on the Radio
Songs over Seven Minutes

Honeymoon's Great (Wish You Were Her)
Josh T. Pearson

Some songs are great for a bop around the kitchen. While others require a mug of tea, an armchair and – in the case of this track – a full 13 minutes of listening, allowing some extra time for digestion. Texan singer Josh T. Pearson admits that writing his 2011 album *Last of the Country Gentlemen* was a bit like talking to a priest, "so no one else hears you". And in *Honeymoon's Great ...*, it's easy to see why. With painful honesty, the track describes the story of a man recently married, who can only think of one thing. As you may have guessed from the title, his preoccupation is certainly female, but just not the lady lying next to him: "I'm in love with an amazing woman, she just is not my wife / What will I tell my pastor, friends, my family or said blushin' bride?" Filling almost a quarter of an hour, the song takes twists and turns worthy of a peculiarly gripping novel. Probably not the best track for a quiet, cross-country drive with your significant other.

Riders on the Storm
The Doors

In his late teens, Jim Morrison used to regularly hitchhike across Florida, keeping sketchbooks which he filled with often-violent images of a mysterious drifter. Almost a decade later, and by now a superstar, Jim introduced us to a murderous hitchhiker in the seven-minute-long *Riders on the Storm* (1971). Fans argue the character is based on infamous killer Billy Cook, who murdered six people while he was hitchhiking to California. Whether Jim's inspiration was real life or his own dark imaginings, the song paints a picture of one Traveling Wilbury who you certainly don't want to pick up: "If you give this man a ride / Sweet family will die / Killer on the road ..."

From this creepy premise, Jim then takes the song into quite a profound musing on the nature of our existence: "Riders on the storm / Into this house we're born / Into this world we're thrown / Like a dog without a bone". The song's eeriness is magnified by the fact that it was released very shortly before Jim's death, entering the Billboard Hot 100 on the same week that Jim unexpectedly died. And if that doesn't unsettle you sufficiently, listen closely to hear the sinister whispering that Jim added in to accompany his vocals, described by Jim's bandmate as "the last thing he ever did".

American Pie
Don McLean

At almost nine minutes, *American Pie* (1971) is the longest song to ever reach number one in the US. And it, too, reads like a novel. After many years of refusing to comment on the lyrics, in 2015 McLean finally offered some insights. Written at the start of the 70s, McLean has said that the song is about "things ... heading in the wrong direction". The hazy days of the 50s and 60s are no more: "Drove my Chevy to the levee but the levee was dry" (the Chevy was the car of choice for baby-boomer teens, while the levee was the hotspot to hang out). The idyllic days of the "good ol' boys" have been replaced by something much more sinister: the death of Buddy Holly ("the day the music died"); a loss of purpose ("a generation lost in space"); the violent death of a young black man, killed by Hell's Angels at a Rolling Stones concert ("fire is the devil's only friend").

When writing the song, McLean could never have known the cultural significance that his song would have. Neither could he have imagined that it would inspire a movie about a teenager who enjoys humping warm pastries.

My Sister
Tindersticks

Ever heard of sleep whisperers? They're people who make a living on YouTube murmuring soft nothings to guide their listeners into peaceful slumber. *My Sister* (1995) starts off in similar fashion: peaceful xylophone accompanying a lovingly-mumbled monologue. That is, until you focus on what is actually being said. Far from a Shakespearean-style ode to his dear sister, the narrator relates a tale more inspired by Hilaire Belloc (whose early-1900s poems for children included gems such as *Matilda: Who Told Lies, and Was Burned to Death*). In this track, the sweet sister carries a Stanley knife, smokes in bed, drinks heavily, loses and regains her eyesight, marries a dickhead at age 15. Somewhere between black comedy and hopeless tragedy, *My Sister* is an outrageous, eight-minute life-journey into the unknown. Let's just hope that its writer was kidding when he described it as "99% true".

From Miles to Herbie
Jazz Tracks that Went Mainstream

Take Five
The Dave Brubeck Quartet

As Beethoven's *Fifth Symphony* is to classical music, and Britney's *Baby One More Time* is to pop, *Take Five* (1959) is the jazz standard for people who might not know much about jazz. Of course, that's not to say the track is anything other than a true classic. And neither does it suggest that *Take Five* is entirely typical of its genre. In fact, the song takes its name from its unusual quintuple time, light cymbals setting the tempo as an upbeat 1-2-3-4-5. The iconic two-chord piano then comes in, making the track instantly recognisable and bringing to mind every Woody Allen movie you've ever watched (and, less excitingly, every furniture store you've ever visited). That unusual quintuple beat was inspired by classical and folk music that the group encountered when they were on a tour of Eurasia in the late 50s. It was so off-the-wall that the label worried that nobody would be able to dance to it and the record would be a total flop. Silly A&R people. *Take Five* went on to become the best-selling jazz single to date.

So What
Miles Davis

As *Take Five* is the most-purchased jazz single of all time, it's often claimed that the best-selling album is Miles Davis' *Kind of Blue* (1959). The album is considered by many to be definitive. In his career, trumpeter Miles started off playing "hot jazz", the frantic, high-paced bebop style that was popular at the time. After years of shakin' and boppin' on the Manhattan club scene, Miles reached his 30s and became more interested in slowing things down. *Kind of Blue* was revolutionary for its "less is more" style, with Miles holding long notes and allowing the spaces to speak. The album was performed by a sextet which included piano, bass, drums and two sax players (including John Coltrane). As was typical for Miles, he just provided a basic outline of each track and told the group to improvise the rest. Undoubtedly, the most recognisable piece on the album is the iconic opener *So What*. And it's the perfect example of each of the six musicians bringing their own personal style to the recording. As for the title of the track, its origin has become the stuff of urban legend. Actor Dennis Hopper once claimed that Miles had taken the expression from a conversation they'd had, in which Dennis kept reacting to Miles with a dismissive "So what?" In his autobiography, Miles suggests that the title might have actually come to him from a time when a female fan was going on about how she had all his albums. A nonplussed Miles interrupted her, and you can guess what he asked.

BIDDY-BIDDY-BOP.

— US3

Cantaloop (Flip Fantasia)

Us3

They say crime never pays, but Us3 would probably beg to differ. The British group started off taking illegal samples of tracks from the iconic jazz label *Blue Note* and using them to make jazz-rap numbers. Once Us3 started getting played on the radio, they soon got a call from label execs. Cold sweats broke out, visions of suited lawyers. Instead, it seemed the label was impressed, signed the group and granted them access to all *Blue Note*'s music, dating back to 1939. It proved to be a good idea. The group's first single, *Cantaloop* (1992), became the first *Blue Note* record to sell over a million in the US. The track sampled various pieces, but mainly the groovy piano of *Cantaloupe Island* by Herbie Hancock. Apparently, when Hancock himself now plays his classic composition at concerts, he jokingly introduces it as a Us3 track. With its fusion of jazz and hip-hop, *Cantaloop (Flip Fantasia)* performed the impossible feat of opening teens' ears to jazz. Its scat-style chorus ("Biddy-biddy-bop") may also have opened the door for the success of the 1994 Eurodance hit *Scatman (Ski-Ba-Bop-Ba-Dop-Bop)*. You can make up your own mind on whether that was a good thing.

Chameleon
Herbie Hancock

Herbie Hancock has been responsible for more than a few jazz anthems. One of his most famous is *Chameleon*, from his genre-bending 1974 album *Head Hunters*. Right off the bat, the track begins with a stonking, elastic bassline to let the listener know that Herbie's new brand of jazz is going to ask you to commit to some funky head bopping. While it initially drew some criticism from jazz purists, the track is now seen as a standard and has become a crowd-pleasing staple of small jazz ensembles around the world. Its hip sound has also been hugely influential, not just in jazz but also in other spheres like hip-hop and pop (any fans of US pop goddesses Fifth Harmony will be reminded of the funky vibes in their 2015 song *Top Down*). Jazz novices beware: 70s jazz was not always the most concise affair. It might be a little easier on the ears to go for the radio edit rather than the whopping 15-minute album version of the track.

Behind the Scenes
Very Successful Producers

Giorgio Moroder (song: *I Feel Love* by Donna Summer)

Back in the 60s, Italian producer Giorgio Moroder set up his own studio in Munich. In the way that the planets have a habit of aligning, American singer Donna Summer also found herself living in the German city in the 70s, where she was working as a session singer. The two began to collaborate and enjoyed success with their 1975 disco hit *Love to Love You Baby*. Then they came up with an idea for a new album, in which each track would take on the feel of a certain decade. After working their way through the 40s, the 50s, the 60s, they wanted the final track to sound futuristic. How to go about it? Well, those typical orchestral disco strings were out of the question. But there was always the increasingly popular Moog synthesiser. And maybe, just maybe, it would sound really cutting edge to use *only* synthesisers. Would it all sound a bit too machine-like? How about getting Donna to sing like a particularly breathy angel? That should soften it out. *I Feel Love* (1977) was completed and released. And nobody had ever heard anything quite like it. David Bowie once recalled how he had been in Berlin around that time, when Brian Eno came running into the room saying that he'd just heard the sound of the future. It seems like Giorgio had achieved his mission, and electronic dance music was born. The track had enormous success around the world, sending Giorgio's career into overdrive. In the following years, he worked with everybody from Bowie to Blondie, even to Daft Punk in later years. He won every award under the sun for movie scores like *Scarface* and *Flashdance* (apparently, his proudest creation is 1983's *What a Feeling*). His sound led to the development of new wave, techno, house, to what any kid these days would understand as being "music". And you know what? In 50 years' time, *I Feel Love* will probably still sound like it was recorded yesterday.

Quincy Jones (song: *Angel* by Aretha Franklin)

Around 1960, Quincy Jones was part of a travelling jazz group. He mainly played trumpet; the rest of the music was taken care of by the group's other 17 members. Yes, 17. They played to enraptured audiences and ecstatic reviews. There was just one problem: they were broke. As Quincy would later say, "We had the best jazz band on the planet, and yet we were literally starving. That's when I discovered that there was music, and there was the music business." Lesson learned, Jones got a job working at *Mercury Records* and soon started composing music for film scores. Within a short time, his work for the movies would truly take off, leading him to go out on his own and develop scores for films like *The Italian Job*. He soon got into producing for big-name singers like Ella Fitzgerald and Sinatra. It was all going swimmingly. That is, until 1974 struck, when Quincy suffered a brain aneurysm. He was so close to death that his family actually planned his funeral. But the great producer was going nowhere: he battled through and ended up attending his own memorial service (it would have been rude to cancel), shaking hands with friends like Marvin Gaye. From the jaws of defeat, Quincy's biggest success was yet to come. In 1979, he produced Michael Jackson's *Off the Wall*, later *Thriller*, then *Bad*; all spectacular triumphs which changed the course of pop. With so many sales under his belt, it's easy to think of Quincy as commercially driven. But to do so would be to understate his talent. This is the man who in 1991 collaborated with Miles Davis for the jazz legend's final album. And let's not forget the timeless, low-key album *Hey Now Hey (The Other Side of the Sky)*, co-produced in 1973 with Aretha Franklin, which spawned the classic hit *Angel*.

T Bone Burnett (song: *My Least Favourite Life* by Lera Lynn)

Getting a job as a guitarist in Bob Dylan's band would be a career highlight for most people. Back in the mid-70s, T Bone Burnett achieved that goal while still in his 20s. Where to go from there? The singer-songwriter started releasing his own material in the 80s and then discovered a knack for producing, going on to work for names like Elvis Costello and Elton John. But it was in the sphere of soundtracks where things really took off. After initial acclaim for his work on movies such as *Great Balls of Fire*, Hollywood developed an insatiable appetite for T Bone. In the following years, the producer won Grammys and Golden Globes for music he developed for movies like *The Big Lebowski*, *O Brother, Where Art Thou?* and *Walk the Line*. For the latter film, Reese Witherspoon thanked T Bone in her Oscar acceptance speech for basically helping her "become" a country singer. His trademark sound involves blues, folk, bluegrass, all of which are especially evident in one of his most outstanding works: the *True Detective* soundtrack. As fans of the TV series will know, the show takes its music seriously. One of the crime drama's most memorable tracks is *My Least Favourite Life* by Lera Lynn. The singer performs the song in a bar scene, playing the role of a blues-singing junkie. Apparently, the show's director instructed Lera and T Bone to come up with something very dark, based on the story of "a lover who dies and comes back as a crow". Umm, tall order. The resulting song was a haunting number about broken wings and a life beyond bleak. So, you know, mission accomplished.

Dr. Dre (song: *Still D.R.E* by Dr. Dre ft. Snoop Dogg)

How to even begin to describe the influence of Dr. Dre? Maybe it's best introduced in his own words, from his track *Still D.R.E*: "Since the last time you heard from me I lost some friends / Well, hell, me and Snoop, we dippin' again / Kept my ear to the streets, signed Eminem / He's triple platinum, doin' 50 a week / Still, I stay close to the heat ..." Released in 1999, the single was a comeback for Dre. In the 80s, he rose to fame rapping with N.W.A, then moved into producing and set up his own label, *Death Row Records*. There, he discovered and produced the biggest names in the industry, like Tupac and Snoop Dogg. By the mid-90s, he was dominating the airwaves both with his own releases (like his album *The Chronic*) and work which he produced for his protégés. In 1996, Dre left *Death Row* after a dispute with colleagues, hence *Still D.R.E*'s claim that he "lost some friends" (though that's likely also a reference to Tupac's murder in the same year). Soon after, he set up a new label and signed newcomers like Eminem and 50 Cent, basically consolidating his position as hip-hop's most bomb player. Dre's style has evolved over the years. Back in the

90s, he popularised G-funk, the bouncing, synthy style that can be heard on rap anthems like Tupac's *California Love*, but also even on pop numbers like The Spice Girls' *Say You'll Be There*. In later years, his approach became simpler, using live instruments. Dre admits that he's not the greatest musician, lyricist or rapper. He surrounds himself with people who he believes in and brings it all together. Again, in his own words: "My greatest talent is knowing exactly what I want to hear."

Mark Ronson (song: *Uptown Funk* by Mark Ronson ft. Bruno Mars)

"I'm too hot (Hot damn!) / Call the police and the fireman / I'm too hot (Hot damn!) / Make a dragon wanna retire man ..." The lyrics from 2014's *Uptown Funk* could really be about Mark Ronson's career. If seeking the 21st-century equivalent of Giorgio or Quincy, it's hard to think of a better contender than Mark. From his early days as a DJ in New York (a baby-faced Ronson actually appeared on the decks in a ridiculous funeral scene in the 2001 comedy *Zoolander*), Mark quickly moved into recording. In 2003, he wrote songs for an album called *Here Comes the Fuzz* and then invited different artists to perform them in studio. Nobody major, just some small fry like Jack White and Sean Paul. From there, he started producing albums for other artists and ended up creating some of the biggest hits of the new millennium for singers like Adele and Lily Allen. And, of course, there was Amy Winehouse's *Back to Black*, the 2007 album which would launch his career to the stratosphere. Its soulful feel was definitely retro, but somehow it all sounded incredibly new. Mark had stumbled upon a winning combo. Since then, Mark has basically been the industry's most wanted man, working with everybody from Queens of the Stone Age to Lady Gaga to (more recently) Vampire Weekend. That mix of old and new is a constant presence, as is Mark's self-acknowledged perfectionism. For example, the recording of *Uptown Funk* involved over 100 takes, performed in studios around the world over a period of months. Towards the end of the process, Ronson says that his hair was falling out and that one highly-strung recording session ended with him vomiting and fainting. Was it all worth it? *Uptown Funk* became one of the best-selling singles of all time. Surely that'll pay for a decent scalp treatment.

Even Better Than the Real Thing? Outstanding Covers

Hurt
Johnny Cash

When the lead singer of Nine Inch Nails was asked his opinion on Johnny Cash's 2003 version of their track *Hurt*, he said that he felt as if the song was now Johnny's. A true musician knows to bow down when it's called for. With lyrics that mention self-harm, possible heroin use and deep depression, it wasn't an obvious choice for Cash. And yet, the sad tale seemed to fit perfectly with the ageing superstar, looking back on his hell-raising past while approaching the end of his life with his demons still in tow. "What have I become / My sweetest friend? / Everyone I know / Goes away in the end". The song's video was ranked by NME as the best video of all time. It shows Cash in the derelict *House of Cash* museum, surrounded by shattered elements of his former glory. Other scenes were shot in his home, where we see his wife, the legendary June Carter. As if the song's tale of regret weren't devastating enough, context makes it even sadder. June died three months after the video was made, Johnny followed suit just four months later. Their family home burned down in 2007. Stock up on the Kleenex.

Respect
Aretha Franklin

It's hard to imagine that *Respect* was ever anybody else's song other than Aretha's. Originally a hit for Otis Redding in 1965, Aretha reworked the song and released her own version just two years later. In some ways, Aretha's cover was an answer song to the original. Otis had written the song from the viewpoint of a man looking for recognition from his lady when he returned from a hard day's work: "I'm about to give you all my money / But all I'm askin', hey / Is a little respect when I get home". Aretha turned the idea on its head, putting herself in the place of the self-sufficient woman who was just about sick of her unappreciative husband: "I'm about to give you all of my money / And all I'm askin' in return, honey / Is to give me my propers when you get home" ("propers" meaning due recognition). The new, no-nonsense, female version struck a chord with the public at a time when feminism and civil rights had recently become mainstream issues. Added to that was the oomph of Aretha's voice, her iconic *R-E-S-P-E-C-T* break and her sisters on backing vocals, insisting on that respect ("Sock it to me, sock it to me ..."). One of the songs of the century was born.

Mad World
Michael Andrews ft. Gary Jules

Who wore it better? Tears For Fears with their 1982 original, synth-pop *Mad World*, or Michael Andrews with his stripped-back piano version from 2003? Hardcore fans of 80s new wave will argue that there's no improving on pop perfection. However, there's no denying that the 2003 cover was a bigger commercial success. Perhaps the bare melody and Gary Jules' clear, unrushed vocals allowed radio listeners to take in the significance of the song's really quite profound lyrics: "... I find it kind of funny / I find it kind of sad / The dreams in which I'm dying / Are the best I've ever had". In contrast to the ominous energy of the original, the *Mad World* cover comes across as a deep sigh as the singer describes a senseless life in which people feel doomed, invisible and apathetic about death. No wonder Brits love playing it so much around Christmas time.

Limit to Your Love
James Blake

There's stripping back and then there's reducing a song to its bare bones. *The Limit to Your Love* was first recorded by Canadian singer Feist in

2007. It was a slow-tempo track, but with ever-building vocals and layers. In 2010, British singer James Blake released his own take on the song, dropping the "The" and featuring stark vocals set against a melody which contains almost as much nothing as something (that's not an existential musing, the song is approximately 50% air). Some call it the new dubstep, others give it a much more technical description as *music for fornication*, which would make an interesting name for an aisle at a record store. The song's lyrics are ambiguous, but let's speculate: might it be the case that James' repeated insistence that "There's a limit to your love" actually means that there isn't a limit to your love? Given the aforementioned genre of the track, that explanation would fit. Not that we need to concern ourselves too much with lyrical intricacies, given that the song seems to be designed for 4 a.m. listening while drunk/naked/aroused/undone (or on a particularly fun night, all of the above).

Mr. Bojangles
Nina Simone

There have been so many covers of *Mr. Bojangles* that it's tough to single one out. But if we're going for pure emotional gut punch, Nina undoubtedly takes the crown. The song was originally written in 1968 as a country number by Jerry Jeff Walker. His inspiration came from a weekend spent in jail after a raucous night in New Orleans. While there, Jerry shared a cell with a homeless man who called himself Mr. Bojangles. The elderly man spoke about his sad life, wandering the land, tap dancing for people to throw a few coins, getting into trouble with the law. Jerry put it all together in just a few verses. In Nina's 1971 version, she swapped country guitar for piano and lush strings. And she let her voice transmit the sheer melancholy of the broken-hearted minstrel: "He spoke with tears of 15 years / How his dog and him travelled about / His dog up and died, he up and died / After 20 years he still grieves ... Mr. Bojangles, dance." As mournful as the song is, at least it eventually brought some joy to its author, Jerry. All those cover versions made sure that his royalty cheques were very healthy indeed. Apparently, he developed something of a coke habit and earned himself the nickname Mr. Blowjangles. Reader, you alone must decide whether that constitutes a happy ending.

It's Oh So Quiet
Björk

Some time in the early 90s, Björk was on a tour of the States with her band. In a roadside store, they discovered an album of old tunes by American divas. It included a little-known gem from 1951 by Hollywood leading lady Betty Hutton, a novelty number about the ups and downs of falling in love. With Betty's juxtaposed whispers and suddenly manic screams, the song quickly became a favourite on the tour bus and Björk decided to take a shot at her own version. And she certainly didn't hold back, magnifying every hush and shriek in the song's rollercoaster ride: "It's, oh, so quiet / It's oh, so still / You're all alone / And so peaceful until / You ring the bell! / Bim bam! / You shout and you yell! / Hi ho!" Of course, Björk could never have guessed that the song's 1995 release would push her into the sphere of global chart-topper. Apparently, she used to get a bit annoyed that her amazing repertoire of boundary-pushing music often gets eclipsed by one silly cover version. Oh well. At least it's a *great* silly cover version.

IT'S, OH, SO QUIET / IT'S OH, SO STILL / YOU'RE ALL ALONE / AND SO PEACEFUL UNTIL …

— BJÖRK

Musical Conversations
Songs about Songs

Killing Me Softly with His Song
Roberta Flack

Long before Katy Perry and Taylor Swift were writing petty diss tracks about each other's music (sigh ...), performers like Roberta Flack were singing about songs that had truly inspired them. *Killing Me Softly ...* was originally recorded by American singer Lori Lieberman in 1971. Soon after, Flack heard it as part of the in-flight music on a plane to New York. She loved it, recorded her own version, and made the track into an international megahit. So, what song provided the inspiration for those lyrics? According to Lieberman, the idea first came to her from an intense experience she'd had while watching McLean perform in LA. Don launched into his track *Empty Chairs*, a weepy number about an abandoned lover, and Lieberman could barely believe how much the sad tale paralleled her own life. In her head, a new song began to take shape, describing the experience of feeling a deep connection to Don's performance: "Strumming my pain with his fingers / Singing my life with his words / Killing me softly with his song ..." If you are under the age of 50 or so, it's probably impossible to listen to the early versions of this track without mentally inserting the sitar chords and "One time!" background-hollering which accompanied the 1998 cover version by The Fugees. Which is not a bad thing.

Melody Noir
Patrick Watson

While haunting melancholy might not be most people's favourite state of mind, there's something about *Melody Noir* (2018) that makes it seem like the most enticing emotion of all. Canadian singer Patrick Watson says the song was inspired by the music of the late Venezuelan singer Simón Díaz, who specialised in the folk music of his homeland. Those traditional *tonadas* were often lovelorn laments that workers used to sing in the fields (perhaps the old-school, Venezuelan equivalent of the builder next door letting loose on a heartfelt Whitney ballad). In particular, *Melody Noir* seems to be a nod towards Díaz's song

Tonada de Luna Llena, a tale of an elusive lover. In Patrick's song, he marvels from afar, each verse closing with the lines, "You are the sweetest melody / I never sung". The song seems steeped in both wonder and sadness. Who is Patrick singing to? A love who he can't be with? The idol that he never got to meet? Or the talent he feels he lacks to create a song as perfect as his idol's? Well, Patrick, you've come close enough.

Your Song
Elton John

OK, enough about songs that talk about other songs. When you're Elton frickin' John, you're allowed to simply reference yourself. *Your Song* (1970) is one of pop's most famous self-referential tracks: "If I was a sculptor, but then again, no / Or a man who makes potions in a travelling show / I know it's not much, but it's the best I can do / My gift is my song, and this one's for you". The young Elton may not have the riches or the handicraft skills to woo his love but, by God, he can bang out a tune to make any fellow weak at the knees. Not that Elton wrote the lyrics here. Most of his hits have been written by long-term collaborator Bernie Taupin. In 1967, 20-year-old Elton and 17-year-old Bernie both responded to an ad by *Liberty Records* looking for singers and songwriters. The label paired the two and thus began their runaway success, Bernie writing, Elton composing and singing. Upon its release, the track was widely praised, with even John Lennon calling it the best new thing since The Beatles' work (humble as ever, John). Bernie Taupin didn't let the whole thing go to his head, bluntly stating, "*Your Song* could only have been written by a 17-year-old who'd never been laid in his life." Why does that seem true of most pop music?

Tower of Song
Leonard Cohen

For most singers, writing a song about the torments of one's own talents would come off as a little pretentious. And yet, Leonard manages to do so with just enough humour to stay on the right side of charming. In *Tower of Song* (1988), he reflects on the lonely ivory tower that his career has put him in, and how it's too late to back out. Such ponderings seem to be brought on by age, with Leonard already in his 50s when he wrote the track: "Well my friends are gone and my hair is grey / I ache in the places where I used to play". Very much a ladies' man in his younger years, might Leonard have been feeling a little, well, delicate in the parts of his body he had previously most enjoyed? He goes on to seek solace in the ghosts of his fellow singers: "I said to Hank Williams, 'How lonely does it get?' / Hank Williams hasn't answered yet". We can assume this is a reference to William's classic country tearjerker *I'm So Lonesome I Could Cry* (1949). Leonard reveals that lonely Hank is in the tower too, but he's a hundred floors up, so he's not the best company. Hank's higher position seems to be simple self-deprecation by Leonard, humbled by Hank's musical abilities. A similar sentiment can be found when Leonard comes to the line, "I was born with the gift of a golden voice". This part of the song often drew cheers at concerts from Leonard's fans, all too aware that Leonard's vocals were far from angelic.

It Wasn't God Who Made Honky Tonk Angels
Kitty Wells

Speaking of Hank Williams, in 1952 he had a huge hit with *The Wild Side of Life*. It was a song about a man whose wife-to-be has cheated on him, choosing instead the lure of the men and the booze of the honky-tonk bars. Hank sings, "I didn't know God made honky-tonk angels", a bitter quip about morally-lacking women. Kitty Wells was having none of it. At the time, she was a struggling country musician, frustrated in a male-dominated industry. When it was suggested to her to record a rebuttal track, she got onboard. To the same melody as Hank's hit, she recorded *It Wasn't God Who Made Honky Tonk Angels*, and set out what was what: "It's a shame that all the blame is on us women / It's not true that only you men feel the same / From the start most every heart that's ever broken / Was because there always was a man to blame". This being the early 50s, conservative radio listeners collectively gasped. While Hank's finger wagging had enjoyed widespread airplay, Kitty's song was quickly banned from many broadcasts for its "suggestive" tone. And yet, the general public lapped it up. Kitty became the first solo woman to top the Billboard Country Charts and ended up outselling Hank's original track. Who said girl power was invented by The Spice Girls?

Enjoy it While it Lasts
Worthwhile One-Hit Wonders

Lovin' You
Minnie Riperton

Some artists fail to repeat their initial success because of the public's short attention span. And others never get the chance. Minnie Riperton was diagnosed with breast cancer in 1976, just a year after hitting number one with *Lovin' You*. Although she went on to record two more albums, her health deteriorated, and she passed away in 1979. Despite not having any other major hits, Minnie is still considered a soul legend. Originally taught as a soprano, her huge range – and whistle tone – caught the attention of the big wigs. Like, oh let's see, Stevie Wonder, who played keyboard on *Lovin' You*. The ballad is clearly addressed to a lover: "Lovin' you is easy 'cause you're beautiful / Makin' love with you is all I wanna do ..." However, Minnie said that the central hook ("la la la la la") came from a lullaby that she had made up for her little daughter, Maya. That daughter would grow up to be the famous comedy actress Maya Rudolph, of *Saturday Night Live* fame. In the album version, Minnie repeatedly sings "Maya, Maya" as the song fades out. One-hit wonders can often be pop at its most meaningless, but Minnie's is one to truly tug on the heart strings.

Play That Funky Music
Wild Cherry

In the mid-70s, Wild Cherry were four white guys who played rock gigs. As they toured the clubs of the Pittsburgh area, they began to notice that patrons seemed keener on disco and funk than plain old rock. The imagined pleas of club-goers soon morphed into an idea for a song: "Play that funky music white boy / Play that funky music right ... Lay down the boogie and play that funky music till you die". In the resulting track, the lyrics were screeched in the singer's best James Brown impression and set to some very funky strumming indeed. And an international smash was born. Wild Cherry never managed to repeat their commercial success, but all was not lost. The group's singer, Rob Parissi is from a small town in Ohio. In 2013, the town named a street after him and (brace yourself) designated August 11th as Rob Parissi Day. Such is the power of a one-hit wonder!

My Sharona
The Knack

The Knack peaked early, their debut single becoming the biggest hit of 1979 in the US. Although the group had modest success with later tracks, they pale in comparison. *My Sharona* was the song that had it all: a killer riff, a bangin' beat and lyrics to make you blush. Singer Doug Fieger said he wrote those lyrics about a girl he had met working in a clothes shop and who went on to become his girlfriend. Her name was Sharona. It all sounds quite romantic except for the fact that Sharona was 17 when she first met Fieger, who was 25 at the time. The questionable dynamic came across in the song's lyrics and caused a hell of a lot of controversy: "Never gonna stop, give it up / Such a dirty mind, always get it up / For the touch of the younger kind". It turned out the "younger kind" was a theme running through quite a few songs on the album, leading to a campaign by certain members of the public to "Knuke The Knack". The group began to fizzle out. And as for Sharona? She moved to LA and became a real estate agent to the stars. Check out her website at (this is not a joke) *mysharona.com*, where you can view luxury condos while rockin' out to the song that she inspired.

There She Goes
The La's

As one-hit wonders go, The La's didn't even enjoy that much of a hit with *There She Goes*. It peaked at number 13 in the UK and number 49 in the US. That's no small feat for some youngsters from Liverpool back in 1990, but it does indicate that most of the song's success came in later years, when it became a cheerful staple for romcom soundtracks, TV commercials and cover versions. The years have seen much discussion about whether the track is just a simple love song or whether the whole thing is actually about ... (you know where this is going, right?) ... about heroin. The ambiguous lyrics have led to plenty of debate: "... There she goes again / Racing through my brain ... Pulsing through my vein". Online forums on the issue are somewhat more frenzied than the norm because of the fact that the most famous cover of the song was by American devotees of Christian rock, Sixpence None the Richer. This leads to plenty of exchanges along the lines of: *Pete from Manchester: "Mate, it's about skank". Carol from Oklahoma: "Bless you, Pete. May love heal you!"*

Hitting the High Notes
Songs Featuring Falsetto

You Should Be Dancing
Bee Gees

It may surprise some to hear that the Bee Gees were not always synonymous with glass-shattering high notes. They began in the late 60s with smooth-voiced, soulful numbers. It wasn't really until the mid-70s that Barry Gibb fully embraced his inner eunuch (why does that sound so disturbing?), coinciding with the group's musical shift towards disco. And thus, a moderately successful group of three English brothers morphed into the international chart-toppers who would define the age of disco. One of the first hits where Barry really let loose was in *You Should Be Dancing* ("My woman takes me hi-i-i-gher / My woman keeps me warm ...") When the track was released in 1976, it became an instant hit. And just to push it into the territory of a true classic, it was then included in the 1977 movie *Saturday Night Fever*. It provided the soundtrack to the legendary scene in which John Travolta somehow looks impossibly cool while doing Russian-style folk dancing while wearing excruciatingly tight flares. Barry's piercing falsetto was only outdone by the shrieks of cinema-going ladies (many gentlemen, too) in all corners of the world.

Tip-Toe thru' the Tulips with Me
Tiny Tim

There is such a fine line between high-pitched and deranged. And Tiny Tim was certainly not shy to tread it. This song was originally written in 1929 and went through various versions before Tim put his own inimitable twist on it in 1968. In falsetto sharp enough to put the finest countertenor to shame, Tim delivered a love song which we can only hope was backed by pure intentions: "Tiptoe through the window / By the window, that is where I'll be / Come tiptoe through the tulips with me". The potential for the track to come across as mildly creepy was only exacerbated by the fact that Tiny Tim was actually 6'1" (that's 1m 85) and used to highlight his brooding features by wearing pale make-up. That said, the public embraced Tim's eccentricity. *Tip-Toe* ... became his biggest hit, reaching number 17 in the US charts. Sadly, it was also Tim's swan song. He suffered a heart attack while performing it in 1996 and died a few hours later.

September
Earth, Wind & Fire

September. The end of summer. The month of dying leaves and the return to the seeping, soul-destroying monotony of your pathetic pretence for a life. So, let's disco! "Hey, hey, hey! / Ba-dee ya, say, do you remember? / Ba-dee ya, dancin' in September / Ba-dee ya, never was a cloudy day ..." As a party song, *September* (1978) has it all: funky guitar, killer horns, soaring strings, and that pitch-perfect falsetto. The group worked with lyricist Allee Willis to prepare the track, who once described the first time she walked into the studio just as the group were playing that iconic intro. She recalls thinking, "Dear God, let this be what they want me to write! Cause it was obviously the happiest-sounding song in the world." How to come up with lyrics to do it justice? Allee says that the group's singer, Maurice White, recommended she read a book on Eastern philosophies. It helped her get into their mindset: an upbeat, positive outlook on life that often led to lyrics about pure joy (that explains the group's other hits, like 1979's *Boogie Wonderland*). And so, *September* became a tale about simply falling head over heels one autumn evening: "Do you remember the 21st night of September?" One part of the lyrics which Allee can't take credit for, however, is the famous "Ba-dee ya" of the chorus. It was Maurice who came up with that jewel. When Allee asked him what the line meant, his response was as breezy as the song itself: "Who the fuck cares?"

Wicked Game
Chris Isaak

"No, I-I don't want to fall in love". Is this one considered falsetto or more of a yodel? Given Isaak's impressive range, it's no wonder he often gets compared to Roy Orbison. The singer says he wrote *Wicked Game* (1990) after he got a booty call from some hot chick who he knew was bad news: "The world was on fire and no one could save me but you / It's strange what desire will make foolish people do..." But Chris has decided not to fall into the trap this time. Like a horned-up tomcat who has decided to take the moral high ground (do tomcats *do* morality??), Chris takes to wailing into the night.

Each soaring "No, I ..." is accompanied by a moody voice of conscience: "This world is only gonna break your heart". Of course, the success of the song was boosted by its ridiculously sexy video featuring shirtless Chris and supermodel Helena Christensen wearing even less, as they frolic in the waves, idly stare and (most importantly) pout heavily. Did Chris set the scene for an entire decade of Calvin Klein ads? Or was it the other way around? It's really a chicken-or-egg type situation.

The Most Wonderful Time of the Year
Alternative Christmas Songs

River
Joni Mitchell

Nothing says *deck the halls* quite like raw heartbreak set to the tune of *Jingle Bells* played in a minor key. In Joni's 1971 classic, the singer is feeling decidedly un-festive as the world around her gets into holiday mode: "It's coming on Christmas / They're cutting down trees / They're putting up reindeer / And singing songs of joy and peace / Oh, I wish I had a river I could skate away on". That latter line (much repeated in the song) is surely a reference to the singer's native Canada, where rivers freeze and skaters skate. So, what troubles does Joni wish she could flee? Well, it seems she's broken up with her beau. And the end of the relationship has sent her into a spiral of questioning the point of her crazy LA existence, while craving the simplicity of the remote, snowy north. Many fans also wonder whether there is a deeper tinge of sadness in those lyrics, considering that Joni had given her baby up for adoption back in Canada before heading to California to become a superstar. It would certainly add a bittersweet twist to Joni's hankering for her homeland. There's nothing quite like Christmas to bring up an unresolved past.

That Was the Worst Christmas Ever!
Sufjan Stevens

Perhaps we can glean a sense of Sufjan's troubled relationship with Christmas from the name that he chose for his 2012 Christmas tour: *Seasonal Affective Disorder Yuletide Disaster Pageant on Ice*. Catchy. Then again, Christmas clearly occupies an important place for the singer, given that he has released two albums dedicated to songs about the festive season. His track *That Was the Worst Christmas Ever!* (2006) is an honest glance back at Christmases past: "Our father yells, throwing the gifts in the wood stove, wood stove / My sister runs away, taking her books to the schoolyard, schoolyard …" No sleigh bells and Mariah-level whistle tone here, just a sweet guitar ballad about that inevitable festive moment when all members of the family might actually kill each other. The song even has (gasp!) some God references, Sufjan himself being interested in matters of spirituality. Who would have ever put Christmas and *religion* together?

Merry Fucking Christmas
Mr. Garrison, the 3rd Grade Teacher

Coming from an album compiled by a talking turd, *Merry Fucking Christmas* was always going to push the boundaries of good taste. The track appeared on a 1999 album from the cartoon *South Park*, a collection of songs put together by Mr. Hankey (who happens to be – literally – a very friendly piece of shit, in case you didn't know). In this song, the character of Mr. Garrison has taken it upon himself to spread the word of peace and goodwill. Well, not exactly. Rather, the righteous teacher finds himself travelling the world to berate all those people who might not be embracing the festive spirit, from Muslims to atheists to the Japanese. How rude of them all not to observe the birth of The Saviour by drinking eggnog. But never fear, Mr. Garrison is here to insist on cultural hegemony and the unquestioned superiority of American traditions: "In case you haven't noticed / There's festive things to do / So let's all rejoice for Jesus / And Merry fucking Christmas to you". Purely for copyright reasons, Hallmark have not yet been able to use those lines as an in-card greeting.

Fairytale of New York
The Pogues
ft. Kirsty MacColl

Readers in the UK and Ireland are probably wondering how on earth our most-played Christmas song could be considered "alternative"? Well, it seems that The Pogues' 1987 classic is not hugely well known internationally (apart from in Scandinavia and New Zealand). Let the Americans keep their dreams of a *White Christmas*, let the Germans toast their glühweins to *Mary's Boy Child*; the Brits and Irish are just fine with a seasonal drunken scrap. No, *Fairytale ...* is not one for the carollers. It is, rather, a diatribe of insults between an ageing couple who've sailed the seas to New York, only to find themselves truly down and out. It may be Christmas, but those dreams of Broadway seem a distant memory from the couple's current, drug-rotted lives. The duet's male character (Shane MacGowan) sings to his lady friend, calling her – in no uncertain terms – a junkie and a slut. But the female character (Kirsty MacColl) is not to be outdone, biting back with commercial radio's most WTF line: "You scumbag, you maggot / You cheap lousy faggot / Happy Christmas, your arse / I pray God it's our last" (is there a couple in existence who have not muttered such sentiments to each other as the in-laws call round for yet another bout of marshmallow roasting?) Although it's impossible to imagine those barbed lines being sung by anyone other than Kirsty, apparently she ended up on the track by accident. She had been asked to record a version to be used as a guide for the eventual singer, but The Pogues liked her take so much that they decided to keep it. As the song concludes, the sorry couple begin to wonder what ever happened to their dreams. Are the two beyond saving? That all depends on the listener's sense of yuletide spirit.

HAPPY CHRISTMAS, YOUR ARSE / I PRAY GOD IT'S OUR LAST.

— THE POGUES

The Call of the Wild
Songs about Animals

Year of the Cat
Al Stewart

Admittedly, *The Year of the Cat* (1976) isn't actually about cats, deserving as our furry little friends may be of their own pop classic. Rather, it's a song about quite a saucy love affair, but of the human variety (how vanilla!) The protagonist is walking around an exotic city when he encounters a beautiful woman who leads him to her quarters where the two of them engage in … activities suggested by wailing guitar and soaring saxophone. The man decides to embrace his fate: "Well morning comes and you're still with her / And the bus and the tourists are gone / And you've thrown away the choice and lost your ticket / So you have to stay on". A romantic notion, even though it turns out their relationship is fleeting. Throughout the song, there are many references to another passing love affair, that of the movie *Casablanca*. In fact, the whole idea of the song seems to be based on transience. The lovers enjoy their time together, but it will only last as long as *The Year of the Cat*. Incidentally, such a year exists solely in the Vietnamese calendar. So, is our protagonist in Morocco or Southeast Asia? Well, does it matter? Just enjoy that mind-blowing piano solo.

Zebra
Beach House

Gorgeous classical guitar, surging backing vocals, the rich voice of lead singer Victoria Legrand: and so begins this classic, dreamy ode to zebras … Ok, update from the editor: apparently zebra whispering is not a thing and Beach House's 2010 track might just be yet another track which claims to be about animals but isn't. Those lyrics have a level of ambiguity that might be beyond the reason of most four-legged beasts. Hell, even those of us two-legged will struggle to understand this one: "Anyway you run / You run before us / Black and white horse / Arching among us". Beach House fans are split down the middle as to what the song might be about. The lyrics keep mentioning the idea of deception. Is Victoria fed up with a certain somebody's lying and zebra-like camouflage? Or is the deception of a fascinating nature, the singer describing her love as a beautiful, wild creature who stands out in a world of monochrome and domestication? It's a tough call: good zebra or bad? But how could a zebra ever be the bad guy?

The Snake
Al Wilson

One animal who is more than happy to play the baddie is the sneaky snake. Al Wilson's 1968 soul classic is a tale about a kind woman who finds a half-frozen snake one morning. She takes him to her home and nurses him. When the animal begins to recover, she clutches him to her bosom, only to receive a deadly bite. As the woman dies and pleads, the snake spells it out for her: "'Oh shut up, silly woman,' said the reptile with a grin / 'You knew damn well I was a snake before you brought me in.'" For some, the song is simply an old yarn about no-good men. Others see it as more political, especially considering that it was originally written in 1963 by a famous civil rights activist named Oscar Brown. Might the snake have represented America's white elite? In 2016, the track got a whole lot more political when Donald Trump regularly read out its lyrics as part of his speeches at campaign rallies, as a metaphor for why the US should "Build the Wall". Brown's daughters asked Trump to stop, but he refused. Somehow, it's difficult to imagine The Donald clutching anything to his bosom other than a double cheeseburger.

Too Many Birds
Bill Callahan

You might expect a song with a bird narrator to be an uplifting affair: boundless freedom, nesty warmth, worm guzzling. Surprising, then, that American lo-fi rocker Bill Callahan's 2009 track is more likely to leave the listener in shuddering, pensive sobs. Bill's blackbird is a mournful little fellow, flying around "without a place to land". He returns to the tree that used to feel like home, only to find it full of too many birds. No, dear reader, this is *not* leading to another crass, Trumpian commentary on immigration. Judging from other songs on the same album, the lyrics are more a reflection on Bill's sadness. Perhaps the teeming tree gives a sense of a restless mind, as Bill hankers for a peace he once had, but which no longer exists. The song concludes with the slowly-building line: "If you could only stop your heartbeat for one heartbeat". As Bill's voice cracks, you get a sense that his powerful emotions, like the birds, are swarming all around. Cue more shuddering sobs.

Papillon
Editors

First things first: what is a papillon? While Google suggests that it is a breed of toy dog, the type that looks adorable but sounds like nails across a blackboard, it's unlikely that Editors had yapping puppies in mind. Rather, it seems that their song *Papillon* (2009) was inspired by the 1969 book of the same name. The famous autobiographical novel was written by Frenchman Henri Charrière, who used to go by the nickname of the title (in French, *papillon* means *butterfly*). The book is basically Henri's real-life tale of being wrongly convicted of murder, getting sent to prison in French Guiana, escaping to the South American mainland and spending the following years getting recaptured and managing to escape again and again. It's a fascinating tale, made into a movie starring Steve McQueen in the 70s, with a remake featuring Charlie Hunnan in 2017. In their song, Editors too seem to have getaways in mind: "Make our escape / You're my own papillon / The world turns too fast / Feel love before it's gone ..." What's the singer running from? A dead relationship? The oppression of the music industry? Impossible to tell. What seems more certain is that he's come to a certain realisation, always coming back to the stark line, "It kicks like a sleep twitch". Suddenly awakened, it's time to move.

And I Ride and I Ride
Songs about Travelling

The Passenger
Iggy Pop

In 1976, Iggy Pop and his friend David Bowie moved to Berlin to try and kick their drug habits. Seriously, guys? Berlin?? They would later admit that the move might not have been exactly cold turkey. But at least they managed to make some great music while there. Iggy's inspiration for *The Passenger* (1977) came from various sources. First, there was his travelling around Berlin on the city's S-Bahn trains: "I am the passenger / And I ride and I ride / I ride through the city's backsides / I see the stars come out of the sky ..." Second, there was the fact that Iggy had recently been touring with Bowie, travelling from city to city in the back of David's car: "Get into the car / We'll be the passenger ..." When it came to writing the song's lyrics, Iggy seemed to be reflecting on his detached, nomadic existence. In a good way. Iggy is not the driver here; he is simply the passenger, sitting back and watching the awesome world whizz by just outside his window, taking it all in. The song's chorus seems like as simple an expression as there can be of a man hellbent on enjoying this crazy ride we call life: "Singin' la la la la la la la la ..." And who better to help him out on backing vocals than his good friend David? *The Passenger* might be one of music's most famous tracks about travelling but, really, maybe it's just as much about friendship.

Around the World
Daft Punk

Why is Daft Punk's 1997 hit titled *Around the World*? There's really no way of knowing. But it was recorded at a time when the duo were starting to get big, performing shows in their native France, around Europe and even in the US. So maybe the track is about globetrotting. Or maybe it's about the international appreciation of a bangin' beat. Well, if they truly were looking for cross-cultural appeal, how better to go about it than to create a track of almost ridiculous simplicity? Musically, *Around the World* was made up of just five basic elements, the most recognisable one being the robot voice which simply repeats the song's title. Add in a disco-like groove inspired by the group's heroes Chic, and the path was paved for a modern classic. One undeniable fan of the track was film director Michel Gondry, who described it as "genius". He got onboard to create a video which has almost become as famous as the song itself. In keeping with the minimalism of the music, Gondry set the whole video on a small, circular stage. Five small groups of dancers move to the music, each group representing a different element of the song: bandaged mummies move to the drum machine; synchronised swimmers dance to the keyboard; tiny-headed athletes represent the bassline; skeletons jolt to the funky guitar; robots shuffle to the vocal. Now that's a party.

Blues Run the Game
Jackson C. Frank

"Catch a boat to England, baby / Maybe to Spain / Wherever I have gone / Wherever I've been and gone / Wherever I have gone / The blues are all the same". In his most famous song, from 1965, Jackson C. Frank sings about an irrefutable truth: you can travel all you want, but there are some things you can't leave behind. When Jackson was just 11, a furnace at his New York school exploded, killing 15 of his fellow pupils and causing him lifelong injuries and scars. While he was recovering, Jackson developed a love for music after a teacher gave him a gift of a guitar. At the age of 21, he received an insurance payout for his injuries, allowing him to follow his dreams and indeed to "catch a boat to England". There, he immersed himself in the folk scene and caught the attention of the big shots. Soon, Jackson was recording an album under the supervision of producer Paul Simon. He was so nervous in the studio that he needed to have special screens placed around him, enabling him to forget his rather intimidating audience comprised of Simon, Garfunkel and Al Stewart. *Blues Run the Game* was the opening track and, sadly, the song's tale of unshakeable sorrow would prove to be more than just a lyric. The track had some initial success in the UK, but Jackson's mental health began to deteriorate. He returned to the States, where he got married and had two kids. But when his son died of cystic fibrosis, Jackson truly spiralled. He spent his later years homeless, and eventually died of pneumonia, aged 56. No silver linings here, The Blues have never been bluer.

WELL IT'S ALL RIGHT, RIDING AROUND IN THE BREEZE / WELL IT'S ALL RIGHT, IF YOU LIVE THE LIFE YOU PLEASE.

— THE TRAVELING WILBURYS

End of the Line
The Traveling Wilburys

Slip off your reading glasses and get ready for a bout of fervent foot tapping, it's time for some Dad Rock. Yes, people, this book is nearing a close and we really are going there. *End of the Line* first appeared in the charts in 1989, a time when commercial music was dominated by shrieking rock and electro cool. That is, until George Harrison set up The Traveling Wilburys with his legendary pals Roy Orbison, Tom Petty, Jeff Lynne and Bob Dylan (although Bob didn't appear on this particular track). As writer Alan Clayson so succinctly put it, the Wilburys' arrival on the scene was like "a Viking longship docking in a hovercraft terminal". But let's not be too harsh on these (by then) middle-aged megastars. Their hits might not have been on-trend at the time, but several have subsequently reached the status of classics. In *End of the Line*, the rockers took it in turns to deliver undeniably feelgood verses about travelling light. And no stuffy old sentiments here, those lyrics are practically worthy of a gay anthem: "Well it's all right, remember to live and let live / Well it's all right, the best you can do is forgive / Well it's all right, riding around in the breeze /

Well it's all right, if you live the life you please ..." With a rhythm that sounds like an old steam train chugging along the track, the message seems to be to just enjoy our shared journey. Because when it comes down to it, life's train has us all headed for the same place (see song's title).

Sailing
Christopher Cross

If the Traveling Wilburys didn't exactly capture the prevailing winds of their era, Christopher Cross had no such problems back in 1980. For many fans of soft rock, his hit *Sailing* defined the style of the time. In subsequent years, people would look back and label the genre as *yacht rock*. That refers to those pensive, melodic ballads that ruled the airwaves in the early 80s, featuring crisp vocals and lyrics usually on some vague theme of escape (think Chicago's *Hard to Say I'm Sorry*). The term *yacht rock* began as a joke, poking fun at those old hits as the type of music some flash, middle-aged git might listen to on his yacht. In more recent years, however, the genre has become cool again. And with due cause. *Sailing* may be polished, but in a way that brings it close to pop perfection. Iconic guitar chords, simple strings, vocals that sound like a sunny day, all telling a simple tale: "Sailing / Takes me away to where I've always heard it could be / Just a dream and the wind to carry me / Soon I will be free ..." Christopher says that he grew up in quite chaotic circumstances, and that a kindly older neighbour used to take him sailing to escape from the madness. And so, those lyrics seem to be about simply drifting away from it all, at least for a while. *Yacht rock* it may be, but loud and proud. Apparently, even John Lennon was a fan.

SAILING / TAKES ME AWAY TO WHERE I'VE ALWAYS HEARD IT COULD BE ...

— CHRISTOPHER CROSS

On the Road
Songs about the Open Highway

Born to Be Wild
Steppenwolf

"Get your motor runnin' / Head out on the highway / Looking for adventure / In whatever comes our way ..." The open road, an empty horizon of infinite possibilities; *Born to Be Wild*, the coolest song that ever was. While the 1968 track became a huge hit in its own right, its legendary status was cemented a year later when it appeared in the movie *Easy Rider*. During the film's opening credits, it accompanies a scene of Peter Fonda and Dennis Hopper, stuffed to the gills with dirty drug-money, riding their Harleys like the undeniable studs that they were. The movie ensured that the song would become the all-time anthem of bikers the world over. But in 2018, songwriter Dennis Edmonton admitted that his inspiration may have been slightly less rock 'n' roll. As a young man, he bought himself a very sensible Ford Falcon which he used to drive around the mountains near LA (he points out that he did so "with the windows down", which is vaguely cooler but not really). And it was these adventures in his trusty old Ford that gave him the idea for the song. Incidentally, on one such drive, a huge thunderstorm broke out. Dennis noticed that the sky was like the colour of lead, which inspired the line, "I like smoke and lightnin' / Heavy metal thunder ..." Thoroughly unscientific records show that this may have been the first time that the term "heavy metal" was used in the context of rock music. Dennis had unwittingly coined a new phrase, and *Born to Be Wild* has gone down in history as the early instigator of heavy metal music.

The Road's My Middle Name
Bonnie Raitt

Want to know what life is like on the road? Bonnie Raitt can tell you a thing or two. The huskiest woman in music has been gigging since the early 70s, bringing blues to the world. In *The Road's My Middle Name* (1989), Bonnie spells it out to her gentleman friend not to get any ideas about settling down: "Guess the road is in my blood / 'Cause I'm my daddy's kid / Just have to learn how to let me go / Just like my momma did … I gotta go / 'Cause the road's my middle name." The song kind of sounds like it was recorded in some smoky roadhouse blues shack in the Deep South, which seems about right considering its context. The 80s were tough for Bonnie. After initial success in the 70s, Bonnie's sales slowed and in 1983, she got dropped from her label. No longer able to afford a backing band, she took to performing solo acoustic gigs to make ends meet. Basically, she went off the rails. Around the same time, she met producer Don Was. The two agreed to make an album, no frills, minimal expenses. Bonnie had the voice of a gravelly goddess and guitar skills to boot. What more did they need? The result was *Nick of Time*, Bonnie's timeless album which would go on to win three gongs at the 1989 Grammys and sell millions. It also introduced a new generation to this petite, red-haired lady who sang the blues and mastered the slide guitar like she was the long-lost daughter of John Lee Hooker. Where does she get it from? Bonnie once told an interviewer, "I'm fully admitting that I'm from Los Angeles and last time I looked, I was still white." Sounds like not even the legend herself can explain it.

Motorcycle Emptiness
Manic Street Preachers

OK, Manic Street Preachers are never going to be the band to write some rollickin' number about the boundless joy of the open road. But jeez, do they know how to write a killer riff. For *Motorcycle Emptiness* (1992), lead singer James Dean Bradfield says that guitar hook came to him in a dream, and may even have found some unlikely inspiration in the strings from ABBA's *Dancing Queen*. As for the motorcycle reference, the lyrics don't exactly yell "Road Trip!" The Manics say the song was inspired by the 1975 novel *Rumble Fish*, by S.E. Hinton. The book is basically about violent biker gangs. At one point, a character sees some fish in a tank and names them "rumble fish", because in their captive environment, they'd kill each other if they could. The song too seems to describe a type of captivity. But in this case, the trap is a consumerist society that thrives on our misery: "From feudal serf to spender / This wonderful world of purchase power / Just like lungs sucking on air / Survivals natural as sorrow, sorrow …" Yes, the lyrics get a bit complex, but just wait for that (ironically) euphoric chorus, that repeated, stadium-filling line: "Under neon loneliness, motorcycle emptine-e-ess". Might the neon be referring to the silly electronics we use to distract ourselves from our underlying sorrow? Might the dreams of the rebel biker be just a pointless fantasy in a world where we don't have any real power? No wonder this track hasn't yet made its way onto any Honda commercials.

I've Been Everywhere
Johnny Cash

In the opening verse of *I've Been Everywhere* (1996), we find Johnny hitching a ride in an old canvas-covered carriage. The driver asks him if he's ever seen such a dusty road before. Mister Coachman, you will regret asking that question. Johnny takes a deep breath, ... and lets loose:

"I've been everywhere, man / I've been everywhere, man / Crossed the deserts bare, man / I've breathed the mountain air, man / Of travel I've a-had my share, man / I've been everywhere." Another breath ... "I've been to Reno, Chicago, Fargo, Minnesota / Buffalo, Toronto, Winslow, Sarasota ..." And so begins a mighty unleashing of just some of the places The Man in Black has graced with his presence. The song has been in existence since 1959, when it was first written as a country ditty about a jaunt around Australia ("Been to Tullamore, Seymour, Lismore, Mooloolaba ...") Over the years, different versions have appeared by singers from the UK, Finland, New Zealand and beyond, always changing those place names to fit the country. But it's undoubtedly Johnny's take which has had most success. Recorded in his later years, Johnny's version is a knee-slappin' rundown of the crazy ride that was his life: a glinting glance over his shoulder before setting his eyes on the road ahead. And off he rode into the sunset.

Acknowledgements

I want to say a massive **thank you** to everybody who helped with this book, directly or indirectly:

— to all the singers and musicians featured in this book, for creating songs worth talking about;

— to my friends and family, for making sure to ask "How's the book going?", and for managing to look interested as I answer;

— to Jaime, for (truly) endless patience, and for being the world's most modest music buff;

— to my editor, Tania Van de Vondel, for a great opportunity, and for introducing me to some of the coolest songs on the planet;

— to Claudia Ros, for wonderful advice;

— to Isabelle Kliger, for being my sister from another mister (also from another missus, but that one's tougher to rhyme);

— to Leah Crowley, for being the Laurel to my Hardy; the Tina to my Amy;

— ... and to the special guest star on this list of acknowledgements, my good friend Mark Cloostermans, the man who made it all possible. Mark, sometimes only a Golden Girls line will do: *Thank you for being a friend.*

Bibliography

Beginnings
Songs with an Amazing Intro

Blue Monday – New Order • Nicolson, B. (2015, Jan 22). New Order – How We Wrote 'Blue Monday'. Retrieved from www.nme.com: https://www.nme.com/blogs/nme-blogs/new-order-how-we-wrote-blue-monday-762505

Setting the Scene
Iconic Opening Lines

The Sound of Silence – Simon & Garfunkel • Eliot, Marc (2010). Paul Simon: A Life. John Wiley and Sons. ISBN 978-0-470-43363-8

Stand by Your Man – Tammy Wynette • Tammy Wynette; Joan Dew (1979). Stand by Your Man. Simon & Schuster. ISBN 978-0-671-22884-2

Tom Traubert's Blues (Four Sheets to the Wind in Copenhagen) – Tom Waits • Humphries, Patrick (2007). The Many Lives of Tom Waits, pg 97. Omnibus Press. ISBN 978-1-84772-509-7

Chin-Chin!
Songs about Drinks

Milkshake – Kelis • Lewis, P. (n.d.). Kelis talks 'Milkshake' and 'Tasty' hits. B&S Issue 1092. Retrieved from www.bluesandsoul.com: http://www.bluesandsoul.com/feature/249/kelis_talks_milkshake_and_tasty_hits/

Lipstick Marks
Songs about the Other Woman

Call Your Girlfriend – Robyn • Snapes, L. (2018, Sept 28). The long read: How Robyn transformed pop. Retrieved from www.theguardian.com: https://www.theguardian.com/music/2018/sep/28/how-robyn-transformed-pop-music-honey

Jolene – Dolly Parton • Vitale, T. (2008, Oct 9). In character: Dolly Parton's 'Jolene' Still Haunts Singers. Retrieved from www.npr.org: https://www.npr.org/2008/10/09/95520570/dolly-partons-jolene-still-haunts-singers?t=1552331108216

The Green-Eyed Monster
Songs about Jealousy

I'd Rather Go Blind – Etta James • Inman, D. (2012, Jan 23). Lyric of the Week. Retrieved from www.americansongwriter.com: https://americansongwriter.com/2012/01/etta-james-id-rather-go-blind/

It's Not You, It's Me
Songs about Getting Dumped

Crying – Roy Orbison • Dylan, B. (2004). Chronicles: Volume One. Simon & Schuster. ISBN 0-7432-2815-4

I Can't Make You Love Me – Bonnie Raitt • Creswell , T. (2006) 1001 Songs: The Great Songs of All Time and the Artists, Stories and Secrets Behind Them. Thunder's Mouth Press. ISBN-10: 1560259159

Someone Like You – Adele • Montgomery, J. (2011, Feb 18). Adele Says 21 Has People Thinking 'I'm Sort Of A Manic-Depressive'. MTV News. MTV Networks. Retrieved 23 July 2011.

Someone Like You – Adele • Wikipedia contributors (2017) Focus On: 100 Most Popular Billboard Adult Contemporary Number-one Singles. Focus On; 1 edition. ASIN: B0788ZNJD6

Over and Out
Songs about Saying Goodbye

November Rain – Guns N' Roses • Fandom Contributors. Guns N' Roses Wiki. Retrieved from www.guns-n-roses.fandom.com: https://guns-n-roses.fandom.com/wiki/November_Rain

It Is What it Is
Songs about Acceptance

You Can't Always Get What You Want – The Rolling Stones • NME. (2007, Apr 3). Exclusive: Keith Richards – 'I snorted my dad's ashes'. Retrieved from www.nme.com: https://www.nme.com/news/music/the-rolling-stones-433-1341398

Both Sides Now – Joni Mitchell • Bellow, S. (1985). Henderson the Rain King. Penguin Books. p. 280. ISBN 0-14-007269-1.

Ladies (and Gentlemen) of the Night
Songs about Prostitution

Private Dancer – Tina Turner • Blogging team (2010, Feb 5). The worst guitar solo in the world. Retrieved from www.stuff.co.nz: http://www.stuff.co.nz/entertainment/blogs/3294741/The-worst-guitar-solo-in-the-world

Making Ends Meet

Songs about Being Broke

Town Called Malice – The Jam • Wilson, J. (2008, May 15). Chasing the blues away. Retrieved from www.newstatesman.com: https://www.newstatesman.com/music/2008/05/paul-weller-jam-album-song

Ever the Optimist

Songs about Maintaining Hope

Don't Give Up – Peter Gabriel ft. Kate Bush • Vanity Fair. (2012, Oct 24). The Proust Questionnaire: Dolly Parton. Retrieved from www.vanityfair.com: https://www.vanityfair.com/culture/2012/11/dolly-parton-proust-questionnaire

Throwing in the Towel

Songs about Giving Up Hope

Love Is a Losing Game – Amy Winehouse • Dixon, P. (2008, Oct 9). Interview: Mark Ronson. Retrieved from www.thenationalstudent.com: https://www.thenationalstudent.com/Music/2008-10-09/Interview_Mark_Ronson.html

The Bright Lights

Songs about Cities

Walking in Memphis – Marc Cohn • Cohn, M. (2014, Apr 8). Song Stories: Walking in Memphis. Retrieved from www.keyboardmag.com: https://www.keyboardmag.com/artists/song-stories-walking-in-memphis

Detroit Calling

Big Motown Hits

Dancing in the Street – Martha and The Vandellas • Simpson, D. (2016, Feb 9). How We Made Dancing in the Street. Retrieved from www.theguardian.com: https://www.theguardian.com/culture/2016/feb/09/how-we-made-dancing-in-the-street-martha-reeves-and-the-vandellas

Don't Matter If You're Black or White

Songs about Racial Discrimination

A Change Is Gonna Come – Sam Cooke • Rolling Stone. (2011, Apr 7). 500 Greatest Songs of All Time. Retrieved from www.rollingstone.com: https://www.rollingstone.com/music/music-lists/500-greatest-songs-of-all-time-151127/sam-cooke-a-change-is-gonna-come-72334/

A Change Is Gonna Come – Sam Cooke • Agerholm, H. (2017, Nov 5). Barack Obama's electrifying speech remembered on anniversary of historic election win. Retrieved from www.independent.co.uk: https://www.independent.co.uk/news/world/americas/us-politics/barack-obama-victory-speech-video-nine-years-anniversary-yes-we-can-a8038326.html

Clandestino – Manu Chao • Cartwright, G. (2007, Oct 1). The wild rover. Retrieved from www.theguardian.com: https://www.theguardian.com/music/2007/oct/01/worldmusic1

People, Rise up

Protest Songs

Fight the Power – Public Enemy • Rosenberg, E. (2019, Feb 20). 'I believe in white supremacy': John Wayne's notorious 1971 Playboy interview goes viral on Twitter. Retrieved from www.washingtonpost.com: https://www.washington-post.com/arts-entertainment/2019/02/20/i-believe-white-supremacy-john-waynes-notorious-playboy-interview-goes-viral-twitter/?noredirect=on&utm_term=.d83e12043c5e

Heading into Combat

Songs about War

A Hard Rain's A-Gonna Fall – Bob Dylan • Rolling Stone. (2011, May 11). 10 Greatest Bob Dylan Songs. Retrieved from www.rollingstone.com: https://www.rollingstone.com/music/music-lists/10-greatest-bob-dylan-songs-152077/a-hard-rains-a-gonna-fall-159663/

They Paved Paradise

Songs about Environmental Matters

4 Degrees – Anohni • Pareles, J. (2016, Apr 21). Anohni: Embracing a New Name, and Sound. Retrieved from www.nytimes.com: https://www.nytimes.com/2016/04/24/arts/music/anohni-embracing-a-new-name-and-sound.html

Virtual Insanity – Jamiroquai • BBC News. (n.d.). On This Day. Retrieved from www.news.bbc.co.uk: http://news.bbc.co.uk/onthisday/hi/dates/stories/february/22/newsid_4245000/4245877.stm

Praying for Time – George Michael • Holden, S. (1990, Sep 16). Recordings; George Michael on Fame and 'Freedom'. Retrieved from www.nytimes.com: https://www.nytimes.

com/1990/09/16/arts/recordings-george-michael-on-fame-and-freedom.html

According to the Scriptures
Songs with Biblical References

1 Corinthians 15:55 – Johnny Cash • Urbanski, D. (2003), The Man Comes Around: The Spiritual Journey of Johnny Cash. New York, NY: Relevant Books. ISBN 978-0-9729276-7-3

Hallelujah – Jeff Buckley • Rolling Stone (9 December 2004.) Hallelujah – Jeff Buckley. Rolling Stone. New York City: Wenner Media LLC.

The Father and the Son
Songs about God and Jesus

God's Song – Randy Newman • The Telegraph. (2015, Sep 18). Randy Newman's 20 Essential Songs. Retrieved from www.telegraph.co.uk: https://www.telegraph.co.uk/music/artists/randy-newman-20-essential-songs/gods-song-thats-why-i-love-mankind-1972/

Where Everybody Knows Your Name
Iconic Theme Tunes of TV Series

How Soon Is Now? – The Smiths • Simpson, M. (2006) Saint Morrissey: A Portrait of This Charming Man by an Alarming Fan. Touchstone. p.63. ISBN-10: 074328481X

Falling – Julee Cruise • Ivie, D. (2017, May 12). Angelo Badalamenti Tells the Stories Behind 5 Twin Peaks Songs. Retrieved from www.vulture.com: https://www.vulture.com/2016/09/twin-peaks-songs-stories-angelo-badalamenti.html

Suicide Is Painless – The Mash • Myers, M. (2008, Oct 24). Interview: Johnny Mandel (Part 5). Retrieved from www.jazzwax.com: https://www.jazzwax.com/2008/10/interview-joh-5.html

Bet You Think This Song Is About You
Songs Inspired by Actors or Actresses

Barbra Streisand – Duck Sauce • Ruark, R. (1963, Jan 18). The Blue's Angel. Pasadena Independent. p. 9

The Silver Screen
Songs about Films

Debaser – Pixies • Simmons, B. (n.d.). The Sports Guy. Retrieved from www.espn.com: http://www.espn.com/espn/page2/story?page=simmons/020611

You Can Choose Your Friends ...
Songs about Parents

Down by the Water – PJ Harvey • Maerz, M. (2005, Oct). PJ Harvey: Shedding light on British rock's electrifying dark star. Spin. 21 (10): 82. Retrieved 4 July 2012.

Ode to My Family – The Cranberries • Contributors. (n.d.). Ode to My Family. Retrieved from cranberriesworld.com: http://cranberriesworld.com/music/song-list-a-z/ode-to-my-family/

Sisters (and Brothers) in Arms
Songs about Siblings

The Mother We Share – Chvrches • 3voor12 (2003, Aug 12). Song Stories: Chvrches – The Mother We Share. Via YouTube: https://www.youtube.com/watch?v=RxqZKIkmN8o

As the Miller Told His Tale
Songs Inspired by Legends

A Whiter Shade of Pale – Procol Harum • Chaucer, G.; edited by Benson, L. (1987). The Riverside Chaucer. Boston: Houghton Mifflin Co. ASIN: B00BT03K34

Corpus Christi Carol – Jeff Buckley • Kane, R. (1998, 1999). The Kingdom for A Kiss Jeff Buckley F.A.Q. Archived 8 May 2006 at the Wayback Machine. Retrieved from www.web.archive.org: https://web.archive.org/web/20060508002054/http://jeffbuckley.com/rfuller/buckley/faq/13grace.html

Heathcliff, it's Me, it's Cathy!
Songs Inspired by Novels

Wuthering Heights – Kate Bush • Brontë, Emily (1847). Wuthering Heights. Thomas Cautley Newby. ISBN 0-486-29256-8.

Scentless Apprentice – Nirvana • Goodman, W. (2018, Sep 21). Nirvana's Menacing Last Testament 'In Utero' Turns 25. Retrieved from www.billboard.com: https://www.billboard.com/articles/news/8476245/nirvanas-in-utero-turns-25

Paranoid Android – Radiohead • Rolling Stone. (2011, Apr 7). 500 Greatest Songs of All Time. Retrieved from www.rollingstone.com: https://www.rollingstone.com/music/music-lists/500-greatest-songs-of-all-time-151127/radiohead-paranoid-android-2-51624/

Star-Cross'd Lovers (and Haterz)

Songs with Shakespearean References

I Am the Walrus – The Beatles • Davies, H. (1968). The Beatles: The Authorised Biography. Heinemann (UK), McGraw-Hill (US)

Isn't it Good, Norwegian Wood?

Songs Featuring in Haruki Murakami's Novels

Sinfonietta – Leoš Janáček (novel: 1Q84, 2009) • Anderson, S. (2011, Oct 21). The Fierce Imagination of Haruki Murakami. Retrieved from www.nytimes.com: https://www.nytimes.com/2011/10/23/magazine/the-fierce-imagination-of-haruki-murakami.html

The Unreliable Narrator

Songs that We Can't Quite Believe

I'm Not in Love – 10cc • Buskin, R. (June 2005). "Classic Tracks: 10cc – 'I'm Not in Love'". Sound on Sound. Cambridge, England: SOS Publications: 62–69.

Putting it on Paper

Books by Musicians

Things the Grandchildren Should Know (song: Things the Grandchildren Should Know by Eels) • Everett, M. (2008). Things the Grandchildren Should Know. Little, Brown. ISBN 978-0-316-02787-8.

Mo' Meta Blues: The World According to Questlove (song: You Got Me by The Roots ft. Erykah Badu & Eve) • Ahmir "Questlove" Thompson; Ben Greenman (2013, June 18). Mo' Meta Blues: The World According to Questlove. Grand Central Publishing. ISBN 978-1-4555-0136-6.

Just Kids (song: Gloria: In Excelsis Deo by Patti Smith) • Smith, P. (2010). Just Kids. Ecco. ISBN 978-0-06-621131-2.

How Music Works (song: Once in a Lifetime by Talking Heads) • Byrne, D. (2012). How Music Works. McSweeney's. ISBN 1936365537.

Tell Me about it

Spoken-Word Songs

Everything Is Everything – Bootsy Collins • McCormick, N. (2008, Jul 3). Paul Heaton: angry man who sings like a bird. Retrieved from www.telegraph.co.uk: https://www.telegraph.co.uk/culture/music/3555617/Paul-Heaton-angry-man-who-sings-like-a-bird.html

This Mortal Coil

Songs about Dying

Death with Dignity – Sufjan Stevens • Dombal, R. (2015, Feb 16). True Myth: A Conversation With Sufjan Stevens. Retrieved from www.pitchfork.com: https://pitchfork.com/features/interview/9595-true-myth-a-conversation-with-sufjan-stevens/

Joanne – Lady Gaga • Moukarbel, C (director). (2017) Gaga: Five Foot Two. Live Nation Productions. Distributed by Netflix.

Short 'n' Sweet

Songs under Two Minutes

The Letter – The Box Tops • McKeen, W. (2000). Rock and Roll Is Here to Stay: An Anthology (1st ed.). New York City: W. W. Norton. pp. 495–496. ISBN 0-393-04700-8.

They'll Never Play That on the Radio

Songs over Seven Minutes

Honeymoon's Great (Wish You Were Her) – Josh T. Pearson • Segal, V. (April 2010). New Albums. Introducing Josh T. Pearson. Q&A. Q magazine. p. 105

American Pie – Don McLean • Hawksley, R. (April 7, 2015). American Pie: 6 crazy conspiracy theories. The Daily Telegraph.

Riders on the Storm – The Doors • Preston, A. (2018, Apr 9). Doors: Riders On The Storm on Classic Cuts today at 3:20pm. Retrieved from www.gaterrocks.iheart.com: https://gaterrocks.iheart.com/content/2018-04-09-doors-riders-on-the-storm-on-classic-cuts-today-at-320pm/

My Sister – Tindersticks • Johnson, S. (2012, Mar 8). Q&A: Tindersticks. Retrieved from www.musicomh.com: https://www.musicomh.com/features/interviews/interview-tindersticks

Behind the Scenes

Very Successful Producers

Quincy Jones (song: Angel by Aretha Franklin) • Gleason, R.J. (2016). Conversations in Jazz: The Ralph J. Gleason Interviews. Yale University Press. ISBN 978-0-300-21452-9.

T Bone Burnett (song: My Least Favourite Life by Lera Lynn) • Niles, J. (2015, Jun 26). Songwriter Lera Lynn Talks 'True Detective' Season 2 Music & More! Retrieved from www.musictimes.com: https://www.musictimes.com/articles/41686/20150626/exclusive-interview-songwriter-lera-lynn-talks-true-detective-season-2.htm

Dr. Dre (song: Still D.R.E by Dr. Dre) • Tyrangiel, J. (2001, Sep 15). In the Doctor's House. TIME. 158 (14). Archived from the original on August 31, 2010.

Musical Conversations
Songs about Songs

Your Song – Elton John • Rolling Stone. (2011, Apr 7). 500 Greatest Songs of All Time . Retrieved from www.rollingstone.com: https://www.rollingstone.com/music/music-lists/500-greatest-songs-of-all-time-151127/elton-john-your-song-66306/

It Wasn't God Who Made Honky Tonk Angels – Kitty Wells • Kingsbury, P. (1995). The Grand Ole Opry History of Country Music: 70 Years of the Songs, the Stars and the Stories. Villard Books/Random House. ISBN-10: 0679435565

Hitting the High Notes
Songs Featuring Falsetto

September – Earth, Wind & Fire • NPR. (2014, Sep 19). The Song That Never Ends: Why Earth, Wind & Fire's 'September' Sustains. Retrieved from www.cpr.org: https://www.cpr org/2014/09/19/the-song-that-never-ends-why-earth-wind-fires-september-sustains/

And I Ride and I Ride
Songs about Travelling

Around the World – Daft Punk • Directors Label (2003). Volume 3: The Work of Director Michel Gondry. Palm Pictures.

End of the Line – Traveling Wilburys • Clayson, A. (2003). George Harrison. London: Sanctuary. ISBN 1-86074-489-3.

On the Road
Songs about the Open Highway

Born to Be Wild – Steppenwolf • Simpson, D. (2018, Jul 31). How we made Steppenwolf's Born to Be Wild. Retrieved from www.theguardian.com: https://www.theguardian.com/music/2018/jul/31/how-we-made-steppenwolf-born-to-be-wild

The Road's My Middle Name – Bonnie Raitt • Weiner, N. (2019, Mar 21). 30 Years of 'Nick of Time': How Bonnie Raitt's 'Underdog Record' Swept the Grammys & Saved Her Career. Retrieved from www.billboard.com: https://www.billboard.com/articles/columns/rock/8503466/bonnie-raitt-nick-of-time-oral-history-30th-anniversary

Information about the songs in this book was also found on the following websites:

www.wikipedia.com
www.reddit.com
www.songfacts.com
www.genius.com
www.youtube.com
www.theguardian.com
www.rollingstone.com
www.americansongwriter.com
www.songmeanings.com

Index